NUCLEARPEDIA

KEY DOCUMENTS
ON NUCLEAR NON-PROLIFERATION,
SAFEGUARDS, AND SECURITY

NNSS CONSULTING LLC

MICHAEL D. ROSENTHAL

ISBN: 149920003X
ISBN 13: 9781499200034
Library of Congress Control Number: 2014907418
CreateSpace Independent Publishing Platform
North Charleston, South Carolina

Preface

Together with other staff at Brookhaven National Laboratory, I offered a course on Nuclear Non-proliferation, Safeguards and Security in the 21st Century from 2009-2013. The course was sponsored by the National Nuclear Security Administration under its Next Generation Safeguards Initiative. Thanks to NNSA, it will be offered again in the summer of 2014.

The course is the impetus for this book. It grows from two lessons learned during the course: one is the value of having key documents available to students, both in and out of class; the second is that students (and many others) like "paper." Hence this collection.

It is clear that no volume could contain all of the documents that could be considered to be "key" in the context of nuclear non-proliferation, safeguards, and security. Nonetheless, it is hoped that the collection here will be useful. It is also clear that errors may have crept into some documents for which apologies are made in advance.

Readers interested in nuclear non-proliferation and international safeguards will also find of interest two other books prepared by Brookhaven National Laboratory:

One is *Deterring Nuclear Proliferation – The Importance of IAEA Safeguards*. A review copy of the textbook is available at http://www.bnl.gov/gars/nns/IAEAtextbook.php.

The second is a three-volume analysis of the negotiation of the IAEA Model Protocol: *Review of the Negotiation of the Model Protocol Additional to the Agreement(s) between State(s) and the International Atomic Energy Agency for the Application of Safeguards (INFCIRC/540 (Corrected)*.

Volume I covers the period from 1991-1996, during which the stage was set for the negotiation of the Model Protocol. It is available at: http://www.bnl.gov/isd/documents/71012.pdf.

Volume II covers major issues that arose during 1996-1997 negotiation of the Model Protocol. It is available at: http://www.bnl.gov/isd/documents/71014.pdf.

Volume III is a detailed article-by- article review of the negotiation. It is available at: http://www.bnl.gov/isd/documents/71015.pdf.

Introduction

The desire to control the spread of nuclear weapons emerged almost as soon as the discovery of fission in 1938. Scientists recognized immediately both the potential of fission to release enormous amounts of energy and the ability to use this energy for either military or peaceful purposes. This duality creates an intrinsic tension between the pursuit of peaceful uses of nuclear energy and any effort to control their spread. This reference guide contains documents that illuminate efforts to limit the proliferation of nuclear weapons among countries, i.e., nuclear non-proliferation.

Section I contains two parts. Part A covers events that led to the conclusion of the Treaty on the Non-Proliferation of Nuclear Weapons (NPT) in 1968. The NPT is the central element of the international, nuclear non-proliferation regime and is impressively successful. Today, only four countries stand outside the NPT – India, Israel, North Korea, and Pakistan.

In light of this central role, Part B includes key conclusions of the parties to the NPT that were reached by consensus at NPT Review Conferences. They have been held every five years from 1975 through 2010. Part B cites key results from the Conferences held in 1995, 2000, and 2010.

This part also includes a section on negative and positive security assurances. These rose to prominence in the context of the 1995 decision on the extension of the NPT. As a result, the five NPT nuclear-weapon states issued statements that set forth their national positions. The United Nations Security Council also adopted a relevant resolution.

Since the early 1990s the IAEA and the United Nations Security Council have addressed instances of non-compliance with NPT safeguards agreements. In 2009 the United Nations Security Council adopted Resolution 1887, "Maintenance of international peace and security: Nuclear non-proliferation and nuclear disarmament," which, among other elements of importance to the NPT, insisted on compliance with all non-proliferation obligations and emphasized the importance of international mechanisms established to ensure that effective, non-proliferation controls are in place everywhere.

Section II is on international safeguards. It covers efforts contemporaneous with the development of the NPT that resulted in the creation of the International Atomic Energy Agency (IAEA) in 1957. The IAEA has two roles. One is to "accelerate and enlarge" peaceful uses of nuclear energy, and the second is to ensure, when called upon, that nuclear energy is not used to "further any military purpose," which is understood to exclude the manufacture of nuclear explosive devices. To fulfill the latter role, the Statute of the IAEA gives it the authority to send inspectors into states and provides them, in principle, with extraordinary rights of access. The NPT takes advantage of this capability by obligating non-nuclear-weapon states to accept a system of comprehensive IAEA safeguards.

Section III covers nuclear cooperation. It contains key documents that describe efforts made by the international community to ensure that the benefits of peaceful uses of nuclear energy are made available under sound non-proliferation conditions. A key to these efforts is nuclear export controls, about which the NPT imposes specific requirements.

It is recognized that treatment of the NPT and IAEA safeguards separately is somewhat artificial. Nonetheless, the International Atomic Energy Agency was created well before the NPT was adopted, and it seems more useful to describe these paths in two sections, rather than one.

Section IV reflects the emergence of the threat that nuclear terrorists might seek to use nuclear or other radioactive material to achieve their aims. Key steps to combat this threat have been taken in the United Nations, through the adoption of international conventions, through convening of nuclear security summits, and through regional and domestic efforts.

Key conventions are:

- The Convention on the Physical Protection of Nuclear Material (CPPNM), which is the only legally binding international agreement covering the area of physical protection of nuclear material. The Convention covers nuclear material in international transport. It entered into force in 1987;
- In 2005 Parties to the CPPNM adopted an amendment to the CPPNM that extended its reach to domestic circumstances. It requires its parties to protect nuclear facilities and nuclear material in peaceful domestic use, storage, or transport. As of March, 2014, the amendment had yet to obtain the necessary approvals of two thirds of the States Parties that is required for it to enter into force;
- International Convention for the Suppression of Acts of Nuclear Terrorism (Convention on Nuclear Terror): The Convention reflects the rise of nuclear smuggling events and international concern about the extraordinary potential for harm if nuclear weapons or material should fall into terrorist hands. It is one of about a dozen terrorist conventions. It entered into force in 2007.

Two resolutions of the United Nations Security Council are of special interest from the perspective of terrorism, S/RES/1373 (2001) and S/RES/1540 (2004). Both were adopted under Chapter VII of the Charter of the United Nations.

In the former, the United Nations Security Council decided that states should take a wide variety of actions, including, for example steps to disrupt terrorist financing, criminalize terrorist offences, provide early warning to others, and deny safe haven.

The latter created legally binding obligations on all UN Member States to have and enforce appropriate and effective measures against the proliferation of nuclear, chemical, and biological weapons (WMD), and their delivery systems, including by establishing controls.

It requires UN Member States to:

- Prohibit support to non-state actors seeking WMD and their means of delivery;

- Adopt and enforce effective laws prohibiting activities involving the proliferation of WMD and their means of delivery to non-state actors; and,

- Have and enforce effective measures to reduce the vulnerability of many legitimate activities to misuse in ways that would foster the proliferation of WMD and their means of delivery to non-state actors.

The threat of nuclear and radiological terrorism prompted President Obama to convene a Nuclear Summit in 2010. Numerous heads of State attended. A second Summit was held in Seoul in 2012 and a third in 2014 in the Netherlands.

The three Nuclear Security Summits issued statements that are reproduced in this section.

TABLE OF CONTENTS

SECTION I

TREATY ON THE NON-PROLIFERATION OF NUCLEAR WEAPONS

Background

This section contains documents that reflect the origins and formation of the international nuclear non-proliferation regime and led to the conclusion of the Treaty on the Non-Proliferation of Nuclear Weapons (NPT) in 1968. Part A ends with the text of the NPT, which entered into force in 1970 and forms the core of international efforts to prevent the spread of nuclear weapons.

Because of their importance Part B includes statements that were agreed by consensus at NPT Review Conferences, which have been held every five years since 1970. It also contains statements made by the five NPT nuclear-weapon states on their policies concerning the use or the threat to use nuclear weapons against non-nuclear-weapon states parties to the NPT.

The first document is the 1939 letter from Albert Einstein to President Roosevelt. It warned the President of the risk that Germany had initiated a nuclear program and urged him to initiate a coordinated U.S. program.

The second is the joint declaration by President Truman and the Prime Ministers of the United Kingdom, C. R. Attlee, and Canada, W. L. Mackenzie King in 1945.[1] It presaged the themes that have dominated discussion of nuclear non-proliferation: taking advantage of the benefits of peaceful uses while reducing their dangers and using effective safeguards to protect against non-compliance with international norms. The Declaration also foresaw a regime for international control.

Soon after, the very first resolution of the UN General Assembly reproduced the key elements of the declaration and established a United Nations Atomic Energy Commission.

In the United States, the 1946 Acheson-Lilienthal Report[2] also contained these elements, stating that a new international organization should implement a "workable system of safeguards [to] remove from individual nations or their citizens the legal right to

---

1 http://www.un.org/disarmament/publications/documents_on_disarmament/1945-1959/DoD_1945-1959_VOL_I.pdf

2 The Acheson-Lilienthal Report – Report on The International Control of Atomic Energy, Prepared for the Secretary of State's Committee on Atomic Energy by a Board of Consultants, Chester I. Barnard, Dr. J. R. Oppenheimer, Dr. Charles A. Thomas, Harry A. Winne, David E. Lilienthal, Chairman. U. S. Government Printing Office, Washington, D. C., March 16, 1946, p. 1. The report is available at http://www.learnworld.com/ZNW/LWText.Acheson-Lilienthal.html. (February 21, 2012.)

engage in certain well-defined activities" that were "intrinsically dangerous" because they were "steps in the production of atomic bombs." This would include mining and the sensitive technologies of uranium enrichment and plutonium separation. The authority would not control activities that were not considered "dangerous". The international organization would also promote peaceful uses of nuclear energy, which the Report concluded, were "within reach of actuality." In transmitting the Report to the Secretary of State, the Acheson Committee noted that it was, "in particular, impressed by the great advantages of an international agency with affirmative powers and functions coupled with powers of inspection and supervision...."

Early efforts to promote international control foundered as the United States and the Soviet Union failed to agree on how to proceed (or even whether to proceed) towards this goal.

Failing this objective, efforts turned towards the non-proliferation of nuclear weapons.

Concerns about nuclear proliferation were reflected in President John F. Kennedy's worries in 1960 that that, "There are indications because of new inventions, that 10, 15, or 20 nations will have a nuclear capacity, including Red China, by the end of the Presidential office in 1964. This is extremely serious . . . I think the fate not only of our own civilization, but I think the fate of the world and the future of the human race is involved in preventing a nuclear war."[3]

It was only in 1961, though, that the UN General Assembly adopted a resolution, 1665(XVI) that commanded the support of France, the Soviet Union, the United Kingdom, and the United States that called for the negotiation of a treaty to prevent the spread of nuclear weapons. (Introduced by Ireland, it is known as the "Irish Resolution.")[4]

This was followed by the adoption of a resolution in 1965 in the UN General Assembly, 2028 (XX), which spelled out the ground-rules for a non-proliferation treaty.[5]

This triggered the negotiation of the Nuclear Non-proliferation Treaty, which was completed in 1968 and entered into force in 1970.

The Treaty provides for conferences to be convened every five years to review the operation of the Treaty. Four of these Review Conferences reached a consensus on a Final Document – in 1975, 1985, 2000, and 2010. In 1995, the Review Conference, although it did not agree on a Final Document, did take four decisions, the most important of which was the decision to extend the NPT indefinitely.

This section contains the consensus decisions taken in 1995 as well as important elements of the Final Documents that were agreed in 2000 and 2010.

---

3   Third Nixon-Kennedy Presidential Debate, October 13, 1960. From http://carnegieendowment. org/2003/11/17/jfk-on-nuclear-weapons-and-non-proliferation/3zcu. (July 17, 2012).

4   http://daccess-dds-ny.un.org/doc/RESOLUTION/GEN/NR0/167/18/IMG/NR016718.pdf?OpenElement

5   http://daccess-dds-ny.un.org/doc/RESOLUTION/GEN/NR0/217/91/IMG/NR021791.pdf?OpenElement

A. TOWARDS THE CREATION OF THE NUCLEAR NON-PROLIFERATION TREATY

Letter from Albert Einstein to President Roosevelt

Albert Einstein
Old Grove Rd.
Nassau Point
Peconic, Long Island

August 2nd 1939

F.D. Roosevelt
President of the United States
White House
Washington, D.C.

Sir:

Some recent work by E. Fermi and L. Szilard, which has been communicated to me in manuscript, leads me to expect that the element uranium may be turned into a new and important source of energy in the immediate future. Certain aspects of the situation which has arisen seem to call for watchfulness and, if necessary, quick action on the part of the Administration. I believe therefore that it is my duty to bring to your attention the following facts and recommendations:

In the course of the last four months it has been made probable - through the work of Joliot in France as well as Fermi and Szilard in America - that it may become possible to set up a nuclear chain reaction in a large mass of uranium, by which vast amounts of power and large quantities of new radium-like elements would be generated. Now it appears almost certain that this could be achieved in the immediate future.

This new phenomenon would also lead to the construction of bombs, and it is conceivable - though much less certain - that extremely powerful bombs of a new type may thus be constructed. A single bomb of this type, carried by boat and exploded in a port, might very well destroy the whole port together with some of the surrounding territory. However, such bombs might very well prove to be too heavy for transportation by air.

The United States has only very poor ores of uranium in moderate quantities. There is some good ore in Canada and the former Czechoslovakia, while the most important source of uranium is Belgian Congo.

In view of the situation you may think it desirable to have more permanent contact maintained between the Administration and the group of physicists working on chain reactions in America. One possible way of achieving this might be for you to entrust with this task a person who has your confidence and who could perhaps serve in an inofficial [stet] capacity. His task might comprise the following:

a) To approach Government Departments, keep them informed of further development, and put forward recommendations for Government action, giving particular attention to the problem of securing a supply of uranium ore for the United States;

b) To speed up the experimental work, which is at present being carried on within the limits of the budgets of University laboratories, by providing funds, if such funds be required, through his contacts with private persons who are willing to make contributions for this cause, and perhaps also by obtaining the co-operation of industrial laboratories which have the necessary equipment.

I understand that Germany has actually stopped the sale of uranium from the Czechoslovakian mines which she has taken over. That she should have taken such early action might perhaps be understood on the ground that the son of the German Under-Secretary of State, von Weizsäcker, is attached to the Kaiser-Wilhelm-Institut in Berlin where some of the American work on uranium is now being repeated.

Yours very truly,

(Albert Einstein)

Declaration on atomic bomb by President Truman and Prime Ministers Attlee and King[6]

Washington, November 15, 1945

The President of the United States, the Prime Minister of the United Kingdom, and the Prime Minister of Canada, have issued the following statement:

(1)   We recognize that the application of recent scientific discoveries to the methods and practice of war has placed at the disposal of mankind means of destruction hitherto unknown, against which there can be no adequate military defense, and in the employment of which no single nation can in fact have a monopoly.

(2)   We desire to emphasize that the responsibility for devising means to insure that the new discoveries shall be used for the benefit of mankind, instead of as a means of destruction, rests not on our nations alone but upon the whole civilized world. Nevertheless, the progress that we have made in the development and use of atomic energy demands that we take an initiative in the matter, and we have accordingly met together to consider the possibility of international action:

(a)   To prevent the use of atomic energy for destructive purposes.

(b)   To promote the use of recent and future advances in scientific knowledge, particularly in the utilization of atomic energy, for peaceful and humanitarian ends.

(3)   We are aware that the only complete protection for the civilized world from the destructive use of scientific knowledge lies in the prevention of war. No system of safeguards that can be devised will of itself provide an effective guarantee against production of atomic weapons by a nation bent on aggression. Nor can we ignore the possibility of the development of other weapons, or of new methods of warfare, which may constitute as great a threat to civilization as the military use of atomic energy.

(4)   Representing as we do, the three countries which possess the knowledge essential to the use of atomic energy, we declare at the outset our willingness, as a first contribution, to proceed with the exchange of fundamental scientific information and the interchange of scientists and scientific literature for peaceful ends with any nation that will fully reciprocate.

(5)   We believe that the fruits of scientific research should be made available to all nations, and that freedom of investigation and free interchange of ideas are essential to the progress of knowledge. In pursuance of this policy, the basic

---

6   http://www.un.org/disarmament/publications/documents_on_disarmament/1945-1959/DoD_1945-1959_VOL_I.pdf

scientific information essential to the development of atomic energy for peaceful purposes has already been made available to the world. It is our intention that all further information of this character that may become available from time to time shall be similarly treated. We trust that other nations will adopt the same policy, thereby creating an atmosphere of reciprocal confidence in which political agreement and cooperation will flourish.

(6) We have considered the question of the disclosure of detailed information concerning the practical industrial application of atomic energy. The military exploitation of atomic energy depends, in large part, upon the same methods and processes as would be required for industrial uses.

We are not convinced that the spreading of the specialized information regarding the practical application of atomic energy, before it is possible to devise effective, reciprocal, and enforceable safeguards acceptable to all nations, would contribute to a constructive solution of the problem of the atomic bomb.

On the contrary we think it might have the opposite effect. We are, however, prepared to share, on a reciprocal basis with others of the United Nations, detailed information concerning the practical industrial application of atomic energy just as soon as effective enforceable safeguards against its use for destructive purposes can be devised.

(7) In order to attain the most effective means of entirely eliminating the use of atomic energy for destructive purposes and promoting its widest use for industrial and humanitarian purposes, we are of the opinion that at the earliest practicable date a commission should be set up under the United Nations Organization to prepare recommendations for submission to the organization.

The commission should be instructed to proceed with the utmost dispatch and should be authorized to submit recommendations from time to time dealing with separate phases of its work.

In particular the commission should make specific proposals:

(a) For extending between all nations the exchange of basic scientific information for peaceful ends,

(b) For control of atomic energy to the extent necessary to insure its use only for peaceful purposes,

(c) For the elimination from national armaments of atomic weapons and of all other major weapons adaptable to mass destruction,

(d)   For effective safeguards by way of inspection and other means to protect complying states against the hazards of violations and evasions.

(8)   The work of the commission should proceed by separate stages, the successful completion of each one of which will develop the necessary confidence of the world before the next stage is undertaken. Specifically, it is considered that the commission might well devote its attention first to the wide exchange of scientists and scientific information, and as a second stage to the development of full knowledge concerning natural resources of raw materials.

(9)   Faced with the terrible realities of the application of science to destruction, every nation will realize more urgently than before the overwhelming need to maintain the rule of law among nations and to banish the scourge of war from the earth This can only be brought about by giving wholehearted support to the United Nations Organization and by consolidating and extending its authority, thus creating conditions of mutual trust in which all peoples will be free to devote themselves to the arts of peace. It is our firm resolve to work without reservation to achieve these ends

The City of Washington,
    THE WHITE HOUSE
        November 15, 1945.

HARRY S. TRUMAN
President of the United States
C. R. ATTLEE
Prime Minister of the United Kingdom
W. L. MacKENZIE KING
Prime Minister of Canada

Establishment of a Commission to deal with the problems raised by the discovery of atomic energy: United Nations General Assembly Resolution 1(I).

Resolved by the General Assembly of the United Nations to establish a Commission, with the composition and competence set out hereunder, to deal with the problem raised by the discovery of atomic energy and other related matters:

1. ESTABLISHMENT OF THE COMMISSION

A Commission is hereby established by the General Assembly with the terms of reference set out under section 5 below.

2. RELATIONS OF THE COMMISSION WITH THE ORGANS OF THE UNITED NATIONS

(a)   The Commission shall submit its reports and recommendations to the Security Council, and such reports and recommendations shall be made public unless the Security Council, in the interest of peace and security, otherwise directs. In the appropriate cases the Security Council should transmit these report to the General Assembly and the Members of the United Nations, as well as to the Economic and Social Council and other organs within the framework of the United Nations.

b)   In view of the Security Council's primary responsibility under the Charter of the United Nations for the maintenance of international peace and security, the Security Council shall issue directions to the Commission in matters affecting security. On these matters the Commission shall be accountable for its work to the Security Council.

3. COMPOSITION OF THE COMMISSION

The Commission shall be composed of one representative from each of those States represented on the Security Council, and Canada when that State is not a member of the Security Council. Each representative on the Commission may have such assistance as he may desire.

4. RULES OF PROCEDURE

The Commission shall have whatever staff it may deem necessary, and shall make recommendations for its rules of procedure to the Security Council, which shall approve them as a procedural matter.

5. TERMS OF REFERENCE OF THE COMMISSION

The Commission shall proceed with the utmost despatch and enquire into all phases of the problem, and make such recommendations from time to time with respect to them as it finds possible. In particular, the Commission shall make specific proposals:

(a)   for extending between all nations the exchange of basic scientific information for peaceful ends;

(b)   for control of atomic energy to the extent necessary to ensure its use only for peaceful purposes;

(c)   for the elimination from national armaments of atomic weapons and of all other major weapons adaptable to mass destruction;

(d)   for effective safeguards by way of inspection and other means to protect complying States against the hazards of violations and evasions.

The work of the Commission should proceed by separate stages, the successful completion of each of which will develop the necessary confidence of the world before the next stage is undertaken.

The Commission shall not infringe upon the responsibilities of any organ of the United Nations, but should present recommendations for the consideration of those organs in the performance of their tasks under the terms of the United Nations Charter.

Seventeenth plenary meeting, 24 January 1946.

Excerpts from the Acheson-Lilienthal Report - Report on the international control of atomic energy

Report of the Board of Consultants[7] of the Committee on Atomic Energy[8]

(March 17, 1946)

On the need for international control of atomic energy

…, we were inescapably driven to two conclusions:

(a) the facts preclude any reasonable reliance upon inspection as the primary safeguard against violations of conventions prohibiting atomic weapons, yet leaving the exploitation of atomic energy in national hands;

(b) the facts suggest quite clearly a reasonable and workable system that may provide security, and even beyond security, foster beneficial and humanitarian uses of atomic energy.

What should be the Characteristics of an Effective System of Safeguards?

It may be helpful to summarize the characteristics that are desirable and indeed essential to an effective system of safeguards; in other words, the criteria for any adequate plan for security.

a. Such a plan must reduce to manageable proportions the problem of enforcement of an international policy against atomic warfare.

b. It must be a plan that provides unambiguous and reliable danger signals if a nation takes steps that do or may indicate the beginning of atomic warfare. Those danger signals must flash early enough to leave time adequate to permit other nations–alone or in concert–to take appropriate action.

---

7 The members of the Board of Consultants were David E. Lilienthal, Chairman of the Tennessee Valley Authority, Chester I. Barnard, President of the New Jersey Bell Telephone Company, J. Robert Oppenheimer, of the California Institute of Technology and the University of California, Charles Allen Thomas, Vice President and Technical Director, Monsanto Chemical Company, and Harry A. Winne, Vice-President in Charge of Engineering Policy, General Electric Company.

8 The Committee on Atomic Energy was established by Secretary of State James Byrnes and chaired by Undersecretary of State Dean Acheson. Other members included Vannevar Bush, James B. Conant, General Leslie Groves, and John J. McCloy.

c. The plan must be one that if carried out will provide security; but such that if it fails or the international situation collapses, any nation such as the United States will still be in a relatively secure position, compared to any other nation.

d. To be genuinely effective for security, the plan must be one that is not wholly negative, suppressive, and police-like. We are not dealing simply with a military or scientific problem but with a problem in statecraft and the ways of the human spirit. Therefore the plan must be one that will tend to develop the beneficial possibilities of atomic energy and encourage the growth of fundamental knowledge, stirring the constructive and imaginative impulses of men rather than merely concentrating on the defensive and negative. It should, in short, be a plan that looks to the promise of man's future well-being as well as to his security.

e. The plan must be able to cope with new dangers that may appear in the further development of this relatively new field. In an organizational sense therefore the plan must have flexibility and be readily capable of extension or contraction.

f. The plan must involve international action and minimize rivalry between nations in the dangerous aspects of atomic development.

On the need to control "intrinsically dangerous" activities

————————

It has become clear to us that if the element of rivalry between nations were removed by assignment of the intrinsically dangerous phases of the development of atomic energy to an international organization responsible to all peoples, a reliable prospect would be afforded for a system of security. For it is the element of rivalry and the impossibility of policing the resulting competition through inspection alone that make inspection unworkable as a sole means of control. With that factor of international rivalry removed, the problem becomes both hopeful and manageable.

To restate the conclusion: It is essential that a workable system of safeguards remove from individual nations or their citizens the legal right to engage in certain well defined activities in respect to atomic energy which we believe will be generally agreed to be intrinsically dangerous because they are or could be made steps in the production of atomic bombs. We schematically describe what we regard as intrinsically dangerous steps later in Chapter V. Those activities thus classified as dangerous we conclude are far less dangerous when carried on not by competing nations but by an international organization whose obligation it is to act for all nations. They can, in our opinion, be rendered sufficiently less dangerous to provide an adequate measure of security.

————————

We have therefore reached these two conclusions:

(a)   that only if the dangerous aspects of atomic energy are taken out of national hands and placed in international hands is there any reasonable prospect of devising safeguards against the use of atomic energy for bombs, and

(b)   only if the international agency was engaged in development and operation could it possibly discharge adequately its functions as a safeguarder of the world's future. Such a development function also seems essential in terms of attracting to the international agency the kind of scientists and technicians that this problem requires, recognizing that a mere policing, inspecting or suppressing function would neither attract nor hold them.

On "dangerous activities"

A word may be in order about our views on what constitute "dangerous activities"--those that, in our opinion, ought to be subject to an international monopoly. It will be appreciated at the outset that this distinction between the "safe" and the "dangerous" can be useful without being completely sharp or fixed for all time. In our view, any activity is dangerous which offers a solution either in the actual fact of its physical installation, or by subtle alterations thereof, to one of the three major problems of making atomic weapons:

•   The provision of raw materials,

•   The production in suitable quality and quantity of the fissionable materials plutonium and U 235, and

•   The use of these materials for the making of atomic weapons.

Among the activities which we would at the present time classify as those dangerous for national exploitation are the following:

•   Prospecting, mining, and refining of uranium, and, to a lesser extent, thorium.
•   The enrichment of the isotope 235 by any methods now known to us.
•   The operation of the various types of reactors for making plutonium, and of separation plants for extracting the plutonium.
•   Research and development in atomic explosives.

SUMMARY

1.   If nations or their citizens carry on intrinsically dangerous activities it seems to us that the chances for safeguarding the future are hopeless.

2.   If an international agency is given responsibility for the dangerous activities, leaving the non-dangerous open to nations and their citizens and if the international agency is given and carries forward affirmative development responsibility, furthering among other things the beneficial uses of atomic energy and enabling itself to comprehend and therefore detect the misuse of atomic energy, there is good prospect of security.

———————

Summary of Proposed Plan-- The proposal contemplates an international agency conducting all intrinsically dangerous operations in the nuclear field, with individual nations and their citizens free to conduct, under license and a minimum of inspection, all non-dangerous, or safe, operations.

The international agency might take any one of several forms, as a UNO Commission, or an international corporation or authority. We shall refer to it as Atomic Development Authority. It must have authority to own and lease property; and to carry on mining, manufacturing, research, licensing, inspecting, selling, or any other necessary operations.

———————

In the field of raw materials-- The first purpose of the agency will be to bring under its complete control world supplies of uranium and thorium. Wherever these materials are found in useful quantities the international agency must own them or control them under effective leasing arrangements.

———————

Production Plants -- The second major function of the Authority would be the construction and operation of useful types of atomic reactors and separation plants.

———————

Research Activities-- We have already referred to the research that the Authority will conduct to extend the field of knowledge in relation to recoverable raw materials. We have referred to research in power development. There will be many other forms of research in which the Authority will have to engage, relating to simplifying reactors and the like.

Here we desire to emphasize that the field of research in its broadest sense is the field in which the greatest opportunities present themselves for national and private activities. For research in relation to the application of discoveries relating to atomic energy is a great area of work which in the context of the general plan of safeguards herein proposed is non-dangerous. For the reasons already indicated the Authority itself will have to engage in a wide variety of research activities.

Inspection Activities-- Throughout this report we have recorded our conviction that international agreements to foreswear the military use of atomic weapons cannot be enforced solely by a system of inspection--that they cannot be enforced in a system which leaves the development of essentially dangerous activities in the field of atomic energy in national hands and subject to national rivalry, and, to insure against diversion of these activities to aggressive ends, relies upon supervision by an agency which has no other function. But inspection in a wide variety of forms has its proper place in the operations of the Atomic Development Authority--it has a proper and essential place. Sometimes it may take a form scarcely recognizable as inspection, but that may be regarded as one of the virtues of the proposal.

Prevention of the wider dissemination of nuclear weapons: United Nations General Assembly Resolution 1665 (XVI) (1961)

The General Assembly,

Recalling its resolutions 1380 (XIV) of 20 November 1959 and 1576 (XV) of 20 December 1960,

Convinced that an increase in the number of States possessing nuclear weapons is growing more imminent and threatens to extend and intensify the arms race and to increase the difficulties of avoiding war and of establishing international peace and security based on the rule of law,

Believing in the necessity of an international agreement, subject to inspection and control, whereby the states producing nuclear weapons would refrain from relinquishing control of such weapons to any nation not possessing them and whereby states not possessing such weapons would refrain from manufacturing them,

1. *Calls upon all States,* and in particular upon the States at present possessing nuclear weapons, to use their best endeavours to secure the conclusion of an international agreement containing provisions under which the nuclear States would undertake to refrain from relinquishing control of nuclear weapons and from transmitting the information necessary for their manufacture to States not possessing such weapons, and provisions under which States not possessing nuclear weapons would undertake not to manufacture or other wise acquire control of such weapons ;

2. *Urges* all States to co-operate to those ends.

1070th plenary meeting,
4 December 1961

Non-proliferation of nuclear weapons: United Nations General Assembly Resolution 2028 (XX). (1965)

The General Assembly,

Conscious of its responsibility under the Charter of the United Nations for disarmament and the consolidation of peace,

Mindful of its responsibility in accordance with Article 11, paragraph 1, of the Charter, which stipulates that the General Assembly may consider the general principles of co-operation in the maintenance of inter national peace and security, including the principles governing disarmament and the regulation of armaments, and may make recommendations with regard to such principles to the Members or to the Security Council or to both,

Recalling its resolutions 1665 (XVI) of 4 December 1961 and 1908 (XVIII) of 27 November 1963,

Recognizing the urgency and great importance of the question of preventing the proliferation of nuclear weapons,

Noting with satisfaction the efforts of Brazil, Burma, Ethiopia, India, Mexico, Nigeria, Sweden and the United Arab Republic to achieve the solution of the problem of non-proliferation of nuclear weapons, as contained in their joint memorandum of 15 September 1965,[1]

Convinced that the proliferation of nuclear weapons would endanger the security of all States and make more difficult the achievement of general and complete disarmament under effective international control,

Noting the declaration adopted by the Assembly of Heads of State and Government of the Organization of African Unity at its first regular session, held at Cairo in July 1964,[2] and the Declaration entitled "Programme for Peace and International Co-operation"[3] adopted by the Second Conference of Heads of State or Government of Non-Aligned Countries, held at Cairo in October 1964,

Noting also the draft treaties to prevent the proliferation of nuclear weapons submitted by the United States of America[4] and the Union of Soviet Socialist Republics,[5] respectively,

---

1 Official Records of the Disarmament Commission, Supplement for January to December 1965, *document DC/227, annex I, sect. E.*

2 For the resolution entitled "Denuclearization of Africa" adopted by the Assembly of Heads of State and Government: see Official Records of the General Assembly, Twentieth Session, Annexes, agenda item 105, document A/5975.

3 *See A/5763.*

4 *Official Records of the Disarmament Commission, Supplement for January to December 1965, document* DC/227, annex I, sect. A.

5 *Official Records of the General Assembly, Twentieth Session, Annexes, agenda item* 106, document A/5976.

Noting further that a draft unilateral non-acquisition declaration has been submitted by Italy,[6]

Convinced that General Assembly resolutions 1652 (XVI) of 24 November 1961 and 1911 (XVIII) of 27 November 1963 aim at preventing the proliferation of nuclear weapons,

Believing that it is imperative to exert further efforts to conclude a treaty to prevent the proliferation of nuclear weapons,

1. *Urges* all States to take all steps necessary for the early conclusion of a treaty to prevent the proliferation of nuclear weapons;

2. *Calls* upon the Conference of the Eighteen-Nation Committee on Disarmament to give urgent consideration to the question of non-proliferation of nuclear weapons and to that end, to reconvene as early as possible with a view to negotiating an international treaty to prevent the proliferation of nuclear weapons, based on the following main principles:

   (a) The treaty should be void of any loopholes which might permit nuclear or non-nuclear Powers to proliferate, directly or indirectly, nuclear weapons in any form;

   (b) The treaty should embody an acceptable balance of mutual responsibilities and obligations of the nuclear and non-nuclear Powers;

   (c) The treaty should be a step towards the achievement of general and complete disarmament and, more particularly, nuclear disarmament;

   (d) There should be acceptable and workable provisions to ensure the effectiveness of the treaty;

   (e) Nothing in the treaty should adversely affect the right of any group of States to conclude regional treaties in order to ensure the total absence of nuclear weapons in their respective territories;

3. *Transmits* the records of the First Committee relating to the discussion of the item entitled "Nonproliferation of nuclear weapons", together with all other relevant documents, to the Eighteen-Nation Committee for its consideration;

4. *Requests* the Eighteen-Nation Committee to submit to the General Assembly at an early date a report on the results of its work on a treaty to prevent the proliferation of nuclear weapons.

---

6 Official Records of the Disarmament Commission, Supplement for January to December 1965, *document DC/227, annex 1, sect. D.*

The Treaty on the Non-Proliferation of Nuclear Weapons
(Entered into force on March 5, 1970)

The States concluding this Treaty, hereinafter referred to as the Parties to the Treaty,

Considering the devastation that would be visited upon all mankind by a nuclear war and the consequent need to make every effort to avert the danger of such a war and to take measures to safeguard the security of peoples,

Believing that the proliferation of nuclear weapons would seriously enhance the danger of nuclear war,

In conformity with resolutions of the United Nations General Assembly calling for the conclusion of an agreement on the prevention of wider dissemination of nuclear weapons,

Undertaking to co-operate in facilitating the application of International Atomic Energy Agency safeguards on peaceful nuclear activities,

Expressing their support for research, development and other efforts to further the application, within the framework of the International Atomic Energy Agency safeguards system, of the principle of safeguarding effectively the flow of source and special fissionable materials by use of instruments and other techniques at certain strategic points,

Affirming the principle that the benefits of peaceful applications of nuclear technology, including any technological by-products which may be derived by nuclear-weapon States from the development of nuclear explosive devices, should be available for peaceful purposes to all Parties to the Treaty, whether nuclear-weapon or non-nuclear-weapon States,

Convinced that, in furtherance of this principle, all Parties to the Treaty are entitled to participate in the fullest possible exchange of scientific information for, and to contribute alone or in co-operation with other States to, the further development of the applications of atomic energy for peaceful purposes,

Declaring their intention to achieve at the earliest possible date the cessation of the nuclear arms race and to undertake effective measures in the direction of nuclear disarmament,

Urging the co-operation of all States in the attainment of this objective,

Recalling the determination expressed by the Parties to the 1963 Treaty banning nuclear weapons tests in the atmosphere, in outer space and under water in its Preamble to seek to achieve the discontinuance of all test explosions of nuclear weapons for all time and to continue negotiations to this end,

Desiring to further the easing of international tension and the strengthening of trust between States in order to facilitate the cessation of the manufacture of nuclear weapons, the liquidation of all their existing stockpiles, and the elimination from national arsenals of nuclear weapons and the means of their delivery pursuant to a Treaty on general and complete disarmament under strict and effective international control,

Recalling that, in accordance with the Charter of the United Nations, States must refrain in their international relations from the threat or use of force against the territorial integrity or political independence of any State, or in any other manner inconsistent with the Purposes of the United Nations, and that the establishment and maintenance of international peace and security are to be promoted with the least diversion for armaments of the world's human and economic resources,

Have agreed as follows:

Article I

Each nuclear-weapon State Party to the Treaty undertakes not to transfer to any recipient whatsoever nuclear weapons or other nuclear explosive devices or control over such weapons or explosive devices directly, or indirectly; and not in any way to assist, encourage, or induce any non-nuclear-weapon State to manufacture or otherwise acquire nuclear weapons or other nuclear explosive devices, or control over such weapons or explosive devices.

Article II

Each non-nuclear-weapon State Party to the Treaty undertakes not to receive the transfer from any transferor whatsoever of nuclear weapons or other nuclear explosive devices or of control over such weapons or explosive devices directly, or indirectly; not to manufacture or otherwise acquire nuclear weapons or other nuclear explosive devices; and not to seek or receive any assistance in the manufacture of nuclear weapons or other nuclear explosive devices.

Article III

1. Each non-nuclear-weapon State Party to the Treaty undertakes to accept safeguards, as set forth in an agreement to be negotiated and concluded with the International Atomic Energy Agency in accordance with the Statute of the International Atomic Energy Agency and the Agency's safeguards system, for the exclusive purpose of verification of the fulfilment of its obligations assumed under this Treaty with a view to preventing diversion of nuclear energy from peaceful uses to nuclear weapons or other nuclear explosive devices. Procedures for the safeguards required by this Article shall be followed with respect to source or special fissionable material whether it is being produced, processed or used in any principal nuclear facility or is outside any such facility.

The safeguards required by this Article shall be applied on all source or special fissionable material in all peaceful nuclear activities within the territory of such State, under its jurisdiction, or carried out under its control anywhere.

2. Each State Party to the Treaty undertakes not to provide: (a) source or special fissionable material, or (b) equipment or material especially designed or prepared for the processing, use or production of special fissionable material, to any non-nuclear-weapon State for peaceful purposes, unless the source or special fissionable material shall be subject to the safeguards required by this Article.

3. The safeguards required by this Article shall be implemented in a manner designed to comply with Article IV of this Treaty, and to avoid hampering the economic or technological development of the Parties or international co-operation in the field of peaceful nuclear activities, including the international exchange of nuclear material and equipment for the processing, use or production of nuclear material for peaceful purposes in accordance with the provisions of this Article and the principle of safeguarding set forth in the Preamble of the Treaty.

4. Non-nuclear-weapon States Party to the Treaty shall conclude agreements with the International Atomic Energy Agency to meet the requirements of this Article either individually or together with other States in accordance with the Statute of the International Atomic Energy Agency. Negotiation of such agreements shall commence within 180 days from the original entry into force of this Treaty. For States depositing their instruments of ratification or accession after the 180-day period, negotiation of such agreements shall commence not later than the date of such deposit. Such agreements shall enter into force not later than eighteen months after the date of initiation of negotiations.

Article IV

1. Nothing in this Treaty shall be interpreted as affecting the inalienable right of all the Parties to the Treaty to develop research, production and use of nuclear energy for peaceful purposes without discrimination and in conformity with Articles I and II of this Treaty.

2. All the Parties to the Treaty undertake to facilitate, and have the right to participate in, the fullest possible exchange of equipment, materials and scientific and technological information for the peaceful uses of nuclear energy. Parties to the Treaty in a position to do so shall also co-operate in contributing alone or together with other States or international organizations to the further development of the applications of nuclear energy for peaceful purposes, especially in the territories of non-nuclear-weapon States Party to the Treaty, with due consideration for the needs of the developing areas of the world.

Article V

Each Party to the Treaty undertakes to take appropriate measures to ensure that, in accordance with this Treaty, under appropriate international observation and through appropriate international procedures, potential benefits from any peaceful applications of nuclear explosions will be made available to non-nuclear-weapon States Party to the Treaty on a non-discriminatory basis and that the charge to such Parties for the explosive devices used will be as low as possible and exclude any charge for research and development. Non-nuclear-weapon States Party to the Treaty shall be able to obtain such benefits, pursuant to a special international agreement or agreements, through an appropriate international body with adequate representation of non-nuclear-weapon States. Negotiations on this subject shall commence as soon as possible after the Treaty enters into force. Non-nuclear-weapon States Party to the Treaty so desiring may also obtain such benefits pursuant to bilateral agreements.

Article VI

Each of the Parties to the Treaty undertakes to pursue negotiations in good faith on effective measures relating to cessation of the nuclear arms race at an early date and to nuclear disarmament, and on a treaty on general and complete disarmament under strict and effective international control.

Article VII

Nothing in this Treaty affects the right of any group of States to conclude regional treaties in order to assure the total absence of nuclear weapons in their respective territories.

Article VIII

1. Any Party to the Treaty may propose amendments to this Treaty. The text of any proposed amendment shall be submitted to the Depositary Governments which shall circulate it to all Parties to the Treaty. Thereupon, if requested to do so by one-third or more of the Parties to the Treaty, the Depositary Governments shall convene a conference, to which they shall invite all the Parties to the Treaty, to consider such an amendment.

2. Any amendment to this Treaty must be approved by a majority of the votes of all the Parties to the Treaty, including the votes of all nuclear-weapon States Party to the Treaty and all other Parties which, on the date the amendment is circulated, are members of the Board of Governors of the International Atomic Energy Agency. The amendment shall enter into force for each Party that deposits its instrument of ratification of the amendment upon the deposit of such instruments of ratification by a majority of all the Parties, including the instruments of ratification of all nuclear-weapon States Party to the Treaty and all other

Parties which, on the date the amendment is circulated, are members of the Board of Governors of the International Atomic Energy Agency. Thereafter, it shall enter into force for any other Party upon the deposit of its instrument of ratification of the amendment.

3. Five years after the entry into force of this Treaty, a conference of Parties to the Treaty shall be held in Geneva, Switzerland, in order to review the operation of this Treaty with a view to assuring that the purposes of the Preamble and the provisions of the Treaty are being realised. At intervals of five years thereafter, a majority of the Parties to the Treaty may obtain, by submitting a proposal to this effect to the Depositary Governments, the convening of further conferences with the same objective of reviewing the operation of the Treaty.

Article IX

1. This Treaty shall be open to all States for signature. Any State which does not sign the Treaty before its entry into force in accordance with paragraph 3 of this Article may accede to it at any time.

2. This Treaty shall be subject to ratification by signatory States. Instruments of ratification and instruments of accession shall be deposited with the Governments of the United Kingdom of Great Britain and Northern Ireland, the Union of Soviet Socialist Republics and the United States of America, which are hereby designated the Depositary Governments.

3. This Treaty shall enter into force after its ratification by the States, the Governments of which are designated Depositaries of the Treaty, and forty other States signatory to this Treaty and the deposit of their instruments of ratification. For the purposes of this Treaty, a nuclear-weapon State is one which has manufactured and exploded a nuclear weapon or other nuclear explosive device prior to 1 January 1967.

4. For States whose instruments of ratification or accession are deposited subsequent to the entry into force of this Treaty, it shall enter into force on the date of the deposit of their instruments of ratification or accession.

5. The Depositary Governments shall promptly inform all signatory and acceding States of the date of each signature, the date of deposit of each instrument of ratification or of accession, the date of the entry into force of this Treaty, and the date of receipt of any requests for convening a conference or other notices.

6. This Treaty shall be registered by the Depositary Governments pursuant to Article 102 of the Charter of the United Nations.

Article X

1. Each Party shall in exercising its national sovereignty have the right to withdraw from the Treaty if it decides that extraordinary events, related to the subject matter of this Treaty, have jeopardized the supreme interests of its country. It shall give notice of such withdrawal to all other Parties to the Treaty and to the United Nations Security Council three months in advance. Such notice shall include a statement of the extraordinary events it regards as having jeopardized its supreme interests.

2. Twenty-five years after the entry into force of the Treaty, a conference shall be convened to decide whether the Treaty shall continue in force indefinitely, or shall be extended for an additional fixed period or periods. This decision shall be taken by a majority of the Parties to the Treaty.

Article XI

This Treaty, the English, Russian, French, Spanish and Chinese texts of which are equally authentic, shall be deposited in the archives of the Depositary Governments. Duly certified copies of this Treaty shall be transmitted by the Depositary Governments to the Governments of the signatory and acceding States.

IN WITNESS WHEREOF the undersigned, duly authorized, have signed this Treaty.

DONE in triplicate, at the cities of London, Moscow and Washington, the first day of July, one thousand nine hundred and sixty-eight.

B. NUCLEAR NON-PROLIFERATION TREATY REVIEW CONFERENCES

Background

Articles VIII.3 and X.2 of the NPT require that conferences of Parties to the Treaty be held as follows:

> **Review Conferences**: Article VIII.3. Five years after the entry into force of this Treaty, a conference of Parties to the Treaty shall be held in Geneva, Switzerland, in order to review the operation of this Treaty with a view to assuring that the purposes of the Preamble and the provisions of the Treaty are being realised. At intervals of five years thereafter, a majority of the Parties to the Treaty may obtain, by submitting a proposal to this effect to the Depositary Governments, the convening of further conferences with the same objective of reviewing the operation of the Treaty.

> **Extension Conference**: Article X.2. Twenty-five years after the entry into force of the Treaty, a conference shall be convened to decide whether the Treaty shall continue in force indefinitely, or shall be extended for an additional fixed period or periods. This decision shall be taken by a majority of the Parties to the Treaty.

In accordance with Article VIII.3, the first conference to "review the operation of [the] Treaty" was held in Geneva in 1975 (five years after the Treaty entered into force in 1970). "NPT Review Conferences" have been held every five years since then.

Although not required by the Treaty, conference participants have always attempted to forge a consensus among the participants on a so-called "Final Document," one that would reflect a common view on the extent to which "the provisions of the Treaty are being realized."[9] Two substantive issues dominate the discussion in review conferences. Both stem from the differentiated obligations in the NPT between non-nuclear-weapon states and nuclear-weapon states. One, by far the most difficult, is the extent to which the NPT nuclear-weapon states have met their obligations under Article VI of the Treaty. The second is the implementation of IAEA safeguards. How to address regional issues, particularly in the Middle East, has also been controversial.

An excellent review of how NPT Review Conferences have addressed these and other issues is in *The Evolution of NPT Review Conference Final Documents, 1975-2000* by Carlton Stoiber.[10]

---

9 The Review Conferences in 1975, 1985, 2000, and 2010 agreed on Final Documents.

10 Carlton Stoiber, The Evolution of NPT Review Conference Final Documents, 1975-2000, The Nonproliferation Review/Fall-Winter 2003, p. 126-166. (http://cns.miis.edu/npr/pdfs/103stoi.pdf March 8, 2014)

The conference of the most moment was held in 1995, 25 years after the NPT entered into force. In accordance with the Treaty, it convened bot to review the implementation of the Treaty and to decide on the future of the Treaty, i.e., whether it should "continue in force indefinitely, or shall be extended for an additional fixed period or periods." A single Review and Extension Conference was held that year.

The 19995 NPT Review and Extension Conference agreed to extend the Treaty indefinitely.

In 2000, the NPT Review Conference agreed on thirteen steps on disarmament that it recommended be pursued in order for the nuclear-weapon states to meet their obligations contained in Article VI of the NPT in the near-term.

In 2010, the NPT Review Conference agreed on a forward-looking action plan.

B.1 1995 NPT Review and Extension Conference

Decision 1 - Strengthening the review process for the Treaty[11]

1. The Conference of the Parties to the Treaty on the Non-Proliferation of Nuclear Weapons examined the implementation of article VIII, paragraph 3, of the Treaty and agreed to strengthen the review process for the operation of the Treaty with a view to assuring that the purposes of the Preamble and the provisions of the Treaty are being realized.

2. The States party to the Treaty participating in the Conference decided, in accordance with article VIII, paragraph 3, that Review Conferences should continue to be held every five years and that, accordingly, the next Review Conference should be held in the year 2000.

3. The Conference decided that, beginning in 1997, the Preparatory Committee should hold, normally for a duration of 10 working days, a meeting in each of the three years prior to the Review Conference. If necessary, a fourth preparatory meeting may be held in the year of the Conference.

4. The purpose of the Preparatory Committee meetings would be to consider principles, objectives and ways in order to promote the full implementation of the Treaty, as well as its universality, and to make recommendations thereon to the Review Conference. These include those identified in the decision on principles and objectives for nuclear non-proliferation and disarmament, adopted on 11 May 1995. These meetings should also make the procedural preparations for the next Review Conference.

5. The Conference also concluded that the present structure of three Main Committees should continue and the question of an overlap of issues being discussed in more than one Committee should be resolved in the General Committee, which would coordinate the work of the Committees so that the substantive responsibility for the preparation of the report with respect to each specific issue is undertaken in only one Committee.

6. It was also agreed that subsidiary bodies could be established within the respective Main Committees for specific issues relevant to the Treaty, so as to provide for a focused consideration of such issues. The establishment of such subsidiary bodies would be recommended by the Preparatory Committee for each Review Conference in relation to the specific objectives of the Review Conference.

7. The Conference further agreed that Review Conferences should look forward as well as back. They should evaluate the results of the period they are reviewing,

---

11 NPT/CONF.1995/32 (Part 1), Annex

including the implementation of undertakings of the States parties under the Treaty, and identify the areas in which, and the means through which, further progress should be sought in the future. Review Conferences should also address specifically what might be done to strengthen the implementation of the Treaty and to achieve its universality.

Decision 2 - Principles and Objectives for Nuclear Non-Proliferation and Disarmament

The Conference of the Parties to the Treaty on the Non-Proliferation of Nuclear Weapons,

Reaffirming the preamble and articles of the Treaty on the Non-Proliferation of Nuclear Weapons,

Welcoming the end of the cold war, the ensuing easing of international tension and the strengthening of trust between States,

Desiring a set of principles and objectives in accordance with which nuclear non-proliferation, nuclear disarmament and international cooperation in the peaceful uses of nuclear energy should be vigorously pursued and progress, achievements and shortcomings evaluated periodically within the review process provided for in article VIII, paragraph 3, of the Treaty, the enhancement and strengthening of which is welcomed,

Reiterating the ultimate goals of the complete elimination of nuclear weapons and a treaty on general and complete disarmament under strict and effective international control,

The Conference affirms the need to continue to move with determination towards the full realization and effective implementation of the provisions of the Treaty, and accordingly adopts the following principles and objectives:

Universality

1. Universal adherence to the Treaty on to the Treaty is an urgent priority. All States not yet party to the Treaty are called upon to accede to the Treaty at the earliest date, particularly those States that operate unsafeguarded nuclear facilities. Every effort should be made by all States parties to achieve this objective.

Non-proliferation

2. The proliferation of nuclear weapons would seriously increase the danger of nuclear war. The Treaty on the Non-Proliferation of Nuclear Weapons has a vital role to play in preventing the proliferation of nuclear weapons. Every effort should be made to implement the Treaty in all its aspects to prevent the proliferation of nuclear weapons and other nuclear explosive devices, without hampering the peaceful uses of nuclear energy by States parties to the Treaty.

Nuclear disarmament

3. Nuclear disarmament is substantially facilitated by the easing of international tension and the strengthening of trust between States which have prevailed

following the end of the cold war. The undertakings with regard to nuclear disarmament as set out in the Treaty on the Non-Proliferation of Nuclear Weapons should thus be fulfilled with determination. In this regard, the nuclear-weapon States reaffirm their commitment, as stated in Article VI, to pursue in good faith negotiations on effective measures relating to nuclear disarmament.

4. The achievement of the following measures is important in the full realization and effective implementation of Article VI, including the programme of action as reflected below:

    (a) The completion by the Conference on Disarmament of the negotiations on a universal and internationally and effectively verifiable Comprehensive Nuclear-Test-Ban Treaty no later than 1996. Pending the entry into force of a Comprehensive Test-Ban Treaty, the nuclear-weapon States should exercise utmost restraint;

    (b) The immediate commencement and early conclusion of negotiations on a non-discriminatory and universally applicable convention banning the production of fissile material for nuclear weapons or other nuclear explosive devices, in accordance with the statement of the Special Coordinator of the Conference on Disarmament and the mandate contained therein;

    (c) The determined pursuit by the nuclear-weapon States of systematic and progressive efforts to reduce nuclear weapons globally, with the ultimate goals of eliminating those weapons, and by all States of general and complete disarmament under strict and effective international control.

Nuclear-weapon-free zones

5. The conviction that the establishment of internationally recognized nuclear-weapon-free zones, on the basis of arrangements freely arrived at among the States of the region concerned, enhances global and regional peace and security is reaffirmed.

6. The development of nuclear-weapon-free zones, especially in regions of tension, such as in the Middle East, as well as the establishment of zones free of all weapons of mass destruction, should be encouraged as a matter of priority, taking into account the specific characteristics of each region. The establishment of additional nuclear-weapon-free zones by the time of the Review Conference in the year 2000 would be welcome.

7. The cooperation of all the nuclear-weapon States and their respect and support for the relevant protocols is necessary for the maximum effectiveness of such nuclear-weapon-free zones and the relevant protocols.

Security assurances

8. Noting United Nations Security Council resolution 984 (1995), which was adopted unanimously on 11 April 1995, as well as the declarations of the nuclear-weapon States concerning both negative and positive security assurances, further steps should be considered to assure non-nuclear-weapon States party to the Treaty against the use or threat of use of nuclear weapons. These steps could take the form of an internationally legally binding instrument.

Safeguards

9. The International Atomic Energy Agency is the competent authority responsible to verify and assure, in accordance with the statute of the Agency and the Agency's safeguards system, compliance with its safeguards agreements with States parties undertaken in fulfilment of their obligations under article III, paragraph 1, of the Treaty, with a view to preventing diversion of nuclear energy from peaceful uses to nuclear weapons or other nuclear explosive devices. Nothing should be done to undermine the authority of the International Atomic Energy Agency in this regard. States parties that have concerns regarding non-compliance with the safeguards agreements of the Treaty by the States parties should direct such concerns, along with supporting evidence and information, to the Agency to consider, investigate, draw conclusions and decide on necessary actions in accordance with its mandate.

10. All States parties required by article III of the Treaty to sign and bring into force comprehensive safeguards agreements and which have not yet done so should do so without delay.

11. International Atomic Energy Agency safeguards should be regularly assessed and evaluated. Decisions adopted by its Board of Governors aimed at further strengthening the effectiveness of Agency safeguards should be supported and implemented and the Agency's capability to detect undeclared nuclear activities should be increased. Also, States not party to the Treaty on the Non-Proliferation of Nuclear Weapons should be urged to enter into comprehensive safeguards agreements with the Agency.

12. New supply arrangements for the transfer of source or special fissionable material or equipment or material especially designed or prepared for the processing, use or production of special fissionable material to non-nuclear-weapon States should require, as a necessary precondition, acceptance of the Agency's full-scope safeguards and internationally legally binding commitments not to acquire nuclear weapons or other nuclear explosive devices.

13. Nuclear fissile material transferred from military use to peaceful nuclear activities should, as soon as practicable, be placed under Agency safeguards in the framework of the voluntary safeguards agreements in place with the

nuclear-weapon States. Safeguards should be universally applied once the complete elimination of nuclear weapons has been achieved.

Peaceful uses of nuclear energy

14. Particular importance should be attached to ensuring the exercise of the inalienable right of all the parties to the Treaty to develop research, production and use of nuclear energy for peaceful purposes without discrimination and in conformity with articles I, II as well as III of the Treaty.

15. Undertakings to facilitate participation in the fullest possible exchange of equipment, materials and scientific and technological information for the peaceful uses of nuclear energy should be fully implemented.

16. In all activities designed to promote the peaceful uses of nuclear energy, preferential treatment should be given to the non-nuclear-weapon States party to the Treaty, taking the needs of developing countries particularly into account.

17. Transparency in nuclear-related export controls should be promoted within the framework of dialogue and cooperation among all interested States party to the Treaty.

18. All States should, through rigorous national measures and international cooperation, maintain the highest practicable levels of nuclear safety, including in waste management, and observe standards and guidelines in nuclear materials accounting, physical protection and transport of nuclear materials.

19. Every effort should be made to ensure that the International Atomic Energy Agency has the financial and human resources necessary to meet effectively its responsibilities in the areas of technical cooperation, safeguards and nuclear safety. The Agency should also be encouraged to intensify its efforts aimed at finding ways and means for funding technical assistance through predictable and assured resources.

20. Attacks or threats of attack on nuclear facilities devoted to peaceful purposes jeopardize nuclear safety and raise serious concerns regarding the application of international law on the use of force in such cases, which could warrant appropriate action in accordance with the provisions of the Charter of the United Nations.

The Conference requests that the President of the Conference bring the present decision, the decision on strengthening the review process for the Treaty and the decision on the extension of the Treaty on the Non-Proliferation of Nuclear Weapons, to the attention of the heads of State or Government of all States and seek their full cooperation on these documents and in the furtherance of the goals of the Treaty.

Decision 3 - Extension of the Treaty on the Non-Proliferation of Nuclear Weapons

The Conference of the Parties to the Treaty on the Non-Proliferation of Nuclear Weapons,

Having convened in New York from 17 April to 12 May 1995, in accordance with article VIII, paragraph 3, and article X, paragraph 2, of the Treaty on the Non-Proliferation of Nuclear Weapons,

Having reviewed the operation of the Treaty and affirming that there is a need for full compliance with the Treaty, its extension and its universal adherence, which are essential to international peace and security and the attainment of the ultimate goals of the complete elimination of nuclear weapons and a treaty on general and complete disarmament under strict and effective international control,

Having reaffirmed article VIII, paragraph 3, of the Treaty and the need for its continued implementation in a strengthened manner and, to this end, emphasizing the decision on strengthening the review process for the Treaty and the decision on principles and objectives for nuclear non-proliferation and disarmament, also adopted by the Conference,

Having established that the Conference is quorate in accordance with article X, paragraph 2, of the Treaty,

Decides that, as a majority exists among States party to the Treaty for its indefinite extension, in accordance with article X, paragraph 2, the Treaty shall continue in force indefinitely.

Resolution on the Middle East

The Conference of the Parties to the Treaty on the Non-Proliferation of Nuclear Weapons,

Reaffirming the purpose and provisions of the Treaty on the Non-Proliferation of Nuclear Weapons,

Recognizing that, pursuant to article VII of the Treaty, the establishment of nuclear-weapon-free zones contributes to strengthening the international non-proliferation regime,

Recalling that the Security Council, in its statement of 31 January 1992, a/ affirmed that the proliferation of nuclear and all other weapons of mass destruction constituted a threat to international peace and security,

Recalling also General Assembly resolutions adopted by consensus supporting the establishment of a nuclear-weapon-free zone in the Middle East, the latest of which is resolution 49/71 of 15 December 1994,

Recalling further the relevant resolutions adopted by the General Conference of the International Atomic Energy Agency concerning the application of Agency safeguards in the Middle East, the latest of which is GC(XXXVIII)/RES/21 of 23 September 1994, and noting the danger of nuclear proliferation, especially in areas of tension,

Bearing in mind Security Council resolution 687 (1991) and in particular paragraph 14 thereof,

Noting Security Council resolution 984 (1995) and paragraph 8 of the decision on principles and objectives for nuclear non-proliferation and disarmament adopted by the Conference on 11 May 1995,

Bearing in mind the other decisions adopted by the Conference on 11 May 1995,

1. Endorses the aims and objectives of the Middle East peace process and recognizes that efforts in this regard, as well as other efforts, contribute to, inter alia, a Middle East zone free of nuclear weapons as well as other weapons of mass destruction;

2. Notes with satisfaction that, in its report (NPT/CONF.1995/MC.III/1), Main Committee III of the Conference recommended that the Conference "call on those remaining States not parties to the Treaty to accede to it, thereby accepting an international legally binding commitment not to acquire nuclear weapons or nuclear explosive devices and to accept International Atomic Energy Agency safeguards on all their nuclear activities";

3. Notes with concern the continued existence in the Middle East of unsafeguarded nuclear facilities, and reaffirms in this connection the recommendation contained in section VI, paragraph 3, of the report of Main Committee III urging those non-parties to the Treaty on the Non-Proliferation of Nuclear Weapons that operate unsafeguarded nuclear facilities to accept full-scope International Atomic Energy Agency safeguards;

4. Reaffirms the importance of the early realization of universal adherence to the Treaty, and calls upon all States of the Middle East that have not yet done so, without exception, to accede to the Treaty as soon as possible and to place their nuclear facilities under full-scope International Atomic Energy Agency safeguards;

5. Calls upon all States in the Middle East to take practical steps in appropriate forums aimed at making progress towards, inter alia, the establishment of an effectively verifiable Middle East zone free of weapons of mass destruction, nuclear, chemical and biological, and their delivery systems, and to refrain from taking any measures that preclude the achievement of this objective;

6. Calls upon all States party to the Treaty on the Non-Proliferation of Nuclear Weapons, and in particular the nuclear-weapon States, to extend their cooperation and to exert their utmost efforts with a view to ensuring the early establishment by regional parties of a Middle East zone free of nuclear and all other weapons of mass destruction and their delivery systems.

a/   S/23500.

B.2 2000 NPT Review Conference

Background

The language of Article VI is general. It does not stipulate how the nuclear-weapon states should pursue nuclear disarmament or in what timeframe. Regardless, non-nuclear-weapon states are critical of the nuclear-weapon states because, in their view, the steps taken by the nuclear-weapon states to move toward nuclear disarmament are both too little and too slow. In NPT review conferences, the issue of nuclear disarmament is often the most contentious.

There is a growing body of statements and documents that highlight the salience of Article VI issues in the international community. For example:

- The 1995 "Principles and Objectives for Nuclear Non-Proliferation and Disarmament" includes a number of specific targets for nuclear disarmament.[12]

- Responding to a 1994 United Nations General Assembly resolution, the International Court of Justice issued several advisory opinions on the legality of nuclear weapons and in so doing took into account Article VI of the NPT. The Court unanimously agreed that, "there exists an obligation to pursue in good faith and bring to a conclusion negotiations leading to nuclear disarmament in all its aspects under strict and effective international control."[13]

- At the 2000 NPT Review Conference the five NPT nuclear-weapon states agreed to take thirteen "practical steps" to implement Article VI, including an "unequivocal undertaking … to accomplish the total elimination of their nuclear arsenals leading to nuclear disarmament, to which all States parties are committed under Article VI."[14]

---

12 1995 Review and Extension Conference of the Parties to the Treaty on the Non-Proliferation of Nuclear Weapons. Final Document, Part I, Annex. Decision 2, "Principles and Objectives for Nuclear Non-Proliferation and Disarmament," (NPT/CONF.1995/32 (Part I)).

13 Legality of the Threat or Use of Nuclear Weapons (Request by the United Nations General Assembly), ICJ Advisory Opinion, 8 July 1966, paragraph 105 F. See also Laurence Boisson de Chazournes and Philippe Sands, editors, *International Law, the International Court of Justice and Nuclear Weapons* (Cambridge, UK: Cambridge University Press, 1999). The United States does not subscribe to the ICJ.

14 2000 Review Conference of the Parties to the Treaty on Non-Proliferation of Nuclear Weapons. Final Document. Volume I Review of the Operation of the Treaty, taking into account the decisions and the resolution adopted by the 1995 Review and Extension Conference, Article VI and eighth to twelfth preambular paragraphs, paragraph 15.6. (NPT/CONF.2000/28 (Parts I and II)). This is one of the 13 "practical steps" agreed upon to implement Article VI.
http://daccess-dds-ny.un.org/doc/UNDOC/GEN/G11/605/15/PDF/G1160515.pdf?OpenElement.

Thirteen "Practical Steps for the Systematic and Progressive Efforts to Implement Article VI of the Treaty on the Non-Proliferation of Nuclear Weapons"[15]

15. The Conference agrees on the following practical steps for the systematic and progressive efforts to implement article VI of the Treaty on the Non-Proliferation of Nuclear Weapons and paragraphs 3 and 4 (c) of the 1995 Decision on "Principles and Objectives for Nuclear Non-Proliferation and Disarmament":

1. The importance and urgency of signatures and ratifications, without delay and without conditions and in accordance with constitutional processes, to achieve the early entry into force of the Comprehensive Nuclear-Test-Ban Treaty.

2. A moratorium on nuclear-weapon-test explosions or any other nuclear explosions pending entry into force of that Treaty.

3. The necessity of negotiations in the Conference on Disarmament on a non-discriminatory, multilateral and internationally and effectively verifiable treaty banning the production of fissile material for nuclear weapons or other nuclear explosive devices in accordance with the statement of the Special Coordinator in 1995 and the mandate contained therein, taking into consideration both nuclear disarmament and nuclear non-proliferation objectives. The Conference on Disarmament is urged to agree on a programme of work which includes the immediate commencement of negotiations on such a treaty with a view to their conclusion within five years.

4. The necessity of establishing in the Conference on Disarmament an appropriate subsidiary body with a mandate to deal with nuclear disarmament. The Conference on Disarmament is urged to agree on a programme of work which includes the immediate establishment of such a body.

5. The principle of irreversibility to apply to nuclear disarmament, nuclear and other related arms control and reduction measures.

6. An unequivocal undertaking by the nuclear-weapon States to accomplish the total elimination of their nuclear arsenals leading to nuclear disarmament, to which all States parties are committed under article VI.

7. The early entry into force and full implementation of START II and the conclusion of START III as soon as possible while preserving and strengthening the Treaty on the Limitation of Anti-Ballistic Missile Systems as a cornerstone of strategic stability and as a basis for further reductions of strategic offensive weapons, in accordance with its provisions.

---

15 NPT/CONF.2000/28 (Parts I and II)

8. The completion and implementation of the Trilateral Initiative between the United States of America, the Russian Federation and the International Atomic Energy Agency.

9. Steps by all the nuclear-weapon States leading to nuclear disarmament in a way that promotes international stability, and based on the principle of undiminished security for all:

   a. Further efforts by the nuclear-weapon States to reduce their nuclear arsenals unilaterally;

   b. Increased transparency by the nuclear-weapon States with regard to the nuclear weapons capabilities and the implementation of agreements pursuant to article VI and as a voluntary confidence-building measure to support further progress on nuclear disarmament;

   c. The further reduction of non-strategic nuclear weapons, based on unilateral initiatives and as an integral part of the nuclear arms reduction and disarmament process;

   d. Concrete agreed measures to further reduce the operational status of nuclear weapons systems;

   e. A diminishing role for nuclear weapons in security policies to minimize the risk that these weapons will ever be used and to facilitate the process of their total elimination;

   f. The engagement as soon as appropriate of all the nuclear-weapon States in the process leading to the total elimination of their nuclear weapons.

10. Arrangements by all nuclear-weapon States to place, as soon as practicable, fissile material designated by each of them as no longer required for military purposes under IAEA or other relevant international verification and arrangements for the disposition of such material for peaceful purposes, to ensure that such material remains permanently outside military programmes.

11. Reaffirmation that the ultimate objective of the efforts of States in the disarmament process is general and complete disarmament under effective international control.

12. Regular reports, within the framework of the strengthened review process for the Non-Proliferation Treaty, by all States parties on the implementation of article VI and paragraph 4 (c) of the 1995 Decision on "Principles and Objectives for Nuclear Non-Proliferation and Disarmament", and recalling the advisory opinion of the International Court of Justice of 8 July 1996.

13. The further development of the verification capabilities that will be required to provide assurance of compliance with nuclear disarmament agreements for the achievement and maintenance of a nuclear-weapon-free.

B.3 2010 NPT Review Conference

"Conclusions and Recommendations for Follow-on Action"[16]

I. Nuclear Disarmament

In pursuit of the full, effective and urgent implementation of article VI of the Treaty on the Non-Proliferation of Nuclear Weapons and paragraphs 3 and 4 (c) of the 1995 decision entitled "Principles and objectives for nuclear non-proliferation and disarmament", and building upon the practical steps agreed to in the Final Document of the 2000 Review Conference of the Parties to the Treaty on the Non-Proliferation of Nuclear Weapons, the Conference agrees on the following action plan on nuclear disarmament which includes concrete steps for the total elimination of nuclear weapons:

A. Principles and objectives

i.   The Conference resolves to seek a safer world for all and to achieve the peace and security of a world without nuclear weapons, in accordance with the objectives of the Treaty.

ii.   The Conference reaffirms the unequivocal undertaking of the nuclear-weapon States to accomplish the total elimination of their nuclear arsenals leading to nuclear disarmament, to which all States parties are committed under article VI.

iii.   The Conference reaffirms the continued validity of the practical steps agreed to in the Final Document of the 2000 Review Conference.

iv.   The Conference reaffirms that significant steps by all the nuclear-weapon States leading to nuclear disarmament should promote international stability, peace and security, and be based on the principle of increased and undiminished security for all.

v.   The Conference expresses its deep concern at the catastrophic humanitarian consequences of any use of nuclear weapons and reaffirms the need for all States at all times to comply with applicable international law, including international humanitarian law.

vi.   The Conference affirms the vital importance of universality of the Treaty on the Non-Proliferation of Nuclear Weapons and calls on all States not parties to the Treaty to accede as non-nuclear-weapon States to the Treaty promptly and without any conditions and to commit to achieving the complete elimination of

---

16   NPT/CONF.2010/50 (Vol. I)
http://www.un.org/ga/search/view_doc.asp?symbol=NPT/CONF.2010/50%20%28VOL.I%29

all nuclear weapons, and calls upon States to promote universal adherence to the Treaty and not to undertake any actions that can negatively affect prospects for the universality of the Treaty.

The Conference resolves that:

- **Action 1**: All States parties commit to pursue policies that are fully compatible with the Treaty and the objective of achieving a world without nuclear weapons.

- **Action 2**: All States parties commit to apply the principles of irreversibility, verifiability and transparency in relation to the implementation of their treaty obligations.

B. Disarmament of nuclear weapons

i. The Conference reaffirms the urgent need for the nuclear-weapon States to implement the steps leading to nuclear disarmament agreed to in the Final Document of the 2000 Review Conference, in a way that promotes international stability, peace and security, and based on the principle of undiminished and increased security for all.

ii. The Conference affirms the need for the nuclear-weapon States to reduce and eliminate all types of their nuclear weapons and encourages, in particular, those States with the largest nuclear arsenals to lead efforts in this regard. iii. The Conference calls on all nuclear-weapon States to undertake concrete disarmament efforts and affirms that all States need to make special efforts to establish the necessary framework to achieve and maintain a world without nuclear weapons. The Conference notes the five-point proposal for nuclear disarmament of the Secretary-General of the United Nations, which proposes, inter alia, consideration of negotiations on a nuclear weapons convention or agreement on a framework of separate mutually reinforcing instruments, backed by a strong system of verification. iv. The Conference recognizes the legitimate interests of non-nuclear-weapon States in the constraining by the nuclear-weapon States of the development and qualitative improvement of nuclear weapons and ending the development of advanced new types of nuclear weapons.

The Conference resolves that:

- **Action 3**: In implementing the unequivocal undertaking by the nuclear-weapon States to accomplish the total elimination of their nuclear arsenals, the nuclear weapon States commit to undertake further efforts to reduce and ultimately eliminate all types of nuclear weapons, deployed and non-deployed, including through unilateral, bilateral, regional and multilateral measures.

- **Action 4**: The Russian Federation and the United States of America commit to seek the early entry into force and full implementation of the Treaty on

Measures for the Further Reduction and Limitation of Strategic Offensive Arms and are encouraged to continue discussions on follow-on measures in order to achieve deeper reductions in their nuclear arsenals.

- **Action 5**: The nuclear-weapon States commit to accelerate concrete progress on the steps leading to nuclear disarmament, contained in the Final Document of the 2000 Review Conference, in a way that promotes international stability, peace and undiminished and increased security. To that end, they are called upon to promptly engage with a view to, inter alia:

    (a)   Rapidly moving towards an overall reduction in the global stockpile of all types of nuclear weapons, as identified in action 3;

    (b)   Address the question of all nuclear weapons regardless of their type or their location as an integral part of the general nuclear disarmament process;

    (c)   To further diminish the role and significance of nuclear weapons in all military and security concepts, doctrines and policies;

    (d)   Discuss policies that could prevent the use of nuclear weapons and eventually lead to their elimination, lessen the danger of nuclear war and contribute to the non-proliferation and disarmament of nuclear weapons;

    (e)   Consider the legitimate interest of non-nuclear-weapon States in further reducing the operational status of nuclear weapons systems in ways that promote international stability and security;

    (f)   Reduce the risk of accidental use of nuclear weapons; and

    (g)   Further enhance transparency and increase mutual confidence

The nuclear-weapon States are called upon to report the above undertakings to the Preparatory Committee at 2014. The 2015 Review Conference will take stock and consider the next steps for the full implementation of article VI.

- **Action 6**: All States agree that the Conference on Disarmament should immediately establish a subsidiary body to deal with nuclear disarmament, within the context of an agreed, comprehensive and balanced programme of work.

C. Security assurances

   i.   The Conference reaffirms and recognizes that the total elimination of nuclear weapons is the only absolute guarantee against the use or threat of use of nuclear weapons and the legitimate interest of non-nuclear-weapon States in receiving unequivocal and legally binding security assurances from nuclear-weapon States which could strengthen the nuclear non-proliferation regime.

ii.   The Conference recalls United Nations Security Council resolution 984 (1995) noting the unilateral statements by each of the nuclear-weapon States, in which they give conditional or unconditional security assurances against the use and the threat of use of nuclear weapons to non-nuclear-weapon States parties to the Treaty and the relevant protocols established pursuant to nuclear-weapon-free zones, recognizing that the treaty-based security assurances are available to such zones.

Without prejudice to efforts within the Treaty on the Non-Proliferation of Nuclear Weapons, the Conference resolves that:

•   **Action 7**: All States agree that the Conference on Disarmament should, within the context of an agreed, comprehensive and balanced programme of work, immediately begin discussion of effective international arrangements to assure non-nuclear-weapon States against the use or threat of use of nuclear weapons, to discuss substantively, without limitation, with a view to elaborating recommendations dealing with all aspects of this issue, not excluding an internationally legally binding instrument. The Review Conference invites the Secretary-General of the United Nations to convene a high-level meeting in September 2010 in support of the work of the Conference on Disarmament.

•   **Action 8**: All nuclear-weapon States commit to fully respect their existing commitments with regard to security assurances. Those nuclear-weapon States that have not yet done so are encouraged to extend security assurances to non-nuclear-weapon States parties to the Treaty.

•   **Action 9**: The establishment of further nuclear-weapon-free zones, where appropriate, on the basis of arrangements freely arrived at among States of the region concerned, and in accordance with the 1999 Guidelines of the United Nations Disarmament Commission, is encouraged. All concerned States are encouraged to ratify the nuclear-weapon-free zone treaties and their relevant protocols, and to constructively consult and cooperate to bring about the entry into force of the relevant legally binding protocols of all such nuclear-weapon free zones treaties, which include negative security assurances. The concerned States are encouraged to review any related reservations.

D. Nuclear testing

i.   The Conference recognizes that the cessation of all nuclear test explosions and all other nuclear explosions, by cons training the development and qualitative improvement of nuclear weapons and ending the development of advanced new types of nuclear weapons, constitutes an effective measure of nuclear disarmament and non-proliferation in all its aspects.

ii.   The Conference reaffirms the vital importance of the entry into force of the Comprehensive Nuclear-Test-Ban Treaty as a core element of the international nuclear disarmament and non-proliferation regime, as well as the determination of the nuclear-weapon States to abide by their respective moratoriums on nuclear test explosions pending the entry into force of the Comprehensive Nuclear-Test-Ban Treaty.

The Conference resolves that:

- **Action 10**: All nuclear-weapon States undertake to ratify the Comprehensive Nuclear-Test-Ban Treaty with all expediency, noting that positive decisions by nuclear-weapon States would have the beneficial impact towards the ratification of that Treaty, and that nuclear-weapon States have the special responsibility to encourage Annex 2 countries, in particular those which have not acceded to the Treaty on the Non-Proliferation of Nuclear Weapons and continue to operate unsafeguarded nuclear facilities, to sign and ratify.

- **Action 11**: Pending the entry into force of the Comprehensive Nuclear-Test-Ban Treaty, all States commit to refrain from nuclear-weapon test explosions or any other nuclear explosions, the use of new nuclear weapons technologies and from any action that would defeat the object and purpose of that Treaty, and all existing moratoriums on nuclear-weapon test explosions should be maintained.

- **Action 12**: All States that have ratified the Comprehensive Nuclear-Test-Ban Treaty recognize the contribution of the conferences on facilitating the entry into force of that Treaty and of the measures adopted by consensus at the Sixth Conference on Facilitating the Entry into Force of the Comprehensive Nuclear-Test-Ban Treaty, held in September 2009, and commit to report at the 2011 Conference on progress made towards the urgent entry into force of that Treaty.

- **Action 13**: All States that have ratified the Comprehensive Nuclear-Test-Ban Treaty undertake to promote the entry into force and implementation of that Treaty at the national, regional and global levels.

- **Action 14**: The Preparatory Commission for the Comprehensive Nuclear-Test-Ban Treaty Organization is to be encouraged to fully develop the verification regime for the Comprehensive Nuclear-Test-Ban Treaty, including early completion and provisional operationalization of the international monitoring system in accordance with the mandate of the Preparatory Commission, which should, upon entry into force of that Treaty, serve as an effective, reliable, participatory and non-discriminatory verification system with global reach, and provide assurance of compliance with that Treaty.

E. Fissile materials

i.   The Conference reaffirms the urgent necessity of negotiating and bringing to a conclusion a non-discriminatory, multilateral and internationally and effectively verifiable treaty banning the production of fissile material for nuclear weapons or other nuclear explosive devices.

The Conference resolves that:

- **Action 15**: All States agree that the Conference on Disarmament should, within the context of an agreed, comprehensive and balanced programme of work, immediately begin negotiation of a treaty banning the production of fissile material for use in nuclear weapons or other nuclear explosive devices in accordance with the report of the Special Coordinator of 1995 (CD/1299) and the mandate contained therein. Also in this respect, the Review Conference invites the Secretary-General of the United Nations to convene a high-level meeting in September 2010 in support of the work of the Conference on Disarmament.

- **Action 16**: The nuclear-weapon States are encouraged to commit to declare, as appropriate, to the International Atomic Energy Agency (IAEA) all fissile material designated by each of them as no longer required for military purposes and to place such material as soon as practicable under IAEA or other relevant international verification and arrangements for the disposition of such material for peaceful purposes, to ensure that such material remains permanently outside military programmes.

- **Action 17**: In the context of action 16, all States are encouraged to support the development of appropriate legally binding verification arrangements, within the context of IAEA, to ensure the irreversible removal of fissile material designated by each nuclear-weapon State as no longer required for military purposes.

- **Action 18**: All States that have not yet done so are encouraged to initiate a process towards the dismantling or conversion for peaceful uses of facilities for the production of fissile material for use in nuclear weapons or other nuclear explosive devices.

F. Other measures in support of nuclear disarmament

i.   The Conference recognizes that nuclear disarmament and achieving the peace and security of a world without nuclear weapons will require openness and cooperation, and affirms the importance of enhanced confidence through increased transparency and effective verification.

The Conference resolves that:

- **Action 19**: All States agree on the importance of supporting cooperation among Governments, the United Nations, other international and regional organizations and civil society aimed at increasing confidence, improving transparency and developing efficient verification capabilities related to nuclear disarmament.

- **Action 20**: States parties should submit regular reports, within the framework of the strengthened review process for the Treaty, on the implementation of the present action plan, as well as of article VI, paragraph 4 (c), of the 1995 decision entitled "Principles and objectives for nuclear non-proliferation and disarmament", and the practical steps agreed to in the Final Document of the 2000 Review Conference, and recalling the advisory opinion of the International Court of Justice of 8 July 1996.

- **Action 21**: As a confidence-building measure, all the nuclear-weapon States are encouraged to agree as soon as possible on a standard reporting form and to determine appropriate reporting intervals for the purpose of voluntarily providing standard information without prejudice to national security. The Secretary-General of the United Nations is invited to establish a publicly accessible repository, which shall include the information provided by the nuclear-weapon States.

- **Action 22**: All States are encouraged to implement the recommendations contained in the report of the Secretary-General of the United Nations (A/57/124) regarding the United Nations study on disarmament and non-proliferation education, in order to advance the goals of the Treaty in support of achieving a world without nuclear weapons.

II. Nuclear non-proliferation

The Conference recalls and reaffirms the decision of the 1995 Review and Extension Conference entitled "Principles and objectives for nuclear non-proliferation and disarmament", noting paragraph 1 of the principles and the elements relevant to article III of the Treaty, in particular paragraphs 9 to 13 and 17 to 19, and to article VII, in particular paragraphs 5 to 7. It also recalls and reaffirms the Resolution on the Middle East adopted at that Conference. The Conference also recalls and reaffirms the outcome of the 2000 Review Conference.

- **Action 23**: The Conference calls upon all States parties to exert all efforts to promote universal adherence to the Treaty, and not to undertake any actions that can negatively affect prospects for the universality of the Treaty.

- **Action 24**: The Conference re-endorses the call by previous review conferences for the application of IAEA comprehensive safeguards to all source or special fissionable material in all peaceful nuclear activities in the States parties in accordance with the provisions of article III of the Treaty.

- **Action 25**: The Conference, noting that 18 States parties to the Treaty have yet to bring into force comprehensive safeguards agreements, urges them to do so as soon as possible and without further delay.

- **Action 26**: The Conference underscores the importance in complying with the non-proliferation obligations, addressing all compliance matters in order to uphold the Treaty's integrity and the authority of the safeguards system.

- **Action 27**: The Conference underscores the importance of resolving all cases of non-compliance with safeguards obligations in full conformity with the IAEA statute and the respective legal obligations of Member States. In this regard, the Conference calls upon Member States to extend their cooperation to the Agency.

- **Action 28**: The Conference encourages all States parties which have not yet done so to conclude and to bring into force additional protocols as soon as possible and to implement them provisionally pending their entry into force.

- **Action 29**: The Conference encourages IAEA to further facilitate and assist the States parties in the conclusion and entry into force of comprehensive safeguards agreements and additional protocols. The Conference calls on States parties to consider specific measures that would promote the universalization of the comprehensive safeguards agreements.

- **Action 30**: The Conference calls for the wider application of safeguards to peaceful nuclear facilities in the nuclear-weapon States, under the relevant voluntary offer safeguards agreements, in the most economic and practical way possible, taking into account the availability of IAEA resources, and stresses that comprehensive safeguards and additional protocols should be universally applied once the complete elimination of nuclear weapons has been achieved.

- **Action 31**: The Conference encourages all States parties with small quantities protocols which have not yet done so to amend or rescind them, as appropriate, as soon as possible.

- **Action 32**: The Conference recommends that IAEA safeguards should be assessed and evaluated regularly. Decisions adopted by the IAEA policy bodies aimed at further strengthening the effectiveness and improving the efficiency of IAEA safeguards should be supported and implemented.

- **Action 33**: The Conference calls upon all States parties to ensure that IAEA continues to have all political, technical and financial support so that it is able to effectively meet its responsibility to apply safeguards as required by article III of the Treaty.

- **Action 34**: The Conference encourages States parties, within the framework of the IAEA statute, to further develop a robust, flexible, adaptive and cost effective international technology base for advanced safeguards through cooperation among Member States and with IAEA.

- **Action 35**: The Conference urges all States parties to ensure that their nuclear related exports do not directly or indirectly assist the development of nuclear weapons or other nuclear explosive devices and that such exports are in full conformity with the objectives and purposes of the Treaty as stipulated, particularly, in articles I, II and III of the Treaty, as well as the decision on principles and objectives of nuclear non-proliferation and disarmament adopted in 1995 by the Review and extension Conference.

- **Action 36**: The Conference encourages States parties to make use of multilaterally negotiated and agreed guidelines and understandings in developing their own national export controls.

- **Action 37**: The Conference encourages States parties to consider whether a recipient State has brought into force IAEA safeguards obligations in making nuclear export decisions.

- **Action 38**: The Conference calls upon all States parties, in acting in pursuance of the objectives of the Treaty, to observe the legitimate right of all States parties, in particular developing States, to full access to nuclear material, equipment and technological information for peaceful purposes.

- **Action 39**: States parties are encouraged to facilitate transfers of nuclear technology and materials and international cooperation among States parties, in conformity with articles I, II, III and IV of the Treaty, and to eliminate in this regard any undue constraints inconsistent with the Treaty.

- **Action 40**: The Conference encourages all States to maintain the highest possible standards of security and physical protection of nuclear materials and facilities.

- **Action 41**: The Conference encourages all States parties to apply, as appropriate, the IAEA recommendations on the physical protection of nuclear material and nuclear facilities (INFCIRC/225/Rev.4 (Corrected)) and other relevant international instruments at the earliest possible date.

- **Action 42**: The Conference calls on all States parties to the Convention on the Physical Protection of Nuclear Material to ratify the amendment to the Convention as soon as possible and encourages them to act in accordance with the objectives and the purpose of the amendment until such time as it enters into force. The Conference also encourages all States that have not yet done so to adhere to the Convention and adopt the amendment as soon as possible.

- **Action 43**: The Conference urges all States parties to implement the principles of the revised IAEA Code of Conduct on the Safety and Security of Radioactive Sources, as well as the Guidance on the Import and Export of Radioactive Sources approved by the IAEA Board of Governors in 2004.

- **Action 44**: The Conference calls upon all States parties to improve their national capabilities to detect, deter and disrupt illicit trafficking in nuclear materials throughout their territories, in accordance with their relevant international legal obligations, and calls upon those States parties in a position to do so to work to enhance international partnerships and capacity-building in this regard. The Conference also calls upon States parties to establish and enforce effective domestic controls to prevent the proliferation of nuclear weapons in accordance with their relevant international legal obligations.

- **Action 45**: The Conference encourages all States parties that have not yet done so to become party to the International Convention for the Suppression of Acts of Nuclear Terrorism as soon as possible.

- **Action 46**: The Conference encourages IAEA to continue to assist the States parties in strengthening their national regulatory controls of nuclear material, including the establishment and maintenance of the State systems of accounting for and control of nuclear material, as well as systems on regional level. The Conference calls upon IAEA Member States to broaden their support for the relevant IAEA programmes.

III. Peaceful uses of nuclear energy

The Conference reaffirms that the Treaty fosters the development of the peaceful uses of nuclear energy by providing a framework of confidence and cooperation within which those uses can take place. The Conference calls upon States parties to act in conformity with all the provisions of the Treaty and to:

- **Action 47**: Respect each country's choices and decisions in the field of peaceful uses of nuclear energy without jeopardizing its policies or international cooperation agreements and arrangements for peaceful uses of nuclear energy and its fuel cycle policies.

- **Action 48**: Undertake to facilitate, and reaffirm the right of States parties to participate in, the fullest possible exchange of equipment, materials and scientific and technological information for the peaceful uses of nuclear energy.

- **Action 49**: Cooperate with other States parties or international organizations in the further development of nuclear energy for peaceful purposes, with due consideration for the needs of the developing areas of the world.

- **Action 50**: Give preferential treatment to the non-nuclear-weapon States parties to the Treaty, taking the needs of developing countries, in particular, into account.

- **Action 51**: Facilitate transfers of nuclear technology and international cooperation among States parties in conformity with articles I, II, III, and IV of the Treaty, and eliminate in this regard any undue constraints inconsistent with the Treaty.

- **Action 52**: Continue efforts, within IAEA, to enhance the effectiveness and efficiency of its technical cooperation programme.

- **Action 53**: Strengthen the IAEA technical cooperation programme in assisting developing States parties in the peaceful uses of nuclear energy.

- **Action 54**: Make every effort and to take practical steps to ensure that IAEA resources for technical cooperation activities are sufficient, assured and predictable.

- **Action 55**: Encourage all States in a position to do so to make additional contributions to the initiative designed to raise 100 million dollars over the next five years as extrabudgetary contributions to IAEA activities, while welcoming the contributions already pledged by countries and groups of countries in support of IAEA activities.

- **Action 56**: Encourage national, bilateral and international efforts to train the necessary skilled workforce needed to develop peaceful uses of nuclear energy.

- **Action 57**: Ensure that, when developing nuclear energy, including nuclear power, the use of nuclear energy must be accompanied by commitments to and ongoing implementation of safeguards as well as appropriate and effective levels of safety and security, consistent with States' national legislation and respective international obligations.

- **Action 58**: Continue to discuss further, in a non-discriminatory and transparent manner under the auspices of IAEA or regional forums, the development of multilateral approaches to the nuclear fuel cycle, including the possibilities of creating mechanisms for assurance of nuclear fuel supply, as well as possible schemes dealing with the back-end of the fuel cycle without affecting rights under the Treaty and without prejudice to national fuel cycle policies, while tackling the technical, legal and economic complexities surrounding these issues, including, in this regard, the requirement of IAEA full scope safeguards.

- **Action 59**: Consider becoming party, if they have not yet done so, to the Convention on Nuclear Safety, the Convention on Early Notification of a Nuclear Accident, the Convention on Assistance in the Case of a Nuclear Accident or Radiological Emergency, the Joint Convention on the Safety of Spent Fuel Management and on the Safety of Radioactive Waste Management, the International Convention for the Suppression of Acts of Nuclear Terrorism, the Convention on the Physical Protection of Nuclear Material, and to ratify its amendment so that it may enter into force at an early date.

- **Action 60**: Promote the sharing of best practices in the area of nuclear safety and security, including through dialogue with the nuclear industry and the private sector, as appropriate.

- **Action 61**: Encourage States concerned, on a voluntary basis, to further minimize highly enriched uranium in civilian stocks and use, where technically and economically feasible.

- **Action 62**: Transport radioactive materials consistent with relevant international standards of safety, security and environmental protection, and to continue communication between shipping and coastal States for the purpose of confidence-building and addressing concerns regarding transport safety, security and emergency preparedness.

- **Action 63**: Put in force a civil nuclear liability regime by becoming party to relevant international instruments or adopting suitable national legislation, based upon the principles established by the main pertinent international instruments.

- **Action 64**: The Conference calls upon all States to abide by the decision adopted by consensus at the IAEA General Conference on 18 September 2009 on prohibition of armed attack or threat of attack against nuclear installations, during operation or under construction.

IV. The Middle East, particularly implementation of the 1995 Resolution on the Middle East

1. The Conference reaffirms the importance of the Resolution on the Middle East adopted by the 1995 Review and Extension Conference and recalls the

affirmation of its goals and objectives by the 2000 Review Conference of the Parties to the Treaty on the Non-Proliferation of Nuclear Weapons. The Conference stresses that the resolution remains valid until the goals and objectives are achieved. The resolution, which was co-sponsored by the depositary States of the Treaty on the Non-Proliferation of Nuclear Weapons (the Russian Federation, the United Kingdom of Great Britain and Northern Ireland and the United States of America), is an essential element of the outcome of the 1995 Conference and of the basis on which the Treaty was indefinitely extended without a vote in 1995. States parties renew their resolve to undertake, individually and collectively, all necessary measures aimed at its prompt implementation.

2. The Conference reaffirms its endorsement of the aims and objectives of the Middle East peace process, and recognizes that efforts in this regard, as well as other efforts, contribute to, inter alia, a Middle East zone free of nuclear weapons as well as other weapons of mass destruction.

3. The Conference takes note of the reaffirmation at the 2010 Review Conference by the five nuclear-weapon States of their commitment to a full implementation of the 1995 Resolution on the Middle East.

4. The Conference regrets that little pr ogress has been achieved towards the implementation of the 1995 Resolution on the Middle East. 5. The Conference recalls the reaffirmation by the 2000 Review Conference of the importance of Israel's accession to the Treaty and the placement of all its nuclear facilities under comprehensive IAEA safe guards. The Conference reaffirms the urgency and importance of achieving universality of the Treaty. The Conference calls on all States in the Middle East that have not yet done so to accede to the Treaty as non-nuclear-weapon States so as to achieve its universality at an early date.

6. The Conference stresses the necessity of strict adherence by all States parties to their obligations and commitments under the Treaty. The Conference urges all States in the region to take relevant steps and confidence-building measures to contribute to the realization of the objectives of the 1995 Resolution on the Middle East and calls upon all States to refrain from undertaking any measures that preclude the achievement of this objective.

7. The Conference emphasizes the importance of a process leading to full implementation of the 1995 Resolution on the Middle East. To that end, the Conference endorses the following practical steps:

(a) The Secretary-General of the United Nations and the co-sponsors of the 1995 Resolution, in consultation with the States of the region, will convene a conference in 2012, to be attended by all States of the Middle East, on the establishment of a Middle East zone free of nuclear weapons and all other weapons of mass destruction, on the basis of arrangements freely arrived at by the States of the region, and with the full support and engagement of the nuclear-weapon States. The 2012 Conference shall take as its terms of reference the 1995 Resolution;

(b) Appointment by the Secretary-General of the United Nations and the co-sponsors of the 1995 Resolution, in consultation with the States of the region, of a facilitator, with a mandate to support implementation of the 1995 Resolution by conducting consultations with the States of the region in that regard and undertaking preparations for the convening of the 2012 Conference. The facilitator will also assist in implementation of follow-on step s agreed by the participating regional States at the 2012 Conference. The facilitator will report to the 2015 Review Conference and its Preparatory Committee meetings;

(c) Designation by the Secretary-General of the United Nations and the co-sponsors of the 1995 Resolution, in consultation with the States of the region, of a host Government for the 2012 Conference;

(d) Additional steps aimed at supporting the implementation of the 1995 Resolution, including that IAEA, the Organisation for the Prohibition of Chemical Weapons and other relevant international organizations be requested to prepare background documentation for the 2012 Conference regarding modalities for a zone free of nuclear weapons and other weapons of mass destruction and their delivery systems, taking into account work previously undertaken and experience gained;

(e) Consideration of all offers aimed at supporting the implementation of the 1995 Resolution, including the offer of the European Union to host a follow-on seminar to that organized in June 2008. 8. The Conference emphasizes the requirement of maintaining parallel progress, in substance and timing, in the process leading to achieving total and complete elimination of all weapons of mass destruction in the region, nuclear, chemical and biological.

9. The Conference reaffirms that all States parties to the Treaty, particularly the nuclear-weapon States and the States in the region, should continue to report on steps taken to implement the 1995 Resolution, through the United Nations Secretariat, to the President of the 2015 Review Conference, as well as to the Chairperson of the Preparatory Committee meetings to be held in advance of that Conference.

10. The Conference further recognizes the important role played by civil society in contributing to the implementation of the 1995 Resolution and encourages all efforts in this regard.

B.4. Negative and Positive Security Assurances

Background

During the negotiation of the NPT, it was clear that five states were to be designated as nuclear-weapon states and allowed under the NPT to retain their nuclear weapons. The states to be designated as non-nuclear-weapon states were keenly aware of the discriminatory outcome to be created by the Treaty, with haves and have-nots. Non-nuclear-weapon states took the view that the nuclear-weapon states should pledge not to attack them with nuclear weapons in exchange for their obligations to eschew nuclear weapons. Despite the efforts of non-nuclear-weapon states to do so, a negative security assurance was not included in the NPT.

During the 1968 United Nations debate on the NPT, concern by a number of states led the Security Council to adopt Resolution 255. Resolution 255 addresses not only negative security assurances but also positive security assurances, i.e., assurances that if an attack or threat of attack with nuclear weapons occurs, action would be taken to assist the victim. The Resolution "welcomes" the intention of "certain states" to provide or support immediate assistance in the event of an attack or threat of attack; no specific action was identified.

In 1978 at the United Nations General Assembly Special Session on Disarmament, the United States presented the first U.S. Presidential statement on negative security assurances. This statement, reaffirmed by subsequent Presidents, gave assurances that the United States would not use nuclear weapons against any non-nuclear-weapon state with a binding legal commitment not to acquire nuclear weapons, except in cases in which such a non-nuclear-weapon state was assisting a nuclear-weapon state or was associated with a nuclear-weapon state in an attack on the United States or its allies.

The other nuclear-weapon states also made negative security assurances, but there were differences between them. For example, the negative security assurance of the Soviet Union excluded states where nuclear weapons were stationed (for example, the Federal Republic of Germany). The Chinese assurance was simple: it committed itself to "no first use" of nuclear weapons.

In the context of the 1995 NPT Review and Extension Conference, the issue of negative security assurances took on new salience. As a result, that year the United States, Britain, France, and Russia were able to agree on a common formulation that generally conforms to the U.S. 1978 statement. China retained its policy of "no first use."

Such assurances were formally recorded in United Nations Security Council documents, and on April 11, 1995, the Security Council adopted Resolution 984, which "takes note" of the statements by the nuclear-weapon states on both negative security assurances and their somewhat less specific statements on positive security assurances.

B.4.1 United Nations Security Council Resolution S/RES/984: Use of Nuclear Weapons (1995)

Resolution adopted by the Security Council at its 3514th meeting, on 11 April 1995[17]

The Security Council,

Convinced that every effort must be made to avoid and avert the danger of nuclear war, to prevent the spread of nuclear weapons, to facilitate international cooperation in the peaceful uses of nuclear energy with particular emphasis on the needs of developing countries, and reaffirming the crucial importance of the Treaty on the Non-Proliferation of Nuclear Weapons to these efforts,

Recognizing the legitimate interest of non-nuclear-weapon States Parties to the Treaty on the Non-Proliferation of Nuclear Weapons to receive security assurances,

Welcoming the fact that more than 170 States have become Parties to the Treaty on the Non-Proliferation of Nuclear Weapons and stressing the desirability of universal adherence to it, Reaffirming the need for all States Parties to the Treaty on the Non-Proliferation of Nuclear Weapons to comply fully with all their obligations,

Taking into consideration the legitimate concern of non-nuclear-weapon States that, in conjunction with their adherence to the Treaty on the Non-Proliferation of Nuclear Weapons, further appropriate measures be undertaken to safeguard their security,

Considering that the present resolution constitutes a step in this direction,

Considering further that, in accordance with the relevant provisions of the Charter of the United Nations, any aggression with the use of nuclear weapons would endanger international peace and security,

1. Takes note with appreciation of the statements made by each of the nuclear-weapon States (S/1995/261, S/1995/262, S/1995/263, S/1995/264, S/1995/265), in which they give security assurances against the use of nuclear weapons to non-nuclear-weapon States that are Parties to the Treaty on the Non-Proliferation of Nuclear Weapons;

2. Recognizes the legitimate interest of non-nuclear-weapon States Parties to the Treaty on the Non-Proliferation of Nuclear Weapons to receive assurances that the Security Council, and above all its nuclear-weapon State permanent members, will act immediately in accordance with the relevant provisions of the Charter of the United Nations, in the event that such States are the victim

---

17 http://www1.umn.edu/humanrts/resolutions/SC95/984SC95.html (March 13, 2014)

of an act of, or object of a threat of, aggression in which nuclear weapons are used;

3. Recognizes further that, in case of aggression with nuclear weapons or the threat of such aggression against a non-nuclear-weapon State Party to the Treaty on the Non-Proliferation of Nuclear Weapons, any State may bring the matter immediately to the attention of the Security Council to enable the Council to take urgent action to provide assistance, in accordance with the Charter, to the State victim of an act of, or object of a threat of, such aggression; and recognizes also that the nuclear-weapon State permanent members of the Security Council will bring the matter immediately to the attention of the Council and seek Council action to provide, in accordance with the Charter, the necessary assistance to the State victim;

4. Notes the means available to it for assisting such a non-nuclear-weapon State Party to the Treaty on the Non-Proliferation of Nuclear Weapons, including an investigation into the situation and appropriate measures to settle the dispute and restore international peace and security;

5. Invites Member States, individually or collectively, if any non-nuclear-weapon State Party to the Treaty on the Non-Proliferation of Nuclear Weapons is a victim of an act of aggression with nuclear weapons, to take appropriate measures in response to a request from the victim for technical, medical, scientific or humanitarian assistance, and affirms its readiness to consider what measures are needed in this regard in the event of such an act of aggression;

6. Expresses its intention to recommend appropriate procedures, in response to any request from a non-nuclear-weapon State Party to the Treaty on the Non-Proliferation of Nuclear Weapons that is the victim of such an act of aggression, regarding compensation under international law from the aggressor for loss, damage or injury sustained as a result of the aggression;

7. Welcomes the intention expressed by certain States that they will provide or support immediate assistance, in accordance with the Charter, to any non-nuclear-weapon State Party to the Treaty on the Non-Proliferation of Nuclear Weapons that is a victim of an act of, or an object of a threat of, aggression in which nuclear weapons are used;

8. Urges all States, as provided for in Article VI of the Treaty on the Non-Proliferation of Nuclear Weapons, to pursue negotiations in good faith on effective measures relating to nuclear disarmament and on a treaty on general and complete disarmament under strict and effective international control which remains a universal goal;

9. Reaffirms the inherent right, recognized under Article 51 of the Charter, of individual and collective self-defence if an armed attack occurs against a member of

the United Nations, until the Security Council has taken measures necessary to maintain international peace and security;

10. Underlines that the issues raised in this resolution remain of continuing concern to the Council.

B.4.2. Statements on Negative and Positive Security Assurances by China, France, Russia, the United Kingdom, and the United States

a. China 1995

From S/1995/265: Statement on security assurances issued on 5 April 1995 by the People's Republic of China.

> For the purpose of enhancing international peace, security and stability and facilitating the realization of the goal of complete prohibition and thorough destruction of nuclear weapons, China hereby declares its position on security assurances as follows:
>
> 1. China undertakes not to be the first to use nuclear weapons at any time or under any circumstances.
>
> 2. China undertakes not to use or threaten to use nuclear weapons against non-nuclear-weapon States or nuclear-weapon-free zones at any time or under any circumstances. This commitment naturally applies to non-nuclear-weapon States parties to the Treaty on the Non-Proliferation of Nuclear Weapons or non-nuclear-weapon States that have entered into any comparable internationally binding commitment not to manufacture or acquire nuclear explosive devices.
>
> 3. China has always held that, pending the complete prohibition and thorough destruction of nuclear weapons, all nuclear-weapon-States should undertake not to be the first to use nuclear weapons and not to use or threaten to use such weapons against non-nuclear-weapon States and nuclear-weapon-free zones at any time or under any circumstances. China strongly calls for the early conclusion of an international convention on no-first-use of nuclear weapons as well as an international legal instrument assuring the non-nuclear-weapon States and nuclear-weapon-free zones against the use or threat of use of nuclear weapons.
>
> 4. China, as a permanent member of the Security Council of the United Nations, undertakes to take action within the Council to ensure that the Council takes appropriate measures to provide, in accordance with the Charter of the United Nations, necessary assistance to any non-nuclear-weapon State that comes under attack with nuclear weapons, and imposes strict and effective sanctions on the attacking State. This commitment naturally applies to any non-nuclear-weapon State party to the Treaty on the Non-Proliferation of Nuclear Weapons or any non-nuclear weapon State that has entered into any comparable internationally-binding commitment not to manufacture or acquire nuclear explosive devices, in the event of an aggression with nuclear weapons or the threat of such aggression against such State.

5. The positive security assurance provided by China, as contained in paragraph 4, does not in any way compromise China's position as contained in paragraph 3 and shall not in any way be construed as endorsing the use of nuclear weapons.

b. France 1995

From S/1995/264: Statement concerning security assurances to non-nuclear-weapon States made by the Permanent Representative of France to the Conference on Disarmament on 6 April 1995.

Firstly, it reaffirms, and clarifies, the negative security assurances which it gave in 1982, specifically:

France reaffirms that it will not use nuclear weapons against non-nuclear-weapon States Parties to the Treaty on the Non-Proliferation of Nuclear Weapons, except in the case of an invasion or any other attack on France, its territory, its armed forces or other troops, or against its allies or a State towards which it has a security commitment, carried out or sustained by such a State in alliance or association with a nuclear-weapon State.

Secondly, and for the first time, France has decided to give positive security assurances to all non-nuclear-weapon States Parties to the Treaty on the Non-Proliferation of Nuclear Weapons. Its accession to the Treaty made this decision both possible and desirable. Accordingly:

"France, as a Permanent Member of the Security Council, pledges that, in the event of attack with nuclear weapons or the threat of such attack against a non-nuclear-weapon State party to the Treaty on the Non-proliferation of Nuclear Weapons, France will immediately inform the Security Council and act within the Council to ensure that the latter takes immediate steps to provide, in accordance with the Charter, necessary assistance to any State which is the victim of such an act or threat of aggression.

c. Russian Federation 1995

From S/1995/261: Statement of the Ministry of Foreign Affairs of the Russian Federation 5 April 1995.

In the event of aggression involving the use of nuclear weapons or the threat of such aggression against a non-nuclear-weapon State party to the Treaty on the Non-Proliferation of Nuclear Weapons, the nuclear Powers which are permanent members of the Security Council will immediately bring the matter to the attention of the Council and will seek to ensure that they provide, in accordance with the Charter, necessary assistance to the State that is a victim of such an act of aggression or that is threatened by such aggression.

Russian Federation will not use nuclear weapons against non-nuclear-weapon States parties to the Treaty on the Non-Proliferation of Nuclear Weapons, except in the case of an invasion or any other attack on the Russian Federation, its territory, its armed forces or other troops, its allies or on a State towards which it has a security commitment, carried out or sustained by such a non-nuclear-weapon State in association or alliance with a nuclear-weapon State.

d. United Kingdom 1995

From S/1995/262: United Kingdom of Great Britain and Northern Ireland declaration on security assurances made in the plenary session of the Conference on Disarmament on 6 April 1995 by Sir Michael Weston, United Kingdom Permanent Representative to the Conference on Disarmament in Geneva.

Recognising the continued concern of non-nuclear-weapon States Parties to the Treaty on the Non-Proliferation of Nuclear Weapons that the assurances given by nuclear-weapon States should be in similar terms, and following consultation with the other nuclear-weapon States, I accordingly give the following undertaking on behalf of my Government:

The United Kingdom will not use nuclear weapons against non-nuclear-weapon States Parties to the Treaty on the Non-Proliferation of Nuclear Weapons except in the case of an invasion or any other attack on the United Kingdom, its dependent territories, its armed forces or other troops, its allies or on a State towards which it has a security commitment, carried out or sustained by such a non-nuclear-weapon State in association or alliance with a nuclear-weapon State.

In giving this assurance the United Kingdom emphasises the need not only for universal adherence to, but also for compliance with, the Treaty on the Non-Proliferation of Nuclear Weapons. In this context, I wish to make clear that Her Majesty's Government does not regard its assurance as applicable if any beneficiary is in material breach of its own non-proliferation obligations under the Treaty on the Non-Proliferation of Nuclear Weapons.

...

I, therefore, recall and reaffirm the intention of the United Kingdom, as a Permanent Member of the United Nations Security Council, to seek immediate Security Council action to provide assistance, in accordance with the Charter, to any non-nuclear-weapon State, party to the Treaty on the Non-Proliferation of

Nuclear Weapons, that is a victim of an act of aggression or an object of a threat of aggression in which nuclear weapons are used.

e. United Kingdom 2010

Statement by John Duncan, Head of the United Kingdom Delegation, to the First Committee of the General Assembly, New York, 19 October 2010.

> We are now able to give an assurance that the UK will not use or threaten to use nuclear weapons against non-nuclear weapon states parties to the NPT. In giving this assurance, we emphasise the need for universal adherence to and compliance with the NPT, and note that this assurance would not apply to any state in material breach of those non-proliferation obligations. We also note that while there is currently no direct threat to the UK or its vital interests from states developing capabilities in other weapons of mass destruction, for example chemical and biological, we reserve the right to review this assurance if the future threat, development and proliferation of these weapons make it necessary.

f. United States 1995

From S/1995/263: Statement issued on 5 April 1995 by the Honourable Warren Christopher, Secretary of State, regarding a declaration by the President on security assurances for non-nuclear-weapon States Parties to the Treaty on the Non-Proliferation of Nuclear Weapons.

It is important that all parties to the Treaty on the Non-Proliferation of Nuclear Weapons fulfil their obligations under the Treaty. In that regard, consistent with generally recognized principles of international law, parties to the Treaty on the Non-Proliferation of Nuclear Weapons must be in compliance with these undertakings in order to be eligible for any benefits of adherence to the Treaty.

> The United States reaffirms that it will not use nuclear weapons against non-nuclear-weapon States Parties to the Treaty on the Non-Proliferation of Nuclear Weapons except in the case of an invasion or any other attack on the United States, its territories, its armed forces or other troops, its allies, or on a State towards which it has a security commitment, carried out or sustained by such a non-nuclear-weapon State in association or alliance with a nuclear-weapon State.

...

> Non-nuclear-weapon States Parties to the Treaty on the Non-Proliferation of Nuclear Weapons have a legitimate desire for assurances that the United Nations Security Council, and above all its nuclear-weapon-State permanent

members, would act immediately in accordance with the Charter, in the event such non-nuclear-weapon States are the victim of an act of, or object of a threat of, aggression in which nuclear weapons are used.

The United States affirms its intention to provide or support immediate assistance, in accordance with the Charter, to any non-nuclear-weapon State Party to the Treaty on the Non-Proliferation of Nuclear Weapons that is a victim of an act of, or an object of a threat of, aggression in which nuclear weapons are used.

g. United States 2010

Since 1995, the United States revised its "negative security assurance" several times. The most recent "negative security assurance' was announced in the Nuclear Posture Review Report issues by the U.S. Department of Defense in April 2010. As stated there:

> ... the role of U.S. nuclear weapons to deter and respond to non-nuclear attacks—conventional, biological, or chemical—has declined significantly. The United States will continue to reduce the role of nuclear weapons in deterring non-nuclear attack.

> To that end, the United States is now prepared to strengthen its long-standing "negative security assurance" by declaring that the United States will not use or threaten to use nuclear weapons against non-nuclear weapons states that are party to the Nuclear Non-Proliferation Treaty (NPT) and in compliance with their nuclear non-proliferation obligations.

> This revised assurance is intended to underscore the security benefits of adhering to and fully complying with the NPT and persuade non-nuclear weapon states party to the Treaty to work with the United States and other interested parties to adopt effective measures to strengthen the non-proliferation regime.

> In making this strengthened assurance, the United States affirms that any state eligible for the assurance that uses CBW against the United States or its allies and partners would face the prospect of a devastating conventional military response—and that any individuals responsible for the attack, whether national leaders or military commanders, would be held fully accountable. Given the catastrophic potential of biological weapons and the rapid pace of biotechnology development, the United States reserves the right to make any adjustment in the assurance that may be warranted by the evolution and proliferation of the biological weapons threat and U.S. capacities to counter that threat.

> In the case of countries not covered by this assurance – states that possess nuclear weapons and states not in compliance with their nuclear non-proliferation obligations – there remains a narrow range of contingencies in which U.S. nuclear weapons may still play a role in deterring a conventional or CBW attack against

the United States or its allies and partners. The United States is therefore not prepared at the present time to adopt a universal policy that the "sole purpose" of U.S. nuclear weapons is to deter nuclear attack on the United States and our allies and partners, but will work to establish conditions under which such a policy could be safely adopted.

Yet this does not mean that our willingness to use nuclear weapons against countries not covered by the new assurance has in any way increased. Indeed, the United States wishes to stress that it would only consider the use of nuclear weapons in extreme circumstances to defend the vital interests of the United States or its allies and partners.

B.4.3. Nuclear- Weapon Free Zones and Negative Security Assurances

Negative security assurances are not necessarily legally binding. The five NPT nuclear-weapon states differ on the character of their individual statements. For example, the United States considers its statement to be politically but not legally binding, while the United Kingdom considers its to be legally binding.

On the other hand, nuclear-weapon free zone treaties (NWFZ) contain provisions that, when in force, obligate nuclear-weapon states not to threaten or use nuclear weapons against parties to the NWFZ. Each NWFZ includes a Protocol to this effect. The status of these commitments as of March 2013 is:[18]

a. Treaty for the Prohibition of Nuclear Weapons in Latin America (Tlatelolco Treaty)

Opened for signature: February 14, 1967
Entered into force: October 23, 2002
Thirty-three States-parties:

Antigua and Barbuda, Argentina, Bahamas, Barbados, Belize, Bolivia, Brazil, Chile, Colombia, Costa Rica, Cuba, Dominica, Dominican Republic, Ecuador, El Salvador, Grenada, Guatemala, Guyana, Haiti, Honduras, Jamaica, Mexico, Nicaragua, Panama, Paraguay, Peru, Saint Kitts and Nevis, Saint Lucia, Saint Vincent and Grenadines, Suriname, Trinidad and Tobago, Uruguay, and Venezuela.

Protocol ratification by nuclear-weapon states:

Text: Additional Protocol II, Article 3:

The Governments represented by the undersigned Plenipotentiaries also undertake not to use or threaten to use nuclear weapons against the

---

18 The text of these treaties (and others) and their status may be found in the "Disarmament Treaties" database of the UN Office of Disarmament affairs at http://www.un.org/disarmament/

Contracting Parties of the Treaty for the Prohibition of Nuclear Weapons in Latin America

Ratified by China, France, the United Kingdom, the United States, and the Soviet Union.

b. South Pacific Nuclear Free Zone Treaty (Treaty of Rarotonga)

Opened for signature: August 6, 1985
Entered into force: December 11, 1986
Thirteen States-parties:

Australia, Cook Islands, Fiji, Kiribati, Nauru, New Zealand, Niue, Papua New Guinea, Samoa, Solomon Islands, Tonga, Tuvalu, and Vanuatu.

Protocol ratification by nuclear-weapon states:

Text Protocol II, Article 1:

Each Party undertakes not to use or threaten to use any nuclear explosive device against:

(a)   Parties to the Treaty; or
(b)   Any territory within the South Pacific Nuclear Free Zone for which a State that has become a Party to Protocol 1 is internationally responsible.

Protocol II (negative security assurances) ratified by China, France, the United Kingdom, and the Soviet Union.

c. Southeast Asia Nuclear Weapon-Free-Zone Treaty (Treaty of Bangkok)

Opened for signature: December 15, 1995
Entered into force: March 27, 1997
Ten State-parties:

Brunei Darussalam, Cambodia, Indonesia, Laos, Malaysia, Myanmar, Philippines, Singapore, Thailand, and Vietnam.

Protocol ratification by nuclear-weapon states:
Text, Protocol, Article 2:

Each State Party undertakes not to use or threaten to use nuclear weapons against any State Party to the Treaty. It further undertakes not to use or threaten to use nuclear weapons within the Southeast Asia Nuclear Weapon-Free Zone.

Protocol has not been ratified by any nuclear-weapon state.

d. African Nuclear Weapon Free Zone Treaty (Treaty of Pelindaba)

Opened for signature: April 11, 1996
Entered into force: July 15, 2009
Thirty-seven States-parties:

Algeria, Benin, Botswana, Burkina Faso, Burundi, Cameroon, Chad, Comoros, Congo, Cote d'Ivoire, Equatorial Guinea, Ethiopia, Gabon, Gambia, Ghana, Guinea, Guinea-Bissau, Kenya, Lesotho, Libyan Arab Jamahiriya, Madagascar, Malawi, Mali, Mauritania, Mauritius, Mozambique, Namibia, Nigeria, Rwanda, Senegal, South Africa, Swaziland, Togo, Tunisia, United Republic of Tanzania, Zambia, and Zimbabwe. (Signatories that have not ratified the treaty are: Angola, Cape Verde, Central African Republic, Democratic Republic of Congo, Djibouti, Egypt, Eritrea, Liberia, Niger, Rwanda, Sao Tome & Principe, Seychelles, Sierra Leone, Somalia, Sudan, and Uganda.)

Protocol ratification by nuclear-weapon states:

Text, Protocol I, Article 1:

Each Protocol Party undertakes not to use or threaten to use a nuclear explosive device against:

(a)   Any Party to the Treaty; or
(b)   Any territory within the African nuclear-weapon-free zone for which a State that has become a Party to Protocol III is internationally responsible as defined in annex I.

Ratified by China, France, Russia, and the United Kingdom.

e. Central Asian Nuclear-Weapon-Free Zone Treaty

Opened for signature: September 8, 2006
Entered into force: March 21, 2009
Five States-parties: Kazakhstan, Kyrgyzstan, Tajikistan, Turkmenistan and Uzbekistan.

Protocol ratification by nuclear-weapon states:

Text, Protocol, Article 1:

Negative Security Assurances: Each Party to this Protocol undertakes not to use or threaten to use a nuclear weapon or other nuclear explosive device against any Party to the Treaty.

The Protocol has not been ratified by any nuclear-weapon state.

SECTION II

NUCLEAR SAFEGUARDS

A. ATOMS FOR PEACE

Background

After WWII, efforts to create an international control regime failed. Nuclear programs were enveloped in secrecy. In the United States, for example, the Atomic Energy Act of 1946 defined and gave to the Atomic Energy Commission the authority to control "restricted data," which included all information on the production of fissionable material or the manufacture or use of atomic weapons. Penalties for transferring such data with the intent to injure the United States were, and remain, severe: life in prison or death.[19] The dissemination of scientific and technical information relating to atomic energy was encouraged. However, cooperation with other countries "with respect to the use of atomic energy for industrial purposes" was prohibited "until Congress declares by joint resolution that effective and enforceable international safeguards against the use of atomic energy for destructive purposes have been established."[20]

In 1953, President Dwight Eisenhower took office and construction began in Britain on the Calder Hall reactor, which would be the world's first nuclear reactor to deliver power in commercial quantities. (The Calder Hall reactor began operations in 1956.)[21] This made concrete the view expressed in 1946 that peaceful uses of nuclear energy represented a plausible dream.

On December 8, 1953 President Eisenhower addressed the United Nations General Assembly. Referring to its resolution of the previous month calling for "the Powers principally involved" to seek a solution to the armaments race, President Eisenhower said that the United States was prepared to engage in such discussions and in doing so would introduce a "new conception," known as "Atoms for Peace." An international atomic energy agency would be established. To this agency, governments would contribute "normal uranium and fissionable material," and the agency would be responsible for storage and protection of the fissionable materials that had been contributed. More importantly, the agency would be responsible for devising and promoting the peaceful uses of nuclear energy.

---

19   Atomic Energy Act of 1946. Public Law 585, 79th Congress. http://www.osti.gov/atomicenergyact.pdf. Section 10(b)(2).

20   Atomic Energy Act of 1946. Public Law 585, 79th Congress. http://www.osti.gov/atomicenergyact.pdf. Sections 10(a)(1) and (2).

21   The first reactor connected to an electrical supply grid went into operation in 1954 at Obninsk in the Soviet Union. It produced about 5 MW of electricity, relatively small compared to the 60 MW of the Calder hall reactor.

Eisenhower's proposal was sketchy, but it was enough to generate serious discussions that led in 1957 to the creation of the International Atomic Energy Agency.

However, in the United States international cooperation would not be possible until the restrictive provisions of the Atomic Energy Act of 1946 were removed. The Atomic Energy Act of 1954 did so.[22]

It called for both "the development and utilization of atomic energy for peaceful purposes" and "a program of international cooperation … to make available … the benefits of peaceful uses of atomic energy." To ensure that nuclear cooperation was not turned to military use, the Act required guarantees by recipient countries that it would be used only for peaceful purposes. The Act also required that the cooperation be under safeguards to ensure compliance with these guarantees. The Act did not, however, require pledges by recipients not to acquire nuclear weapons through their own means.

---

22 For complete text, see NUREG-0980 at http://www.nrc.gov/reading-rm/doc-collections/nuregs/staff/sr0980/

Atoms for Peace: Address by Dwight D. Eisenhower, President of the United States of America

(Given to the 470th Plenary Meeting of the United Nations General Assembly on Tuesday, 8 December 1953)[23]

Madame President, Members of the General Assembly:

When Secretary General Hammarskjold's invitation to address this General Assembly reached me in Bermuda, I was just beginning a series of conferences with the Prime Ministers and Foreign Ministers of Great Britain and of France. Our subject was some of the problems that beset our world.

During the remainder of the Bermuda Conference, I had constantly in mind that ahead of me lay a great honor. That honor is mine today as I stand here, privileged to address the General Assembly of the United Nations.

At the same time that I appreciate the distinction of addressing you, I have a sense of exhilaration as I look upon this assembly.

Never before in history has so much hope for so many people been gathered together in a single organization. Your deliberations and decisions during these somber years have already realized part of those hopes.

But the great tests and the great accomplishments still lie ahead. And in the confident expectation of those accomplishments, I would use the office which, for the time being, I hold, to assure you that the Government of the United States will remain steadfast in its support of this body. This we shall do in the conviction that you will provide a great share of the wisdom of the courage and the faith which can bring to this world lasting peace for all nations and happiness and well-being for all men.

Clearly, it would not be fitting for me to take this occasion to present to you a unilateral American report on Bermuda. Nevertheless, I assure you that in our deliberations on that lovely island we sought to invoke those same great concepts of universal peace and human dignity which are so cleanly etched in your Charter. Neither would it be a measure of this great opportunity merely to recite, however hopefully, pious platitudes.

I therefore decided that this occasion warranted my saying to you some of the things that have been on the minds and hearts of my legislative and executive associates and on mine for a great many months – thoughts I had originally planned to say primarily to the American people.

---

23 Atoms for Peace, Address given by Dwight D. Eisenhower before the General Assembly of the United Nations on Peaceful Uses of Atomic Energy, New York City, December 8, 1953. http://www.eisenhower. archives.gov/research/online_documents/atoms_for_peace.html.

I know that the American people share my deep belief that if a danger exists in the world, it is a danger shared by all - and equally, that if hope exists in the mind of one nation, that hope should be shared by all.

Finally, if there is to be advanced any proposal designed to ease, even by the smallest measure, the tensions of today's world, what more appropriate audience could there be than the members of the General Assembly of the United Nations.

I feel impelled to speak today in a language that, in a sense, is new - one, which I, who have spent so much of my life in the military profession, would have preferred never to use.

That new language is the language of atomic warfare.

The atomic age has moved forward at such a pace that every citizen of the world should have some comprehension, at least in comparative terms, of the extent of this development, of the utmost significance to every one of us. Clearly if the peoples of the world are to conduct an intelligent search for peace, they must be armed with the significant facts of today's existence.

My recital of atomic danger and power is necessarily stated in United States terms, for these are the only incontrovertible facts that I know. I need hardly point out to this assembly, however, that this subject is global, not merely national in character.

On July 16, 1945, the United States set off the world's first atomic test explosion.

Since that date in 1945, the United States has conducted forty-two test explosions.

Atomic bombs today are more than twenty five times as powerful as the weapons with which the atomic age dawned, while hydrogen weapons are in the ranges of millions of tons of TNT equivalent.

Today the United States' stockpile of atomic weapons, which, of course, increase daily, exceeds by many times the explosive equivalent of the total of all bombs and all shells that came from every plane and every gun in every theatre of war through all the years of World War II.

A single air group, whether afloat or land based, can now deliver to any reachable target a destructive cargo exceeding in power all the bombs that fell on Britain in all of World War II.

In size and variety the development of atomic weapons has been no less remarkable. This development has been such that atomic weapons have virtually achieved conventional status within our armed services. In the United States services, the Army, the Navy, the Air Force and the Marine Corps are all capable of putting this weapon to military use.

But the dread secret and the fearful engines of atomic might are not ours alone. In the first place, the secret is possessed by our friends and Allies, Great Britain and Canada, whose scientific genius made a tremendous contribution to our original discoveries and the designs of atomic bombs.

The secret is also known by the Soviet Union.

The Soviet Union has informed us that, over recent years, it has devoted extensive resources to atomic weapons. During this period, the Soviet Union has exploded a series of atomic devices, including at least one involving thermonuclear reactions.

If at one time the United States possessed what might have been called a monopoly of atomic power, that monopoly ceased to exist several years ago. Therefore, although our earlier start has permitted us to accumulate what is today a great quantitative advantage, the atomic realities of today comprehend two facts of even greater significance.

First, the knowledge now possessed by several nations will eventually be shared by others, possibly all others.

Second, even a vast superiority in numbers of weapons, and a consequent capability of devastating retaliation, is no preventive, of itself, against the fearful material damage and toll of human lives that would be inflicted by surprise aggression.

The free world, at least dimly aware of these facts, has naturally embarked on a large program of warning and defense systems. That program will be accelerated and expanded.

But let no one think that the expenditure of vast sums for weapons and systems of defense can guarantee absolute safety for the cities and the citizens of any nation.

The awful arithmetic of the atomic bomb does not permit of such an easy solution.

Even against the most powerful defense, an aggressor in possession of the effective minimum number of atomic bombs for a surprise attack could probably place a sufficient number of his bombs on the chosen targets to cause hideous damage.

Should such an atomic attack be launched against the United States, our reaction would be swift and resolute. But for me to say that the defense capabilities of the United States are such that they could inflict terrible losses upon an aggressor - for me to say that the retaliation capabilities of the United States are so great that such an aggressor's land would be laid waste - all this, while fact, is not the true expression of the purpose and the hope of the United States.

To pause there would be to confirm the hopeless finality of a belief that two atomic colossi are doomed malevolently to eye each other indefinitely across a trembling world.

To stop there would be to accept helplessly the probability of civilization destroyed - the annihilation of the irreplaceable heritage of mankind handed down to us generation from generation - and the condemnation of mankind to begin all over again the age old struggle upward from savagery toward decency and right and justice.

8 December 1953 Atoms for Peace

Surely no sane member of the human race could discover victory in such desolation. Could anyone wish his name to be coupled by history with such human degradation and destruction?

Occasional pages of history do record the faces of the "Great Destroyers" but the whole book of history reveals mankind's never-ending quest for peace and mankind's God-given capacity to build.

It is with the book of history, and not with isolated pages, that the United States will ever wish to be identified. My country wants to be constructive, not destructive.

It wants agreements, not wars, among nations. It wants, itself, to live in freedom and in the confidence that the people of every other nation enjoy equally the right of choosing their own way of life.

So my country's purpose is to help us move out of the dark chamber of horrors into the light, to find a way by which the minds of men, the hopes of men, the souls of men everywhere, can move forward toward peace and happiness and well-being. In this quest, I know that we must not lack patience.

I know that in a world divided, such as ours today, salvation cannot be attained by one dramatic act.

I know that many steps will have to be taken over many months before the world can look at itself one day and truly realize that a new climate of mutually peaceful confidence is abroad in the world.

But I know, above all else, that we must start to take these steps - now.

The United States and its Allies, Great Britain and France, have, over the past months, tried to take some of these steps. Let no one say that we shun the conference table.

On the record has long stood the request of the United States, Great Britain and France, to negotiate with the Soviet Union the problems of a divided Germany. On that record has long stood the request of the same three nations to negotiate an Austrian peace treaty.

On the same record still stands the request of the United Nations to negotiate the problems of Korea. Most recently, we have received from the Soviet Union what is in effect an expression of willingness to hold a four-power meeting.

Along with our Allies, Great Britain and France, we were pleased to see that this note did not contain the unacceptable preconditions previously put forward.

As you already know from our joint Bermuda communiqué, the United States, Great Britain and France have agreed promptly to meet with the Soviet Union. The Government of the United States approaches this conference with hopeful sincerity. We will bend every effort of our minds to the single purpose of emerging from that conference with tangible results toward peace - the only true way of lessening international tension.

We never have, we never will, propose or suggest that the Soviet Union surrender what is rightfully theirs. We will never say that the peoples of Russia are an enemy with whom we have no desire ever to deal or mingle in friendly and fruitful relationship.

On the contrary, we hope that this coming conference may initiate a relationship with the Soviet Union which will eventually bring about a free intermingling of the peoples of the East and of the West - the one sure, human way of developing the understanding required for confident and peaceful relations.

Instead of the discontent which is now setting upon Eastern Germany, occupied Austria and the countries of Eastern Europe, we seek a harmonious family of free European nations, with none a threat to the other, and least of all a threat to the peoples of Russia. Beyond the turmoil and strife and misery of Asia, we seek peaceful opportunity for these peoples to develop their natural resources and to elevate their lot.

These are not idle words of shallow vision. Behind them lies a story of nations lately come to independence, not as a result of war but through free grant or peaceful negotiation. There is a record already written of assistance gladly given by nations of the West to needy peoples and to those suffering the temporary effects of famine, drought and natural disaster.

These are deeds of peace. They speak more loudly than promises or protestations of peaceful intent.

But I do not wish to rest either upon the reiteration of past proposals or the restatement of past deeds. The gravity of the time is such that every new avenue of peace, no matter how dimly discernible, should be explored.

There is at least one new avenue of peace which has not yet been well explored - an avenue now laid out by the General Assembly of the United Nations.

In its resolution of Nov. 18, 1953, this General Assembly suggested-and I quote - "that the Disarmament Commission study the desirability of establishing a subcommittee consisting of representatives of the powers principally involved, which should seek, in private, an acceptable solution - and report such a solution to the General Assembly and to the Security Council not later than 1 September, 1954."

The United States, heeding the suggestion of the General Assembly of the United Nations, is instantly prepared to meet privately with such other countries as may be "principally involved," to seek "an acceptable solution" to the atomic armaments race which overshadows not only the peace but the very life of the world.

We shall carry into these private or diplomatic talks a new conception. The United States would seek more than the mere reduction or elimination of atomic materials for military purposes. It is not enough to take this weapon out of the hands of the soldiers.

It must be put into the hands of those who will know how to strip its military casing and adapt it to the arts of peace.

The United States knows that if the fearful trend of atomic military build-up can be reversed, this greatest of destructive forces can be developed into a great boon for the benefit of all mankind.

The United States knows that peaceful power from atomic energy is no dream of the future. That capability, already proved, is here now - today. Who can doubt, if the entire body of the world's scientists and engineers had adequate amounts of fissionable material with which to test and develop their ideas, that this capability would rapidly be transformed into universal, efficient and economic usage?

To hasten the day when fear of the atom will begin to disappear from the minds of people and the governments of the East and West there are certain steps that can be taken now.

I therefore make the following proposals:

The governments principally involved to the extent permitted by elementary prudence, to begin now and continue to make joint contributions from their stockpiles of normal uranium and fissionable materials to an international atomic energy agency. We would expect that such an agency would be set up under the aegis of the United Nations.

The ratios of contributions, the procedures and other details would properly be within the scope of the "private conversations" I have referred to earlier.

The United States is prepared to undertake these explorations in good faith. Any partner of the United States acting in the same good faith will find the United States a not unreasonable or ungenerous associate.

Undoubtedly initial and early contributions to this plan would be small in quantity. However, the proposal has the great virtue that it can be undertaken without irritations and mutual suspicions incident to any attempt to set up a completely acceptable system of world-wide inspection and control.

The Atomic Energy Agency could be made responsible for the impounding, storage and protection of the contributed fissionable and other materials. The ingenuity of our scientists will provide special, safe conditions under which such a bank of fissionable material can be made essentially immune to surprise seizure.

The more important responsibility of this atomic energy agency would be to devise methods whereby this fissionable material would be allocated to serve the peaceful pursuits of mankind. Experts would be mobilized to apply atomic energy to the needs of agriculture, medicine and other peaceful activities. A special purpose would be to provide abundant electrical energy in the power-starved areas of the world. Thus the contributing powers would be dedicating some of their strength to serve the needs rather than the fears of mankind.

The United States would be more than willing - it would be proud - to take up with others "principally involved" the development of plans whereby such peaceful use of atomic energy would be expedited.

Of those "principally involved" the Soviet Union must of course, be one. I would be prepared to submit to the Congress of the United States, and with every expectation of approval, any such plan that would:

First, encourage world-wide investigation into the most effective peacetime uses of fissionable material; and with the certainty that they had all the material needed for the conduct of all experiments that were appropriate;

Second, begin to diminish the potential destructive power of the world's atomic stockpiles;

Third, allow all peoples of all nations to see that, in this enlightened age, the great powers of the earth, both of the East and of the West, are interested in human aspirations first rather than in building up the armaments of war;

Fourth, open up a new channel for peaceful discussion and initiate at least a new approach to the many difficult problems that must be solved in both private and public conversations if the world is to shake off the inertia imposed by fear and is to make positive progress toward peace.

Against the dark background of the atomic bomb, the United States does not wish merely to present strength, but also the desire and the hope for peace. The coming months will be fraught with fateful decisions. In this Assembly, in the capitals and military headquarters of the world; in the hearts of men everywhere, be they governed or governors, may they be the decisions which will lead this world out of fear and into peace.

To the making of these fateful decisions, the United States pledges before you - and therefore before the world - its determination to help solve the fearful atomic dilemma - to devote its entire heart and mind to find the way by which the miraculous inventiveness of man shall not be dedicated to his death, but consecrated to his life.

I again thank the delegates for the great honor they have done me in inviting me to appear before them and in listening to me so courteously.

Thank you.

Statute of the International Atomic Energy Agency
(As amended through 1989)[24]

---

24 The IAEA Statute entered into force in July 1957.

ARTICLE XXIII: Authentic texts and certified copies

ANNEX: Preparatory Commission[25]

STATUTE

ARTICLE I: Establishment of the Agency

The Parties hereto establish an International Atomic Energy Agency (hereinafter referred to as "the Agency") upon the terms and conditions hereinafter set forth.

ARTICLE II: Objectives

The Agency shall seek to accelerate and enlarge the contribution of atomic energy to peace, health and prosperity throughout the world. It shall ensure, so far as it is able, that assistance provided by it or at its request or under its supervision or control is not used in such a way as to further any military purpose.

ARTICLE III: Functions

A. The Agency is authorized:

    1. To encourage and assist research on, and development and practical application of, atomic energy for peaceful uses throughout the world; and, if requested to do so, to act as an intermediary for the purposes of securing the performance of services or the supplying of materials, equipment, or facilities by one member of the Agency for another; and to perform any operation or service useful in research on, or development or practical application of, atomic energy for peaceful purposes;

---

25 The IAEA General Conference has approved two amendments to the Statute of the IAEA. One is to amend Article VI of the Statute in order to increase the size of the Board from its present membership of 35 to 43. The General Conference approved it in 1999 in Resolution GC(43)/RES/19. As of July 2013, 55 Member Sates had accepted the Amendment. The second is to amend Article XIV.A of the Statute so as to is to permit the establishment of biennial, rather than annual, budgeting. The General Conference approved it in 1999 in Resolution GC(43/RES/8. As of July 2013 52 Member States had informed the IEA of their acceptance of this amendment. Amendments enter into force when two-thirds of the membership of the IAEA accepts them. As of February 2014, the number of Member States was 162, of which 2/3 is 108 Member States. It should be noted that even if the amendment to Article VI enters into force, it will not take effect, by its own terms, until the IAEA "General Conference confirms a list of all Member States of the Agency which has been adopted by the Board, in both cases by ninety per cent of those present and voting, whereby each Member State is allocated to one of [geographic areas contained Article VI.] This may be difficult to achieve since it would require states in the Middle East to agree that Israel is part of the area Middle East and South Asia.

2. To make provision, in accordance with this Statute, for materials, services, equipment, and facilities to meet the needs of research on, and development and practical application of, atomic energy for peaceful purposes, including the production of electric power, with due consideration for the needs of the under-developed areas of the world;

3. To foster the exchange of scientific and technical information on peaceful uses of atomic energy;

4. To encourage the exchange of training of scientists and experts in the field of peaceful uses of atomic energy;

5. To establish and administer safeguards designed to ensure that special fissionable and other materials, services, equipment, facilities, and information made available by the Agency or at its request or under its supervision or control are not used in such a way as to further any military purpose; and to apply safeguards, at the request of the parties, to any bilateral or multilateral arrangement, or at the request of a State, to any of that State's activities in the field of atomic energy;

6. To establish or adopt, in consultation and, where appropriate, in collaboration with the competent organs of the United Nations and with the specialized agencies concerned, standards of safety for protection of health and minimization of danger to life and property (including such standards for labour conditions), and to provide for the application of these standards to its own operation as well as to the operations making use of materials, services, equipment, facilities, and information made available by the Agency or at its request or under its control or supervision; and to provide for the application of these standards, at the request of the parties, to operations under any bilateral or multilateral arrangements, or, at the request of a State, to any of that State's activities in the field of atomic energy;

7. To acquire or establish any facilities, plant and equipment useful in carrying out its authorized functions, whenever the facilities, plant, and equipment otherwise available to it in the area concerned are inadequate or available only on terms it deems unsatisfactory.

B. In carrying out its functions, the Agency shall:

1. Conduct its activities in accordance with the purposes and principles of the United Nations to promote peace and international co-operation, and in conformity with policies of the United Nations furthering the establishment of safeguarded worldwide disarmament and in conformity with any international agreements entered into pursuant to such policies;

2. Establish control over the use of special fissionable materials received by the Agency, in order to ensure that these materials are used only for peaceful purposes;

3. Allocate its resources in such a manner as to secure efficient utilization and the greatest possible general benefit in all areas of the world, bearing in mind the special needs of the under- developed areas of the world;

4. Submit reports on its activities annually to the General Assembly of the United Nations and, when appropriate, to the Security Council: if in connection with the activities of the Agency there should arise questions that are within the competence of the Security Council, the Agency shall notify the Security Council, as the organ bearing the main responsibility for the maintenance of international peace and security, and may also take the measures open to it under this Statute, including those provided in paragraph C of Article XII;

5. Submit reports to the Economic and Social Council and other organs of the United Nations on matters within the competence of these organs.

C. In carrying out its functions, the Agency shall not make assistance to members subject to any political, economic, military, or other conditions incompatible with the provisions of this Statute.

D. Subject to the provisions of this Statute and to the terms of agreements concluded between a State or a group of States and the Agency which shall be in accordance with the provisions of the Statute, the activities of the Agency shall be carried out with due observance of the sovereign rights of States.

ARTICLE IV: Membership

A. The initial members of the Agency shall be those States Members of the United Nations or of any of the specialized agencies which shall have signed this Statute within ninety days after it is opened for signature and shall have deposited an instrument of ratification.

B. Other members of the Agency shall be those States, whether or not Members of the United Nations or of any of the specialized agencies, which deposit an instrument of acceptance of this Statute after their membership has been approved by the General Conference upon the recommendation of the Board of Governors. In recommending and approving a State for membership, the Board of Governors and the General Conference shall determine that the State is able and willing to carry out the obligations of membership in the Agency, giving due consideration to its ability and willingness to act in accordance with the purposes and principles of the Charter of the United Nations.

C.   The Agency is based on the principle of the sovereign equality of all its members, and all members, in order to ensure to all of them the rights and benefits resulting from membership, shall fulfill in good faith the obligation assumed by them in accordance with this Statute.

ARTICLE V: General Conference

A.   A General Conference consisting of representatives of all members shall meet in regular annual session and in such special sessions as shall be convened by the Director General at the request of the Board of Governors or of a majority of members. The sessions shall take place at the headquarters of the Agency unless otherwise determined by the General Conference.

B.   At such sessions, each member shall be represented by one delegate who may be accompanied by alternates and by advisers. The cost of attendance of any delegation shall be borne by the member concerned.

C.   The General Conference shall elect a President and such other officers as may be required at the beginning of each session. They shall hold office for the duration of the session. The General Conference, subject to the provisions of this Statute, shall adopt its own rules of procedure. Each member shall have one vote. Decisions pursuant to paragraph H of article XIV, paragraph C of article XVIII and paragraph B of article XIX shall be made by a two-thirds majority of the members present and voting. Decisions on other questions, including the determination of additional questions or categories of questions to be decided by a two-thirds majority, shall be made by a majority of the members present and voting. A majority of members shall constitute a quorum.

D.   The General Conference may discuss any questions or any matters within the scope of this Statute or relating to the powers and functions of any organs provided for in this Statute, and may make recommendations to the membership of the Agency or to the Board of Governors or to both on any such questions or matters.

E.   The General Conference shall:

  1.   Elect members of the Board of Governors in accordance with article VI;

  2.   Approve States for membership in accordance with article IV;

  3.   Suspend a member from the privileges and rights of membership in accordance with article XIX;

  4.   Consider the annual report of the Board;

5.   In accordance with article XIV, approve the budget of the Agency recommended by the Board or return it with recommendations as to its entirety or parts to the Board, for resubmission to the General Conference;

6.   Approve reports to be submitted to the United Nations as required by the relationship agreement between the Agency and the United Nations, except reports referred to in paragraph C of article XII, or return them to the Board with its recommendations;

7.   Approve any agreement or agreements between the Agency and the United Nations and other organizations as provided in article XVI or return such agreements with its recommendations to the Board, for resubmission to the General Conference;

8.   Approve rules and limitations regarding the exercise of borrowing powers by the Board, in accordance with paragraph G of article XIV; approve rules regarding the acceptance of voluntary contributions to the Agency; and approve, in accordance with paragraph F of article XIV, the manner in which the general fund referred to in that paragraph may be used;

9.   Approve amendments to this Statute in accordance with paragraph C of article XVIII;

10.   Approve the appointment of the Director General in accordance with paragraph A of article VII.

F.   The General Conference shall have the authority:

1.   To take decisions on any matter specifically referred to the General Conference for this purpose by the Board;

2.   To propose matters for consideration by the Board and request from the Board reports on any matter relating to the functions of the Agency.

ARTICLE VI.   Board of Governors

A.   The Board of Governors shall be composed as follows:

1.   The outgoing Board of Governors shall designate for membership on the Board the ten members most advanced in the technology of atomic energy including the production of source materials, and the member most advanced in the technology of atomic energy including the production of source materials in each of the following areas in which none of the aforesaid ten is located:

1.   North America

2.   Latin America

3.   Western Europe

4.   Eastern Europe

5.   Africa

6.   Middle East and South Asia

7.   South East Asia and the Pacific

8.   Far East.

2.   The General Conference shall elect to membership of the Board of Governors:

(a)   Twenty members, with due regard to equitable representation on the Board as a whole of the members in the areas listed in sub-paragraph A. 1 of this article, so that the Board shall at all times include in this category five representatives of the area of Latin America, four representatives of the area of Western Europe, three representatives of the area of Eastern Europe, four representatives of the area of Africa, two representatives of the area of the Middle East and South Asia, one representative of the area of South East Asia and the Pacific, and one representative of the area of the Far East. No member in this category in any one term of office will be eligible for re-election in the same category for the following term of office; and

(b)   One further member from among the members in the following areas:

Middle East and South Asia,
South East Asia and the Pacific,
Far East;

(c)   One further member from among the members in the following areas:

Africa,
Middle East and South Asia,
South East Asia and the Pacific.

B. The designations provided for in sub-paragraph A-1 of this article shall take place not less than sixty days before each regular annual session of the General Conference. The elections provided for in sub-paragraph A-2 of this article shall take place at regular annual sessions of the General Conference.

C. Members represented on the Board of Governors in accordance with sub-paragraph A-1 of this article shall hold office from the end of the next regular annual session of the General Conference after their designation until the end of the following regular annual session of the General Conference.

D. Members represented on the Board of Governors in accordance with sub-paragraph A-2 of this article shall hold office from the end of the regular annual session of the General Conference at which they are elected until the end of the second regular annual session of the General Conference thereafter.

E. Each member of the Board of Governors shall have one vote. Decisions on the amount of the Agency's budget shall be made by a two-thirds majority of those present and voting, as provided in paragraph H of article XIV. Decisions on other questions, including the determination of additional questions or categories of questions to be decided by a two-thirds majority, shall be made by a majority of those present and voting. Two-thirds of all members of the Board shall constitute a quorum.

F. The Board of Governors shall have authority to carry out the functions of the Agency in accordance with this Statute, subject to its responsibilities to the General Conference as provided in this Statute.

G. The Board of Governors shall meet at such times as it may determine. The meetings shall take place at the headquarters of the Agency unless otherwise determined by the Board.

H. The Board of Governors shall elect a Chairman and other officers from among its members and, subject to the provisions of this Statute, shall adopt its own rules of procedure.

I. The Board of Governors may establish such committees as it deems advisable. The Board may appoint persons to represent it in its relations with other organizations.

J. The Board of Governors shall prepare an annual report to the General Conference concerning the affairs of the Agency and any projects approved by the Agency. The Board shall also prepare for submission to the General Conference such reports as the Agency is or may be required to make to the United Nations or to any other organization the work of which is related to that of the Agency. These reports, along with the annual reports, shall be submitted to members of the Agency at least one month before the regular annual session of the General Conference.

ARTICLE VII: Staff

A.   The staff of the Agency shall be headed by a Director General. The Director General shall be appointed by the Board of Governors with the approval of the General Conference for a term of four years. He shall be the chief administrative officer of the Agency.

B.   The Director General shall be responsible for the appointment, organization, and functioning of the staff and shall be under the authority of and subject to the control of the Board of Governors. He shall perform his duties in accordance with regulations adopted by the Board.

C.   The staff shall include such qualified scientific and technical and other personnel as may be required to fulfill the objectives and functions of the Agency. The Agency shall be guided by the principle that its permanent staff shall be kept to a minimum.

D.   The paramount consideration in the recruitment and employment of the staff and in the determination of the conditions of service shall be to secure employees of the highest standards of efficiency, technical competence, and integrity. Subject to this consideration, due regard shall be paid to the contributions of members to the Agency and to the importance of recruiting the staff on as wide a geographical basis as possible.

E.   The terms and conditions on which the staff shall be appointed, remunerated, and dismissed shall be in accordance with regulations made by the Board of Governors, subject to the provisions of this Statute and to general rules approved by the General Conference on the recommendation of the Board.

F.   In the performance of their duties, the Director General and the staff shall not seek or receive instructions from any source external to the Agency. They shall refrain from any action which might reflect on their position as officials of the Agency; subject to their responsibilities to the Agency, they shall not disclose any industrial secret or other confidential information coming to their knowledge by reason of their official duties for the Agency. Each member undertakes to respect the international character of the responsibilities of the Director General and the staff and shall not seek to influence them in the discharge of their duties.

G.   In this article the term "staff" includes guards.

ARTICLE VIII: Exchange of information

A.   Each member should make available such information as would, in the judgement of the member, be helpful to the Agency.

B.   Each member shall make available to the Agency all scientific information developed as a result of assistance extended by the Agency pursuant to article XI.

C.   The Agency shall assemble and make available in an accessible form the information made available to it under paragraphs A and B of this article. It shall take positive steps to encourage the exchange among its members of information relating to the nature and peaceful uses of atomic energy and shall serve as an intermediary among its members for this purpose.

ARTICLE IX: Supplying of materials

A.   Members may make available to the Agency such quantities of special fissionable materials as they deem advisable and on such terms as shall be agreed with the Agency. The materials made available to the Agency may, at the discretion of the member making them available, be stored either by the member concerned or, with the agreement of the Agency, in the Agency's depots.

B.   Members may also make available to the Agency source materials as defined in article XX and other materials. The Board of Governors shall determine the quantities of such materials which the Agency will accept under agreements provided for in article XIII.

C.   Each member shall notify the Agency of the quantities, form, and composition of special fissionable materials, source materials, and other materials which that member is prepared, in conformity with its laws, to make available immediately or during a period specified by the Board of Governors.

D.   On request of the Agency a member shall, from the materials which it has made available, without delay deliver to another member or group of members such quantities of such materials as the Agency may specify, and shall without delay deliver to the Agency itself such quantities of such materials as are really necessary for operations and scientific research in the facilities of the Agency.

E.   The quantities, form and composition of materials made available by any member may be changed at any time by the member with the approval of the Board of Governors.

F.   An initial notification in accordance with paragraph C of this article shall be made within three months of the entry into force of this Statute with respect to the member concerned. In the absence of a contrary decision of the Board of Governors, the materials initially made available shall be for the period of the calendar year succeeding the year when this Statute takes effect with respect to the member concerned. Subsequent notifications shall likewise, in the absence of a contrary action by the Board, relate to the period of the calendar year following the notification and shall be made no later than the first day of November of each year.

G. The Agency shall specify the place and method of delivery and, where appropriate, the form and composition, of materials which it has requested a member to deliver from the amounts which that member has notified the Agency it is prepared to make available. The Agency shall also verify the quantities of materials delivered and shall report those quantities periodically to the members.

H. The Agency shall be responsible for storing and protecting materials in its possession. The Agency shall ensure that these materials shall be safeguarded against

   1. hazards of the weather,

   2. unauthorized removal or diversion,

   3. damage or destruction, including sabotage, and

   4. forcible seizure. In storing special fissionable materials in its possession, the Agency shall ensure the geographical distribution of these materials in such a way as not to allow concentration of large amounts of such materials in any one country or region of the world.

I. The Agency shall as soon as practicable establish or acquire such of the following as may be necessary:

   1. Plant, equipment, and facilities for the receipt, storage, and issue of materials;

   2. Physical safeguards;

   3. Adequate health and safety measures;

   4. Control laboratories for the analysis and verification of materials received;

   5. Housing and administrative facilities for any staff required for the foregoing.

J. The materials made available pursuant to this article shall be used as determined by the Board of Governors in accordance with the provisions of this Statute. No member shall have the right to require that the materials it makes available to the Agency be kept separately by the Agency or to designate the specific project in which they must be used.

ARTICLE X: Services, equipment, and facilities

Members may make available to the Agency services, equipment, and facilities which may be of assistance in fulfilling the Agency's objectives and functions.

ARTICLE XI: Agency projects

A.   Any member or group of members of the Agency desiring to set up any project for research on, or development or practical application of, atomic energy for peaceful purposes may request the assistance of the Agency in securing special fissionable and other materials, services, equipment, and facilities necessary for this purpose. Any such request shall be accompanied by an explanation of the purpose and extent of the project and shall be considered by the Board of Governors.

B.   Upon request, the Agency may also assist any member or group of members to make arrangements to secure necessary financing from outside sources to carry out such projects. In extending this assistance, the Agency will not be required to provide any guarantees or to assume any financial responsibility for the project.

C.   The Agency may arrange for the supplying of any materials, services, equipment, and facilities necessary for the project by one or more members or may itself undertake to provide any or all of these directly, taking into consideration the wishes of the member or members making the request.

D.   For the purpose of considering the request, the Agency may send into the territory of the member or group of members making the request a person or persons qualified to examine the project. For this purpose the Agency may, with the approval of the member or group of members making the request, use members of its own staff or employ suitably qualified nationals of any member.

E.   Before approving a project under this article, the Board of Governors shall give due consideration to:

    1.   The usefulness of the project, including its scientific and technical feasibility;

    2.   The adequacy of plans, funds, and technical personnel to assure the effective execution of the project;

    3.   The adequacy of proposed health and safety standards for handling and storing materials and for operating facilities;

    4.   The inability of the member or group of members making the request to secure the necessary finances, materials, facilities, equipment, and services;

5.   The equitable distribution of materials and other resources available to the Agency;

6.   The special needs of the under-developed areas of the world; and

7.   Such other matters as may be relevant.

F.   Upon approving a project, the Agency shall enter into an agreement with the member or group of members submitting the project, which agreement shall:

1.   Provide for allocation to the project of any required special fissionable or other materials;

2.   Provide for transfer of special fissionable materials from their then place of custody, whether the materials be in the custody of the Agency or of the member making them available for use in Agency projects, to the member or group of members submitting the project, under conditions which ensure the safety of any shipment required and meet applicable health and safety standards;

3.   Set forth the terms and conditions, including charges, on which any materials, services, equipment, and facilities are to be provided by the Agency itself, and, if any such materials, services, equipment, and facilities are to be provided by a member, the terms and conditions as arranged for by the member or group of members submitting the project and the supplying member;

4.   Include undertakings by the member or group of members submitting the project: (a) that the assistance provided shall not be used in such a way as to further any military purpose; and (b) that the project shall be subject to the safeguards provided for in article XII, the relevant safeguards being specified in the agreement;

5.   Make appropriate provision regarding the rights and interests of the Agency and the member or members concerned in any inventions or discoveries, or any patents therein, arising from the project;

6.   Make appropriate provision regarding settlement of disputes;

7.   Include such other provisions as may be appropriate.

G.   The provisions of this article shall also apply where appropriate to a request for materials, services, facilities, or equipment in connection with an existing project.

ARTICLE XII: Agency safeguards

A.   With respect to any Agency project, or other arrangement where the Agency is requested by the parties concerned to apply safeguards, the Agency shall have the following rights and responsibilities to the extent relevant to the project or arrangement:

1.   To examine the design of specialized equipment and facilities, including nuclear reactors, and to approve it only from the view-point of assuring that it will not further any military purpose, that it complies with applicable health and safety standards, and that it will permit effective application of the safeguards provided for in this article;

2.   To require the observance of any health and safety measures prescribed by the Agency;

3.   To require the maintenance and production of operating records to assist in ensuring accountability for source and special fissionable materials used or produced in the project or arrangement;

4.   To call for and receive progress reports;

5.   To approve the means to be used for the chemical processing of irradiated materials solely to ensure that this chemical processing will not lend itself to diversion of materials for military purposes and will comply with applicable health and safety standards; to require that special fissionable materials recovered or produced as a by-product be used for peaceful purposes under continuing Agency safeguards for research or in reactors, existing or under construction, specified by the member or members concerned; and to require deposit with the Agency of any excess of any special fissionable materials recovered or produced as a by-product over what is needed for the above-stated uses in order to prevent stockpiling of these materials, provided that thereafter at the request of the member or members concerned special fissionable materials so deposited with the Agency shall be returned promptly to the member or members concerned for use under the same provisions as stated above.

6.   To send into the territory of the recipient State or States inspectors, designated by the Agency after consultation with the State or States concerned, who shall have access at all times to all places and data and to any person who by reason of his occupation deals with materials, equipment, or facilities which are required by this Statute to be safeguarded, as necessary to account for source and special fissionable materials supplied and fissionable products and to determine whether there is compliance with the undertaking against use in furtherance of any military purpose referred to in sub-paragraph F-4 of article XI, with the health

and safety measures referred to in sub-paragraph A-2 of this article, and with any other conditions prescribed in the agreement between the Agency and the State or States concerned. Inspectors designated by the Agency shall be accompanied by representatives of the authorities of the State concerned, if that State so requests, provided that the inspectors shall not thereby be delayed or otherwise impeded in the exercise of their functions;

7. In the event of non-compliance and failure by the recipient State or States to take requested corrective steps within a reasonable time, to suspend or terminate assistance and withdraw any materials and equipment made available by the Agency or a member in furtherance of the project.

B. The Agency shall, as necessary, establish a staff of inspectors. The Staff of inspectors shall have the responsibility of examining all operations conducted by the Agency itself to determine whether the Agency is complying with the health and safety measures prescribed by it for application to projects subject to its approval, supervision or control, and whether the Agency is taking adequate measures to prevent the source and special fissionable materials in its custody or used or produced in its own operations from being used in furtherance of any military purpose. The Agency shall take remedial action forthwith to correct any non-compliance or failure to take adequate measures.

C. The staff of inspectors shall also have the responsibility of obtaining and verifying the accounting referred to in sub paragraph A-6 of this article and of determining whether there is compliance with the undertaking referred to in sub paragraph F-4 of article XI, with the measures referred to in sub-paragraph A-2 of this article, and with all other conditions of the project prescribed in the agreement between the Agency and the State or States concerned. The inspectors shall report any non-compliance to the Director General who shall thereupon transmit the report to the Board of Governors. The Board shall call upon the recipient State or States to remedy forthwith any non-compliance which it finds to have occurred. The Board shall report the non-compliance to all members and to the Security Council and General Assembly of the United Nations. In the event of failure of the recipient State or States to take fully corrective action within a reasonable time, the Board may take one or both of the following measures: direct curtailment or suspension of assistance being provided by the Agency or by a member, and call for the return of materials and equipment made available to the recipient member or group of members. The Agency may also, in accordance with article XIX, suspend any non-complying member from the exercise of the privileges and rights of membership.

ARTICLE XIII: Reimbursement of members

Unless otherwise agreed upon between the Board of Governors and the member furnishing to the Agency materials, services, equipment, or facilities, the Board shall enter into an agreement with such member providing for reimbursement for the items furnished.

ARTICLE XIV: Finance

A. The Board of Governors shall submit to the General Conference the annual budget estimates for the expenses of the Agency. To facilitate the work of the Board in this regard, the Director General shall initially prepare the budget estimates. If the General Conference does not approve the estimates, it shall return them together with its recommendations to the Board. The Board shall then submit further estimates to the General Conference for its approval.

B. Expenditures of the Agency shall be classified under the following categories:

    1. Administrative expenses: these shall include:

        (a) Costs of the staff of the Agency other than the staff employed in connection with materials, services, equipment, and facilities referred to in sub paragraph B-2 below; costs of meetings; and expenditures required for the preparation of Agency projects and for the distribution of information;

        (b) Costs of implementing the safeguards referred to in article XII in relation to Agency projects or, under sub-paragraph A-5 of article III, in relation to any bilateral or multilateral arrangement, together with the costs of handling and storage of special fissionable material by the Agency other than the storage and handling charges referred to in paragraph E below;

    2. Expenses, other than those included in sub-paragraph 1 of this paragraph, in connection with any materials, facilities, plant, and equipment acquired or established by the Agency in carrying out its authorized functions, and the costs of materials, services, equipment, and facilities provided by it under agreements with one or more members.

C. In fixing the expenditures under sub-paragraph B-1 (b) above, the Board of Governors shall deduct such amounts as are recoverable under agreements regarding the application of safeguards between the Agency and parties to bilateral or multilateral arrangements.

D. The Board of Governors shall apportion the expenses referred to in sub-paragraph B-1 above, among members in accordance with a scale to be fixed by the General Conference. In fixing the scale the General Conference shall be guided by the principles adopted by the United Nations in assessing contributions of Member States to the regular budget of the United Nations.

E. The Board of Governors shall establish periodically a scale of charges, including reasonable uniform storage and handling charges, for materials, services, equipment, and facilities furnished to members by the Agency. The scale shall be designed to produce revenues for the Agency adequate to meet the expenses and costs referred to in sub paragraph B-2 above, less any voluntary contributions which the Board of Governors may, in accordance with paragraph F, apply for this purpose. The proceeds of such charges shall be placed in a separate fund which shall be used to pay members for any materials, services, equipment, or facilities furnished by them and to meet other expenses referred to in sub-paragraph B-2 above which may be incurred by the Agency itself.

F. Any excess of revenues referred to in paragraph E over the expenses and costs there referred to, and any voluntary contributions to the Agency, shall be placed in a general fund which may be used as the Board of Governors, with the approval of the General Conference, may determine.

G. Subject to rules and limitations approved by the General Conference, the Board of Governors shall have the authority to exercise borrowing powers on behalf of the Agency without, however, imposing on members of the Agency any liability in respect of loans entered into pursuant to this authority, and to accept voluntary contributions made to the Agency.

H. Decisions of the General Conference on financial questions and of the Board of Governors on the amount of the Agency's budget shall require a two-thirds majority of those present and voting.

ARTICLE XV: Privileges and immunities

A. The Agency shall enjoy in the territory of each member such legal capacity and such privileges and immunities as are necessary for the exercise of its functions.

B. Delegates of members together with their alternates and advisers, Governors appointed to the Board together with their alternates and advisers, and the Director General and the staff of the Agency, shall enjoy such privileges and immunities as are necessary in the independent exercise of their functions in connection with the Agency.

C. The legal capacity, privileges, and immunities referred to in this article shall be defined in a separate agreement or agreements between the Agency, represented for this purpose by the Director General acting under instructions of the Board of Governors. and the members.

ARTICLE XVI: Relationship with other organizations

A. The Board of Governors, with the approval of the General Conference, is authorized to enter into an agreement or agreements establishing an appropriate relationship between the Agency and the United Nations and any other organizations the work of which is related to that of the Agency.

B. The agreement or agreements establishing the relationship of the Agency and the United Nations shall provide for:

 1. Submission by the Agency of reports as provided for in sub-paragraphs B-4 and B-5 of article III;

 2. Consideration by the Agency of resolutions relating to it adopted by the General Assembly or any of the Councils of the United Nations and the submission of reports, when requested, to the appropriate organ of the United Nations on the action taken by the Agency or by its members in accordance with this Statute as a result of such consideration.

ARTICLE XVII: Settlement of disputes

A. Any question or dispute concerning the interpretation or application of this Statute which is not settled by negotiation shall be referred to the International Court of Justice in conformity with the Statute of the Court, unless the parties concerned agree on another mode of settlement.

B. The General Conference and the Board of Governors are separately empowered, subject to authorization from the General Assembly of the United Nations, to request the International Court of Justice to give an advisory opinion on any legal question arising within the scope of the Agency's activities.

ARTICLE XVIII: Amendments and withdrawals

A. Amendments to this Statute may be proposed by any member. Certified copies of the text of any amendment proposed shall be prepared by the Director General and communicated by him to all members at least ninety days in advance of its consideration by the General Conference.

B. At the fifth annual session of the General Conference following the coming into force of this Statute, the question of a general review of the provisions of this Statute shall be placed on the agenda of that session. On approval by a majority of the members present and voting, the review will take place at the following General Conference. Thereafter, proposals on the question of a general review of this Statute may be submitted for decision by the General Conference under the same procedure.

C. Amendments shall come into force for all members when:

 (i) Approved by the General Conference by a two-thirds majority of those present and voting after consideration of observations submitted by the Board of Governors on each proposed amendment, and

(ii) Accepted by two-thirds of all the members in accordance with their respective constitutional processes. Acceptance by a member shall be effected by the deposit of an instrument of acceptance with the depositary Government referred to in paragraph C of article XXI.

D. At any time after five years from the date when this Statute shall take effect in accordance with paragraph E of article XXI or whenever a member is unwilling to accept an amendment to this Statute, it may withdraw from the Agency by notice in writing to that effect given to the depositary Government referred to in paragraph C of article XXI, which shall promptly inform the Board of Governors and all members.

E. Withdrawal by a member from the Agency shall not affect its contractual obligations entered into pursuant to article XI or its budgetary obligations for the year in which it withdraws.

ARTICLE XIX: Suspension of privileges

A. A member of the Agency which is in arrears in the payment of its financial contributions to the Agency shall have no vote in the Agency if the amount of its arrears equals or exceeds the amount of the contributions due from it for the preceding two years. The General Conference may, nevertheless, permit such a member to vote if it is satisfied that the failure to pay is due to conditions beyond the control of the member.

B. A member which has persistently violated the provisions of this Statute or of any agreement entered into by it pursuant to this Statute may be suspended from the exercise of the privileges and rights of membership by the General Conference acting by a two-thirds majority of the members present and voting upon recommendation by the Board of Governors.

ARTICLE XX: Definitions

As used in this Statute:

1. The term "special fissionable material" means plutonium-239; uranium-233; uranium enriched in the isotopes 235 or 233; any material containing one or more of the foregoing; and such other fissionable material as the Board of Governors shall from time to time deter mine; but the term "special fissionable material" does not include source material.

2. The term "uranium enriched in the isotopes 235 or 233" means uranium containing the isotopes 235 or 233 or both in an amount such that the abundance

ratio of the sum of these isotopes to the isotope 238 is greater than the ratio of the isotope 235 to the isotope 238 occurring in nature.

3.   The term "source material" means uranium containing the mixture of isotopes occurring in nature; uranium depleted in the isotope 235; thorium; any of the foregoing in the form of metal, alloy, chemical compound, or concentrate; any other material containing one or more of the foregoing in such concentration as the Board of Governors shall from time to time determine; and such other material as the Board of Governors shall from time to time determine.

ARTICLE XXI: Signature, acceptance, and entry into force

A.   This Statute shall be open for signature on 26 October 1956 by all States Members of the United Nations or of any of the specialized agencies and shall remain open for signature by those States for a period of ninety days.

B.   The signatory States shall become parties to this Statute by deposit of an instrument of ratification.

C.   Instruments of ratification by signatory States and instruments of acceptance by States whose membership has been approved under paragraph B of article IV of this Statute shall be deposited with the Government of the United States of America, hereby designated as depositary Government.

D.   Ratification or acceptance of this Statute shall be effected by States in accordance with their respective constitutional processes.

E.   This Statute, apart from the Annex, shall come into force when eighteen States have deposited instruments of ratification in accordance with paragraph B of this article, provided that such eighteen States shall include at least three of the following States: Canada, France, the Union of Soviet Socialist Republics, the United Kingdom of Great Britain and Northern Ireland, and the United States of America. Instruments of ratification and instruments of acceptance deposited thereafter shall take effect on the date of their receipt.

F.   The depositary Government shall promptly inform all States signatory to this Statute of the date of each deposit of ratification and the date of entry into force of the Statute. The depositary Government shall promptly inform all signatories and members of the dates on which States subsequently become parties thereto.

G.   The Annex to this Statute shall come into force on the first day this Statute is open for signature.

ARTICLE XXII: Registration with the United Nations

A.   This Statute shall be registered by the depositary Government pursuant to Article 102 of the Charter of the United Nations.

B.   Agreements between the Agency and any member or members, agreements between the Agency and any other organization or organizations, and agreements between members subject to approval of the Agency, shall be registered with the Agency. Such agreements shall be registered by the Agency with the United Nations if registration is required under Article 102 of the Charter of the United Nations.

ARTICLE XXIII: Authentic texts and certified copies

This Statute, done in the Chinese, English, French, Russian and Spanish languages, each being equally authentic, shall be deposited in the archives of the depositary Government. Duly certified copies of this Statute shall be transmitted by the depositary Government to the Governments of the other signatory States and to the Governments of States admitted to membership under paragraph B of article IV.

In witness whereof the undersigned, duly authorized, have signed this Statute.

DONE at the Headquarters of the United Nations, this twenty-sixth day of October, one thousand nine hundred and fifty-six.

ANNEX: Preparatory Commission

A.   A Preparatory Commission shall come into existence on the first day this Statute is open for signature. It shall be composed of one representative each of Australia, Belgium, Brazil, Canada, Czechoslovakia, France, India, Portugal, Union of South Africa, Union of Soviet Socialist Republics, United Kingdom of Great Britain and Northern Ireland, and United States of America, and one representative each of six other States to be chosen by the International Conference on the Statute of the International Atomic Energy Agency. The Preparatory Commission shall remain in existence until this Statute comes into force and thereafter until the General Conference has convened and a Board of Governors has been selected in accordance with article VI.

B.   The expenses of the Preparatory Commission may be met by a loan provided by the United Nations and for this purpose the Preparatory Commission shall make the necessary arrangements with the appropriate authorities of the United Nations, including arrangements for repayment of the loan by the Agency. Should these funds be insufficient, the Preparatory Commission may accept advances from Governments. Such advances may be set off against the contributions of the Governments concerned to the Agency.

C.   The Preparatory Commission shall:

1.   Elect its own officers, adopt its own rules of procedure, meet as often as necessary, determine its own place of meeting and establish such committees as it deems necessary;

2.   Appoint an executive secretary and staff as shall be necessary, who shall exercise such powers and perform such duties as the Commission may determine;

3.   Make arrangements for the first session of the General Conference, including the preparation of a provisional agenda and draft rules of procedure, such session to be held as soon as possible after the entry into force of this Statute;

4.   Make designations for membership on the first Board of Governors in accordance with sub-paragraphs A-1 and A-2 and paragraph B of article VI;

5.   Make studies, reports, and recommendations for the first session of the General Conference and for the first meeting of the Board of Governors on subjects of concern to the Agency requiring immediate attention, including (a) the financing of the Agency; (b) the programmes and budget for the first year of the Agency; (c) technical problems relevant to advance planning of Agency operations; (d) the establishment of a permanent Agency staff; and (e) the location of the permanent headquarters of the Agency;

6.   Make recommendations for the first meeting of the Board of Governors concerning the provisions of a headquarters agreement defining the status of the Agency and the rights and obligations which will exist in the relationship between the Agency and the host Government;

7.   (a) Enter into negotiations with the United Nations with a view to the preparation of a draft agreement in accordance with article XVI of this Statute, such draft agreement to be submitted to the first session of the General Conference and to the first meeting of the Board of Governors; and

(b) make recommendations to the first session of the Conference and to the first meeting of the Board of Governors concerning the relationship of the Agency to other international organizations as contemplated in article XVI of this Statute.

B. IAEA SAFEGUARDS AGREEMENTS

Background

The IAEA first applied safeguards in 1961 under a framework that was agreed by the Board of Governors and published in INFCIRC/66. The framework evolved over time as more complex facilities became subject to safeguards. So-called INFCIRC/66 safeguards agreements are "item-specific." They cover only specific items listed in the "inventory" of the agreement. Inventories include nuclear material but can also include facilities, equipment, and materials, such as heavy water and graphite.

The conclusion of the NPT changed this dramatically. Under the NPT, each non-nuclear-weapon state is required to accept safeguards on all nuclear material in all of its peaceful nuclear activities. Coverage of nuclear material is comprehensive no matter where located. Because it is comprehensive, it was considered unnecessary to also capture other nuclear-fuel-cycle related materials or activities.

After the NPT opened for signature in 1968, the IAEA acted quickly to investigate the technical, legal, and financial ramifications of implementing NPT safeguards. Consultants and experts meetings were convened, and by late 1969, the IAEA had drafted a complete model agreement. The IAEA Board of Governors then established a Safeguards Committee to agree on a model NPT safeguards agreement using the IAEA draft as a starting point.

The Committee met for the first time in April 1970 and completed its work in March 1971. The result was a system of on-site inspection by an international organization of an entire industry and independent verification of the flows and inventories of radioactive and potentially dangerous materials. Reflecting this, the Committee's report to the Board of Governors noted that the model safeguards agreement incorporated "a number of fundamental technical principles, concepts and criteria, some of which were novel and of considerable complexity."

Implementation of the model safeguards agreemen required the development and deployment of new equipment and technology needed to meet the unique requirements of safeguards. Especially important is the need to ensure that the IAEA can draw independent conclusions in an environment where a state may wish to defeat this capability. This imposes challenging requirements on verification equipment and techniques. The IAEA would also need to recruit and train a team of inspectors.

In April 1971, the Board of Governors adopted the model as the basis for negotiation of NPT safeguards agreements between non-nuclear-weapon states and the IAEA. The model agreement is called "The Structure and Content of Agreements Between the Agency and States Required in Connection with the Treaty on the Non-Proliferation of Nuclear Weapons" and is published by the IAEA as Information Circular 153 (INFCIRC/153 (corrected)).

The NPT Model Safeguards Agreement - INFCIRC/153 (Corrected)

INFCIRC/153 (Corrected)

THE STRUCTURE AND CONTENT OF AGREEMENTS BETWEEN THE AGENCY AND STATES REQUIRED IN CONNECTION WITH THE TREATY ON THE NON-PROLIFERATION OF NUCLEAR WEAPONS

CONTENTS

PART I

BASIC UNDERTAKING

1. The Agreement should contain, in accordance with Article III.1 of the Treaty on the Non-Proliferation of Nuclear Weapons,* an undertaking by the State to accept safeguards, in accordance with the terms of the Agreement, on all source or special fissionable material in all peaceful nuclear activities within its territory, under its jurisdiction or carried out under its control any where, for the exclusive purpose of verifying that such material is not diverted to nuclear weapons or other nuclear explosive devices.

APPLICATION OF SAFEGUARDS

2. The Agreement should provide for the Agency's right and obligation to ensure that safeguards will be applied, in accordance with the terms of the Agreement, on all source or special fissionable material in all peaceful nuclear activities within the territory of the State, under its jurisdiction or carried out under its control anywhere, for the exclusive purpose of verifying that such material is not diverted to nuclear weapons or other nuclear explosive devices.

CO-OPERATION BETWEEN THE AGENCY AND THE STATE

3. The Agreement should provide that the Agency and the State should co-operate to facilitate the implementation of the safeguards provided for therein.

IMPLEMENTATION OF SAFEGUARDS

4. The Agreement should provide that safeguards shall be implemented in a manner designed:

    (a) To avoid hampering the economic and technological development of the State or international co-operation in the field of peaceful nuclear activities, including international exchange of *nuclear material;***
    (b) To avoid undue interference in the State's peaceful nuclear activities, and in particular in the operation of *facilities;* and
    (c) To be consistent with prudent management practices required for the economic and safe conduct of nuclear activities.

5. The Agreement should provide that the Agency shall take every precaution to protect commercial and industrial secrets and other confidential information coming to its knowledge in the implementation of the Agreement. The Agency shall not publish or communicate to any State, organization or person

---

* Reproduced in document INFCIRC/140.

** Terms in italics have specialized meanings, which are defined in paragraphs 98-116 below.

any information obtained by it in connection with the implementation of the Agreement, except that specific information relating to such implementation in the State may be given to the Board of Governors and to such Agency staff members as require such knowledge by reason of their official duties in connection with safeguards, but only to the extent necessary for the Agency to fulfil its responsibilities in implementing the Agreement. Summarized information on *nuclear material* being safeguarded by the Agency under the Agreement may be published upon decision of the Board if the States directly concerned agree.

6.   The Agreement should provide that in implementing safeguards pursuant thereto the Agency shall take full account of technological developments in the field of safeguards, and shall make every effort to ensure optimum cost effectiveness and the application of the principle of safeguarding effectively the flow of *nuclear material* subject to safeguards under the Agreement by use of instruments and other techniques at certain *strategic points* to the extent that present or future technology permits. In order to ensure optimum cost effectiveness, use should be made, for example, of such means as:

   (a)   Containment as a means of defining *material balance areas* for accounting purposes;

   (b)   Statistical techniques and random sampling in evaluating the flow of *nuclear material;* and

   (c)   Concentration of verification procedures on those stages in the nuclear fuel cycle involving the production, processing, use or storage of *nuclear material* from which nuclear weapons or other nuclear explosive devices could readily be made, and minimization of verification procedures in respect of other *nuclear material,* on condition that this does not hamper the Agency in applying safeguards under the Agreement.

NATIONAL SYSTEM OF ACCOUNTING FOR AND CONTROL OF NUCLEAR MATERIAL

7.   The Agreement should provide that the State shall establish and maintain a system of accounting for and control of all *nuclear material* subject to safeguards under the Agreement, and that such safeguards shall be applied in such a manner as to enable the Agency to verify, in ascertaining that there has been no diversion of *nuclear material* from peaceful uses to nuclear weapons or other nuclear explosive devices, findings of the State's system. The Agency's verification shall include, inter alia, independent measurements and observations conducted by the Agency in accordance with the procedures specified in Part II below. The Agency, in its verification, shall take due account of the technical effectiveness of the State's system.

PROVISION OF INFORMATION TO TIIE AGENCY

8.   The Agreement should provide that to ensure the effective implementation of safeguards thereunder the Agency shall be provided, in accordance with the provisions set out in Part II below, with information concerning *nuclear material* subject to safeguards under the Agreement and the features of *facilities* relevant to safeguarding such material. The Agency shall require only the minimum amount of information and data consistent with carrying out its responsibilities under the Agreement. Information pertaining to *facilities shall* be the minimum necessary for safeguarding *nuclear material* subject to safeguards under the Agreement. In examining design information, the Agency shall, at the request of the State, be prepared to examine on premises of the State design information which the State regards as being of particular sensitivity. Such information would not have to be physically transmitted to the Agency provided that it remained available for ready further examination by the Agency on premises of the State.

AGENCY INSPECTORS

9.   The Agreement should provide that the State shall take the necessary steps to ensure that Agency inspectors can effectively discharge their functions under the Agreement. The Agency shall secure the consent of the State to the designation of Agency inspectors to that State. If the State, either upon proposal of a designation or at any other time after a designation has been made, objects to the designation, the Agency shall propose to the State an alternative designation or designations. The repeated refusal of a State to accept the designation of Agency inspectors that would impede the inspections conducted under the Agreement would be considered by the Board upon referral by the Director General with a view to appropriate action. The visits and activities of Agency inspectors shall be so arranged as to reduce to a minimum the possible inconvenience and disturbance to the State and to the peaceful nuclear activities inspected, as well as to ensure protection of industrial secrets or any other confidential information coming to the inspectors' knowledge.

PRIVILEGES AND IMMUNITIES

10.   The Agreement should specify the privileges and immunities which shall be granted to the Agency and its staff in respect of their functions under the Agreement. In the case of a State party to the Agreement on the Privileges and Immunities of the Agency,* the provisions thereof, as in force for such State, shall apply. In the case of other States, the privileges and immunities granted should be such as to ensure that:

---

* Reproduced in document INFCIRC/9 / Rev. 2

(a) The Agency and its staff will be in a position to discharge their functions under the Agreement effectively; and

(b) No such State will be placed thereby in a more favourable position than States party to the Agreement on the Privileges and Immunities of the Agency.

TERMINATION OF SAFEGUARDS

Consumption or dilution of nuclear material

11. The Agreement should provide that safeguards shall terminate on *nuclear material* subject to safeguards thereunder upon determination by the Agency that it has been consumed, or has been diluted in such a way that it is no longer usable for any nuclear activity relevant from the point of view of safeguards, or has become practicably irrecoverable.

Transfer of nuclear material out of the State

12. The Agreement should provide, with respect to *nuclear material* subject to safeguards thereunder, for notification of transfers of such material out of the State, In accordance with the provisions set out in paragraphs 92-94 below. The Agency shall terminate safeguards under the Agreement on *nuclear material* when the recipient State has assumed responsibility therefor, as pro vided for in paragraph 91. The Agency shall maintain records indicating each transfer and, where applicable, the re-application of safeguards to the transferred *nuclear material.*

Provisions relating to nuclear material to be used in non-nuclear activities

13. The Agreement should provide that if the State wishes to use *nuclear material* subject to safeguards thereunder in non-nuclear activities, such as the production of alloys or ceramics, it shall agree with the Agency on the cir circumstances under which the safeguards on such *nuclear material* may be terminated.

NON-APPLICATION OF SAFEGUARDS TO NUCLEAR MATERIAL TO BE USED IN NON-PEACEFUL ACTIVITIES

14. The Agreement should provide that if the State intends to exercise its discretion to use *nuclear material* which is required to be safeguarded thereunder in a nuclear activity which does not require the application of safeguards under the Agreement, the following procedures will apply:

(a) The State shall inform the Agency of the activity, making it clear:
   (i) That the use of the *nuclear material* in a non-proscribed military activity will not be in conflict with an undertaking the State may have given and in respect of which Agency safeguards apply, that

the *nuclear material* will be used only in a peaceful nuclear activity; and

(ii) That during the period of non-application of safeguards the *nuclear material* will not be used for the production of nuclear weapons or other nuclear explosive devices;

(b) The Agency and the State shall make an arrangement so that, only while the *nuclear material* is in such an activity, the safeguards pro vided for in the Agreement will not be applied. The arrangement shall identify, to the extent possible, the period or circumstances during which safeguards will not be applied. In any event, the safeguards provided for in the Agreement shall again apply as soon as the *nuclear material* is reintroduced into a peaceful nuclear activity. The Agency shall be kept informed of the total quantity and composition of such unsafeguarded *nuclear material in* the State and of any exports of such material; and

(c) Each arrangement shall be made in agreement with the Agency. The Agency's agreement shall be given as promptly as possible; it shall only relate to the temporal and procedural provisions, reporting arrangements, etc., but shall not involve any approval or classified knowledge of the military activity or relate to the use of the *nuclear material* therein.

FINANCE

15. The Agreement should contain one of the following *sets* of provisions:

(a) An agreement with a Member of the Agency should provide that each party thereto shall bear the expense it incurs in implementing its responsibilities thereunder. However, if the State or persons under its jurisdiction incur extraordinary expenses as a result of a specific request by the Agency, the Agency shall reimburse such expenses provided that it has agreed in advance to do so. In any case the Agency shall bear the cost of any additional measuring or sampling which inspectors may request; or

(b) An agreement with a party not a Member of the Agency should in application of the provisions of Article X IV.C of the Statute, provide that the party shall reimburse fully to the Agency the safeguards expenses the Agency incurs thereunder. However, if the party or persons under its jurisdiction incur extraordinary expenses as a result of a specific request by the Agency, the Agency shall reimburse such expenses provided that it has agreed in advance to do so.

THIRD PARTY LIABILITY FOR NUCLEAR DAMAGE

16. The Agreement should provide that the State shall ensure that any protection against third party liability in respect of nuclear damage, including any insurance or other financial security, which may be available under its laws or regulations shall apply to the Agency and its officials for the purpose of the

implementation of the Agreement, in the same way as that protection applies to nationals of the State.

INTERNATIONAL RESPONSIBILITY

17.   The Agreement should provide that any claim by one party thereto against the other in respect of any damage, other than damage arising out of a nuclear incident, resulting from the implementation of safeguards under the Agreement, shall be settled in accordance with international law.

MEASURES IN RELATION TO VERIFICATION OF NON-DIVERSION

18.   The Agreement should provide that if the Board, upon report of the Director General, decides that an action by the State is essential and urgent in order to ensure verification that *nuclear material* subject to safeguards under the Agreement is not diverted to nuclear weapons or other nuclear explosive devices the Board shall be able to call upon the State to take the required action without delay, irrespective of whether procedures for the settlement of a dispute have been invoked.

19.   The Agreement should provide that if the Board upon examination of relevant information reported to it by the Director General finds that the Agency is not able to verify that there has been no diversion of *nuclear material* required to be safeguarded under the Agreement to nuclear weapons or other nuclear explosive devices, it may make the reports provided for in paragraph C of Article XII of the Statute and may also take, where applicable, the other measures provided for in that paragraph. In taking such action the Board shall take account of the degree of assurance provided by the safeguards measures that have been applied and shall afford the State every reasonable opportunity to furnish the Board with any necessary reassurance.

INTERPRETATION AND APPLICATION OF THE AGREEMENT AND SETTLEMENT OF DISPUTES

20.   The Agreement should provide that the parties thereto shall, at the request of either, consult about any question arising out of the interpretation or application thereof.

21.   The Agreement should provide that the State shall have the right to request that any question arising out of the interpretation or application thereof be considered by the Board; and that the State shall be invited by the Board to participate in the discussion of any such question by the Board.

22.   The Agreement should provide that any dispute arising out of the interpretation or application thereof except a dispute with regard to a finding by the Board under paragraph 19 above or an action taken by the Board pursuant to such a finding which is not settled by negotiation or another procedure agreed to by the parties should, on the request of either party, be submitted to an arbitral tribunal composed as follows: each party would designate one arbitrator,

and the two arbitrators so designated would elect a third, who would be the Chairman. If, within 30 days of the request for arbitration, either party has not designated an arbitrator, either party to the dispute may request the President of the International Court of Justice to appoint an arbitrator. The same procedure would apply if, within 30 days of the designation or appointment of the second arbitrator, the third arbitrator had not been elected. A majority of the members of the arbitral tribunal would constitute a quorum, and all decisions would require the concurrence of two arbitrators. The arbitral procedure would be fixed by the tribunal. The decisions of the tribunal would be binding on both parties.

FINAL CLAUSES

Amendment of the Agreement

23. The Agreement should provide that the parties thereto shall, at the request of either of them, consult each other on amendment of the Agreement. All amendments shall require the agreement of both parties. It might additionally be provided, if convenient to the State, that the agreement of the parties on amendments to Part II of the Agreement could be achieved by recourse to a simplified procedure. The Director General shall promptly inform all Member States of any amendment to the Agreement.

Suspension of application of Agency safeguards under other agreements

24. Where applicable and where the State desires such a provision to appear, the Agreement should provide that the application of Agency safeguards in the State under other safeguards agreements with the Agency shall be suspended while the Agreement is in force. If the State has received assistance from the Agency for a project, the State's undertaking in the Project Agreement not to use items subject thereto in such a way as to further any military purpose shall continue to apply.

Entry into force and duration

25. The Agreement should provide that it shall enter into force on the date on which the Agency receives from the State written notification that the statutory and constitutional requirements for entry into force have been met. The Director General shall promptly inform all Member States of the entry into force.

26. The Agreement should provide for it to remain in force as long as the State is party to the Treaty on the Non-Proliferation of Nuclear Weapons.

PART II

INTRODUCTION

27.　The Agreement should provide that the purpose of Part II thereof is to specify the procedures to be applied for the implementation of the safeguards provisions of Part I.

OBJECTIVE OF SAFEGUARDS

28.　The Agreement should provide that the objective of safeguards is the timely detection of diversion of significant quantities of *nuclear material* from peaceful nuclear activities to the manufacture of nuclear weapons or of other nuclear explosive devices or for purposes unknown, and deterrence of such diversion by the risk of early detection.

29.　To this end the Agreement should provide for the use of material accountancy as a safeguards measure of fundamental importance, with containment and surveillance as important complementary measures.

30.　The Agreement should provide that the technical conclusion of the Agency's verification activities shall be a statement, in respect of each *material balance area,* of the amount of *material unaccounted for* over a specific period, giving the limits of accuracy of the amounts stated.

NATIONAL SYSTEM OF ACCOUNTING FOR AND CONTROL OF NUCLEAR MATERIAL

31.　The Agreement should provide that pursuant to paragraph 7 above the Agency, in carrying out its verification activities, shall make full use of the State's system of accounting for and control of all *nuclear material* subject to safeguards under the Agreement, and shall avoid unnecessary duplication of the State's accounting and control activities.

32.　The Agreement should provide that the State's system of accounting for and control of all *nuclear material* subject to safeguards under the Agreement shall be based on a structure of material balance areas, and shall make pro vision as appropriate and specified in the Subsidiary Arrangements for the establishment of such measures as:

　(a)　A measurement system for the determination of the quantities of *nuclear material* received, produced, shipped, lost or otherwise removed from inventory, and the quantities on inventory;

　(b)　The evaluation of precision and accuracy of measurements and the estimation of measurement uncertainty;

(c)   Procedures for identifying, reviewing and evaluating differences in shipper/ receiver measurements;

(d)   Procedures for taking a *physical inventory;*

(e)   Procedures for the evaluation of accumulations of unmeasured inventory and unmeasured losses;

(f)   A system of records and reports showing, for each *material balance area,* the inventory of *nuclear material* and the changes in that inventory including receipts into and transfers out of the *material balance area;*

(g)   Provisions to ensure that the accounting procedures and arrangements are being operated correctly; and

(h)   Procedures for the provisions of reports to the Agency in accordance with paragraphs 59-69 below.

STARTING POINT OF SAFEGUARDS

33.   The Agreement should provide that safeguards shall not apply thereunder to material in mining or ore processing activities.

34.   The Agreement should provide that:

(a)   When any material containing uranium or thorium which has not reached the stage of the nuclear fuel cycle described in sub paragraph (c) below is directly or indirectly exported to a non-nuclear weapon State, the State shall inform the Agency of its quantity, composition and destination, unless the material is exported for specifically non-nuclear purposes;

(b)   When any material containing uranium or thorium which has not reached the stage of the nuclear fuel cycle described in sub-paragraph (c) below is imported, the State shall inform the Agency of its quantity and composition, unless the material is imported for specifically non nuclear purposes; and

(c)   When any *nuclear material* of a composition and purity suitable for fuel fabrication or for being isotopically enriched leaves the plant or the process stage in which it has been produced, or when such *nuclear material,* or any other *nuclear material* produced at a later stage in the nuclear fuel cycle, is imported into the State, the *nuclear material* shall become subject to the other safeguards procedures specified in the Agreement.

TERMINATION OF SAFEGUARDS

35.   The Agreement should provide that safeguards shall terminate on *nuclear material* subject to safeguards thereunder under the conditions set forth in paragraph 11 above. Where the conditions of that paragraph are not met, but the State considers that the recovery of safeguarded *nuclear material* from residues is not for the time being practicable or desirable, the Agency and the State shall consult on the appropriate safeguards measures to be applied. It should further be provided that safeguards shall terminate on *nuclear material* subject

to safeguards under the Agreement under the conditions set forth in paragraph 13 above, provided that the State and the Agency agree that such *nuclear material* is practicably irrecoverable.

EXEMPTIONS FROM SAFEGUARDS

36. The Agreement should provide that the Agency shall, at the request of the State, exempt *nuclear material* from safeguards, as follows:

    (a) Special fissionable material, when it is used in gram quantities or less as a sensing component in instruments;

    (b) *Nuclear material,* when it is used in non-nuclear activities in accordance with paragraph 13 above, if such *nuclear material* is recoverable; and

    (c) Plutonium with an isotopic concentration of plutonium-238 exceeding 80%.

37. The Agreement should provide that *nuclear material* that would otherwise be subject to safeguards shall be exempted from safeguards at the request of the State, provided that *nuclear material* so exempted in the State may not at any time exceed:

    (a) One kilogram in total of special fissionable material, which may consist of one of more of the following:
       (i) Plutonium;
       (ii) Uranium with an *enrichment* of 0.2 (20%) and above, taken account of by multiplying its weight by its *enrichment;* and
       (iii) Uranium with an *enrichment* below 0.2 (20%) and above that of natural uranium, taken account of by multiplying its weight by five times the square of its *enrichment;*

    (b) Ten metric tons in total of natural uranium and depleted uranium with an *enrichment* above 0.005 (0.5%);

    (c) Twenty metric tons of depleted uranium with an *enrichment* of 0.005 (0.5 %) or below; and

    (d) Twenty metric tons of thorium;
       or such greater amounts as may be specified by the Board of Governors for uniform application.

38. The Agreement should provide that if exempted *nuclear material* is to be processed or stored together with safeguarded *nuclear material,* provision should be made for the re-application of safeguards thereto.

SUBSIDIARY ARRANGEMENTS

39. The Agreement should provide that the Agency and the State shall make Subsidiary Arrangements which shall specify in detail, to the extent necessary to permit the Agency to fulfil its responsibilities under the Agreement in an

effective and efficient manner, how the procedures laid down in the Agreement are to be applied. Provision should be made for the possibility of an extension or change of the Subsidiary Arrangements by agreement between the Agency and the State without amendment of the Agreement.

40. It should be provided that the Subsidiary Arrangements shall enter into force at the same time as, or as soon as possible after, the entry into force of the Agreement. The State and the Agency shall make every effort to achieve their entry into force within 90 days of the entry into force of the Agreement, a later date being acceptable only with the agreement of both parties. The State shall provide the Agency promptly with the information required for completing the Subsidiary Arrangements. The Agreement should also provide that, upon its entry into force, the Agency shall be entitled to apply the procedures laid down therein in respect of the *nuclear material* listed in the inventory provided for in paragraph 41 below.

INVENTORY

41. The Agreement should provide that, on the basis of the initial report referred to in paragraph 62 below, the Agency shall establish a unified inventory of all *nuclear material* in the State subject to safeguards under the Agreement, irrespective of its origin, and maintain this inventory on the basis of subsequent reports and of the results of its verification activities. Copies of the inventory shall be made available to the State at agreed intervals.

DESIGN INFORMATION

General

42. Pursuant to paragraph 8 above, the Agreement should stipulate that design information in respect of existing *facilities* shall be provided to the Agency during the discussion of the Subsidiary Arrangements, and that the time limits for the provision of such information in respect of new *facilities* shall be specified in the Subsidiary Arrangements. It should further be stipulated that such information shall be provided as early as possible before *nuclear material* is introduced into a new *facility*.

43. The Agreement should specify that the design information in respect of each *facility* to be made available to the Agency shall include, when applicable:

(a) The identification of the *facility*, stating its general character, purpose, nominal capacity and geographic location, and the name and address to be used for routine business purposes;

(b) A description of the general arrangement of the *facility* with reference, to the extent feasible, to the form, location and flow of *nuclear material* and to the general layout of important items of equipment which use, produce or process *nuclear material;*

(c) A description of features of the *facility* relating to material account any, containment and surveillance; and

(d) A description of the existing and proposed procedures at the *facility* for *nuclear material* accountancy and control, with special reference to *material balance areas* established by the operator, measurements of flow and procedures for *physical inventory* taking.

44. The Agreement should further provide that other information relevant to the application of safeguards shall be made available to the Agency in respect of each *facility,* in particular on organizational responsibility for material accountancy and control. It should also be provided that the State shall make available to the Agency supplementary information on the health and safety procedures, which the Agency shall observe and with which the inspectors shall comply at the *facility.*

45. The Agreement should stipulate that design information in respect of a modification relevant for safeguards purposes shall be provided for examination sufficiently in advance for the safeguards procedures to be adjusted when necessary.

Purposes of examination of design information

46. The Agreement should provide that the design information made avail able to the Agency shall be used for the following purposes:

(a) To identify the features of *facilities* and *nuclear material* relevant to the application of safeguards to *nuclear material* in sufficient detail to facilitate verification;

(b) To determine *material balance areas* to be used for Agency accounting purposes and to select those *strategic points* which are *key measurement points* and which will be used to determine the *nuclear material* flows and inventories; in determining such *material balance areas* the Agency shall, inter alia, use the following criteria:

(i) The size of the *material balance area* should be related to the accuracy with which the material balance can be established;

(ii) In determining the *material balance area* advantage should be taken of any opportunity to use containment and surveillance to help ensure the completeness of flow measurements and thereby simplify the application of safeguards and concentrate measurement efforts at *key measurement points;*

(iii) A number of *material balance areas* in use at a *facility* or at distinct sites may be combined in one *material balance area* to be used for Agency accounting purposes when the Agency determines that this is consistent with its verification requirements; and

(iv) If the State so requests, a special *material balance area* around a process step involving commercially sensitive information may be established;

(c) To establish the nominal timing and procedures for taking of *physical inventory* for Agency accounting purposes;

(d) To establish the records and reports requirements and records evaluation procedures;

(e) To establish requirements and procedures for verification of the quantity and location of *nuclear material;* and

(f) To select appropriate combinations of containment and surveillance methods and techniques and the *strategic points* at which they are to be applied.

It should further be provided that the results of the examination of the design information shall be included in the Subsidiary Arrangements.

Re-examination of design information

47. The Agreement should provide that design information shall be re examined in the light of changes in operating conditions, of developments in safeguards technology or of experience in the application of verification procedures, with a view to modifying the action the Agency has taken pursuant to paragraph 46 above.

Verification of design information

48. The Agreement should provide that the Agency, in co-operation with the State, may send inspectors to *facilities* to verify the design information provided to the Agency pursuant to paragraphs 42–45 above for the purposes stated in paragraph 46.

INFORMATION IN RESPECT OF NUCLEAR MATERIAL OUTSIDE FACILITIES

49. The Agreement should provide that the following information concerning *nuclear material* customarily used outside *facilities* shall be provided as applicable to the Agency:

(a) A general description of the use of the *nuclear material,* its geographic Location, and the user 's name and address for routine business purposes; and

(b) A general description of the existing and proposed procedures for *nuclear material* accountancy and control, including organizational responsibility for material accountancy and control.

The Agreement should further provide that the Agency shall be informed on a timely basis of any change in the information provided to it under this paragraph.

50. The Agreement should provide that the information made available to the Agency in respect of *nuclear material* customarily used outside *facilities* may be used, to the extent relevant, for the purposes set out in subparagraphs 46(b)-(f) above.

RECORDS SYSTEM

General

51. The Agreement should provide that in establishing a national system of accounting for and control of *nuclear material* as referred to in paragraph 7 above, the State shall arrange that records are kept in respect of each *material balance area*. Provision should also be made that the Subsidiary Arrangements shall describe the records to be kept in respect of each *material balance area*.

52. The Agreement should provide that the State shall make arrangements to facilitate the examination of records by inspectors, particularly if the records are not kept in English, French, Russian or Spanish.

53. The Agreement should provide that the records shall be retained for at least five years.

54. The Agreement should provide that the records shall consist, as appropriate, of:

   (a) Accounting records of all *nuclear material* subject to safeguards under the Agreement; and

   (b) Operating records for *facilities* containing such *nuclear material*.

55. The Agreement should provide that the system of measurements on which the records used for the preparation of reports are based shall either conform to the latest international standards or be equivalent in quality to such standards.

Accounting records

56. The Agreement should provide that the accounting records shall set forth the following in respect of each *material balance area*:

   (a) All *inventory changes,* so as to permit a determination of the *book inventory* at any time;

   (b) All measurement results that are used for determination of the *physical inventory;* and

   (c) All *adjustments* and *corrections* that have been made in respect of *inventory changes, book inventories* and *physical inventories*.

57. The Agreement should provide that for all *inventory changes* and *physical inventories* the records shall show, in respect of each *batch* of *nuclear material:* material

identification, *batch data* and *source data*. Provision should further be included that records shall account for uranium, thorium and plutonium separately in each *batch* of *nuclear material*. Furthermore, the date of the *inventory change* and, when appropriate, the originating *material balance area* and the receiving *material balance area* or the recipient, shall be indicated for each *inventory change*.

Operating records

58. The Agreement should provide that the operating records shall set forth as appropriate in respect of each *material balance area:*

   (a) Those operating data which are used to establish changes in the quantities and composition of *nuclear material;*
   (b) The data obtained from the calibration of tanks and instruments and from sampling and analyses, the procedures to control the quality of measurements and the derived estimates of random and systematic error;
   (c) A description of the sequence of the actions taken in preparing for, and in taking, a *physical inventory,* in order to ensure that it is correct and complete; and
   (d) A description of the actions taken in order to ascertain the cause and magnitude of any accidental or unmeasured loss that might occur.

REPORTS SYSTEM

General

59. The Agreement should specify that the State shall provide the Agency with reports as detailed in paragraphs 60-69 below in respect of *nuclear material* subject to safeguards thereunder.

60. The Agreement should provide that reports shall be made in English, French, Russian or Spanish, except as otherwise specified in the Subsidiary Arrangements.

61. The Agreement should provide that reports shall be based on the records kept in accordance with paragraphs 51-58 above and shall consist, as appropriate, of accounting reports and special reports.

Accounting reports

62. The Agreement should stipulate that the Agency shall be provided with an initial report on all *nuclear material* which is to be subject to safeguards thereunder. It should also be provided that the initial report shall be dispatched by the State to the Agency within 30 days of the last day of the calendar month in which the Agreement enters into force, and shall reflect the situation as of the last day of that month.

63.   The Agreement should stipulate that for each *material balance area* the State shall provide the Agency with the following accounting reports:

   (a)   *Inventory change* reports showing changes in the inventory of *nuclear material*. The reports shall be dispatched as soon as possible and in any event within 30 days after the end of the month in which the *inventory changes* occurred or were established; and

   (b)   Material balance reports showing the material balance based on a *physical inventory* of *nuclear material* actually present in the *material balance area*. The reports shall be dispatched as soon as possible and in any event within 30 days after the *physical inventory* has been taken.

   The reports shall be based on data available as of the date of reporting and may be corrected at a later date as required.

64.   The Agreement should provide that *inventory change* reports shall specify identification and *batch data* for each *batch* of *nuclear material*, the date of the *inventory change* and, as appropriate, the originating *material balance area* and the receiving *material balance area* or the recipient. These reports shall be ac companied by concise notes:

   (a)   Explaining the *inventory changes,* on the basis of the operating data contained in the operating records provided for under subparagraph 58(a) above; and

   (b)   Describing, as specified in the Subsidiary Arrangements, the anticipated operational programme, particularly the taking of a *physical inventory*.

65,   The Agreement should provide that the State shall report each *inventory change, adjustment* and *correction* either periodically in a consolidated list or individually. The *inventory changes* shall be reported in terms of *batches;* small amounts, such as analytical samples, as specified in the Subsidiary Arrangements, may be combined and reported as one *inventory change*.

66.   The Agreement should stipulate that the Agency shall provide the State with semi-annual statements of *book inventory* of *nuclear material* subject to safe guards, for each *material balance area,* as based on the *inventory change* reports for the period covered by each such statement.

67.   The Agreement should specify that the material balance reports shall include the following entries, unless otherwise agreed by the Agency and the State:

   (a)   Beginning *physical inventory;*
   (b)   *Inventory changes* (first increases, then decreases);
   (c)   Ending *book inventory;*
   (d)   *Shipper/ receiver differences;*
   (e)   Adjusted ending *book inventory;*

(f)   Ending *physical inventory;* and

(g)   *Material unaccounted for.*

A statement of the *physical inventory*, listing all *batches* separately and specifying material identification and *batch data* for each *batch*, shall be attached to each material balance report.

Special reports

68.   The Agreement should provide that the State shall make special reports without delay:

(a)   If any unusual incident or circumstances lead the State to believe that there is or may have been loss of *nuclear material* that exceeds the limits to be specified for this purpose in the Subsidiary Arrangements; or

(b)   If the containment has unexpectedly changed from that specified in the Subsidiary Arrangements to the extent that unauthorized removal of *nuclear material* has become possible.

Amplification and clarification of reports

69.   The Agreement should provide that at the Agency's request the State shall supply amplifications or clarifications of any report, in so far as relevant for the purpose of safeguards.

INSPECTIONS

General

70.   The Agreement should stipulate that the Agency shall have the right to make inspections as provided for in paragraphs 71-82 below.

Purposes of inspections

71.   The Agreement should provide that the Agency may make ad hoc inspections in order to:

(a)   Verify the information contained in the initial report on the *nuclear material* subject to safeguards under the Agreement;

(b)   Identify and verify changes in the situation which have occurred since the date of the initial report; and

(c)   Identify, and if possible verify the quantity and composition of, *nuclear material* in accordance with paragraphs 93 and 96 below, before its transfer out of or upon its transfer into the State.

72. The Agreement should provide that the Agency may make routine inspections in order to:

    (a)   Verify that reports are consistent with records;

    (b)   Verify the location, identity, quantity and composition of all *nuclear material* subject to safeguards under the Agreement; and

    (c)   Verify information on the possible causes of *material unaccounted for, shipper/ receiver differences* and uncertainties in the *book inventory*.

73. The Agreement should provide that the Agency may make special inspections subject to the procedures laid down in paragraph 77 below:

    (a)   In order to verify the information contained in special reports; or

    (b)   If the Agency considers that information made available by the State, including explanations from the State and information obtained from routine inspections, is not adequate for the Agency to fulfll its responsibilities under the Agreement.

An inspection shall be deemed to be special when it is either additional to the routine inspection effort provided for in paragraphs 78-82 below, or involves access to information or locations in addition to the access specified in paragraph 76 for ad hoc and routine inspections, or both.

Scope of inspections

74. The Agreement should provide that for the purposes stated in para graphs 71-73 above the Agency may:

    (a)   Examine the records kept pursuant to paragraphs 51-58;

    (b)   Make independent measurements of all *nuclear material* subject to safeguards under the Agreement;

    (c)   Verify the functioning and calibration of instruments and other measuring and control equipment;

    (d)   Apply and make use of surveillance and containment measures; and

    (e)   Use other objective methods which have been demonstrated to be technically feasible.

75. It should further be provided that within the scope of paragraph 74 above the Agency shall be enabled:

    (a)   To observe that samples at *key measurement points* for material balance accounting are taken in accordance with procedures which pr o duce representative samples, to observe the treatment and analysis of the samples and to obtain duplicates of such samples;

(b)   To observe that the measurements of *nuclear material* at *key measurement points* for material balance accounting are representative, and to observe the calibration of the instruments and equipment involved ;

(c)   To make arrangements with the State that, if necessary:

(i)   Additional measurements are made and additional samples taken for the Agency's use;

(ii)   The Agency's standard analytical samples are analysed;

(iii) Appropriate absolute standards are used in calibrating instruments and other equipment; and

(iv)   Other calibrations are carried out;

(d)   To arrange to use its own equipment for independent measurement and surveillance, and if so agreed and specified in the Subsidiary Arrangements, to arrange to install such equipment;

(e)   To apply its seals and other identifying and tamper-indicating devices to containments, if so agreed and specified in the Subsidiary Arrangements; and

(f)   To make arrangements with the State for the shipping of samples taken for the Agency's use.

Access for inspections

76.   The Agreement should provide that:

(a)   For the purposes specified in sub-paragraphs 71(a) and (b) above and until such time as the *strategic points* have been specified in the Subsidiary Arrangements, the Agency's inspectors shall have access to any location where the initial report or any inspections carried out in connection with it indicate that *nuclear material* is present;

(b)   For the purposes specified in sub-paragraph 71(c) above the inspectors shall have access to any location of which the Agency has been notified in accordance with sub-paragraphs 92(c) or 95(c) below;

(c)   For the purposes specified in paragraph 72 above the Agency's inspectors shall have access only to the *strategic points* specified in the Subsidiary Arrangements and to the records maintained pursuant to paragraphs 51-58 ; and

(d)   In the event of the State concluding that any unusual circum stances require extended limitations on access by the Agency, the State and the Agency shall promptly make arrangements with a view to enabling the Agency to discharge its safeguards responsibilities in the light of these limitations. The Director General shall report each such arrangement to the Board.

77.   The Agreement should provide that in circumstances which may lead to special inspections for the purposes specified in paragraph 7 3 above the State and the Agency shall consult forthwith. As a result of such consultations the Agency may make inspections in addition to the routine inspection effort provided for in paragraphs 78-82 below, and may obtain access in agreement with the State

to information or locations in addition to the access specified in paragraph 76 above for ad hoc and routine inspections. Any disagreement concerning the need for additional access shall be resolved in accordance with paragraphs 21 and 22; in case action by the State is essential and urgent, paragraph 18 above shall apply.

Frequency and intensity of routine inspections

78. The Agreement should provide that the number, intensity, duration and timing of routine inspections shall be kept to the minimum consistent with the effective implementation of the safeguards procedures set forth therein, and that the Agency shall make the optimum and most economical use of available inspection resources.

79. The Agreement should provide that in the case of *facilities* and *material balance areas* outside *facilities* with a content or *annual throughput,* whichever is greater, of *nuclear material* not exceeding five *effective kilograms,* routine inspections shall not exceed one per year. For other *facilities* the number, intensity, duration, timing and mode of inspections shall be determined on the basis that in the maximum or limiting case the inspection regime shall be no more intensive than is necessary and sufficient to maintain continuity of knowledge of the flow and inventory of *nuclear material.*

80. The Agreement should provide that the maximum routine inspection effort in respect of *facilities* with a content or *annual throughput* of *nuclear material* exceeding five *effective kilograms* shall be determined as follows:

(a) For reactors and sealed stores, the maximum total of routine inspection per year shall be determined by allowing one sixth of a *man year of inspection* for each such *facility* in the State;

(b) For other *facilities* involving plutonium or uranium enriched to more than 5%, the maximum total of routine inspection per year shall be determined by allowing for each such *facility* $30 \times \{Square\ Root[E]\}$ man-days of inspection per year, where E is the inventory or *annual throughput* of *nuclear material,* whichever is greater, expressed in *effective kilograms.* The maximum established for any such *facility* shall not, however, be less than 1.5 *man-year of inspection;* and

(c) For all other *facilities,* the maximum total of routine inspection per year shall be determined by allowing for each such *facility* one third of a *man-year of inspection* plus $0.4 \times E$ man-days of inspection per year, where E is the inventory or *annual throughput* of *nuclear material,* whichever is greater, expressed in *effective kilograms.*

The Agreement should further provide that the Agency and the State may agree to amend the maximum figures specified in this paragraph upon determination by the Board that such amendment is reasonable.

81. Subject to paragraphs 78-80 above the criteria to be used for deter mining the actual number, intensity, duration, timing and mode of routine inspections of any *facility* shall include:

    (a) The form of *nuclear material,* in particular, whether the material is in bulk form or contained in a number of separate items; its chemical composition and, in the case of uranium, whether it is of low or high *enrichment;* and its accessibility;

    (b) The effectiveness of the State's accounting and control system, including the extent to which the operators of *facilities* are functionally independent of the State's accounting and control system; the extent to which the measures specified in paragraph 32 above have been implemented by the State; the promptness of reports submitted to the Agency; their consistency with the Agency's independent verification; and the amount and accuracy of the *material unaccounted for,* as verified by the Agency;

    (c) Characteristics of the State's nuclear fuel cycle, in particular, the number and types of *facilities* containing *nuclear material* subject to safe guards, the characteristics of such *facilities* relevant to safeguards, notably the degree of containment; the extent to which the design of such *facilities* facilitates verification of the flow and inventory of *nuclear material;* and the extent to which information from different *material balance areas* can be correlated;

    (d) International interdependence, in particular, the extent to which *nuclear material* is received from or sent to other States for use or processing; any verification activity by the Agency in connection therewith; and the extent to which the State's nuclear activities are interrelated with those of other States; and

    (e) Technical developments in the field of safeguards, including the use of statistical techniques and random sampling in evaluating the flow of *nuclear material.*

82. The Agreement should provide for consultation between the Agency and the State if the latter considers that the inspection effort is being deployed with undue concentration on particular *facilities.*

Notice of inspections

83. The Agreement should provide that the Agency shall give advance notice to the State before arrival of inspectors at *facilities* or *material balance areas* out side *facilities,* as follows:

    (a) For ad hoc inspections pursuant to sub-paragraph 71 (c) above, at least 24 hours, for those pursuant to sub-paragraphs 71 (a) and (b), as well as the activities provided for in paragraph 48, at least one week ;

    (b) For special inspections pursuant to paragraph 73 above, as promptly as possible after the Agency and the State have consulted as provided for in paragraph 77, it being understood that notification of arrival normally will constitute part of the consultations; and

(c)   For routine inspections pursuant to paragraph 72 above, at least 24 hours in respect of the *facilities* referred to in sub-paragraph 80(b) and sealed stores containing plutonium or uranium enriched to more than 5%, and one week in all other cases.

Such notice of inspections shall include the names of the inspectors and shall indicate the *facilities* and the *material balance areas* outside *facilities* to be visited and the periods during which they will be visited. If the inspectors are to arrive from outside the State the Agency shall also give advance notice of the place and time of their arrival in the State.

84.   However, the Agreement should also provide that, as a supplementary measure, the Agency may carry out without advance notification a portion of the routine inspections pursuant to paragraph 80 above in accordance with the principle of random sampling. In performing any unannounced inspections, the Agency shall fully take into account any operational programme provided by the State pursuant to paragraph 64(b). Moreover, whenever practicable, and on the basis of the operational programme, it shall advise the State periodically of its general programme of announced and unannounced inspections, specifying the general periods when inspections are foreseen. In carrying out any unannounced inspections, the Agency shall make every effort to minimize any practical difficulties for *facility* operators and the State, bearing in mind the relevant provisions of paragraphs 44 above and 89 below. Similarly the State shall make every effort to facilitate the task of the inspectors.

Designation of inspectors

85.   The Agreement should provide that:

(a)   The Director General shall inform the State in writing of the name, qualifications, nationality, grade and such other particulars as may be relevant, of each Agency official he proposes for designation as an inspector for the State;

(b)   The State shall inform the Director General within 30 days of the receipt of such a proposal whether it accepts the proposal;

(c)   The Director General may designate each official who has been accepted by the State as one of the inspectors for the State, and shall inform the State of such designations; and

(d)   The Director General, acting in response to a request by the State or on his own initiative, shall immediately inform the State of the withdrawal of the designation of any official as an inspector for the State.

The Agreement should also provide, however, that in respect of inspectors needed for the purposes stated in paragraph 48 above and to carry out ad hoc inspections pursuant to sub-paragraphs 71 (a) and (b) the designation procedures shall be completed if possible within 30 days after the entry into force of the Agreement. If such designation appears impossible within this time limit, inspectors for such purposes shall be designated on a temporary basis.

86. The Agreement should provide that the State shall grant or renew as quickly as possible appropriate visas, where required, for each inspector designated for the State.

Conduct and visits of inspectors

87. The Agreement should provide that inspectors, in exercising their functions under paragraphs 48 and 71-75 above, shall carry out their activities in a manner designed to avoid hampering or delaying the construction, commissioning or operation of *facilities,* or affecting their safety. In particular inspectors shall not operate any *facility* themselves or direct the staff of a *facility* to carry out any operation. If inspectors consider that in pursuance of paragraphs 74 and 75, particular operations in a *facility* should be carried out by the operator, they shall make a request therefor.

88. When inspectors require services available in the State, including the use of equipment, in connection with the performance of inspections, the State shall facilitate the procurement of such services and the use of such equipment by inspectors.

89. The Agreement should provide that the State shall have the right to have inspectors accompanied during their inspections by representatives of the State, provided that inspectors shall not thereby be delayed or otherwise impeded in the exercise of their functions.

STATEMENTS ON THE AGENCY'S VERIFICATION ACTIVITIES

90. The Agreement should provide that the Agency shall inform the State of:

    (a) The results of inspections, at intervals to be specified in the Subsidiary Arrangements; and
    (b) The conclusions it has drawn from its verification activities in the State, in particular by means of statements in respect of each *material balance area,* which shall be made as soon as possible after a *physical inventory* has been taken and verified by the Agency and a material balance has been struck.

INTERNATIONAL TRANSFERS

General

91. The Agreement should provide that *nuclear material* subject or required to be subject to safeguards thereunder which is transferred internationally shall, for purposes of the Agreement, be regarded as being the responsibility of the State:

(a)   In the case of import, from the time that such responsibility ceases to lie with the exporting State, and no later than the time at which the *nuclear material* reaches its destination; and

(b)   In the case of export, up to the time at which the recipient State assumes such responsibility, and no later than the time at which the *nuclear material* reaches its destination.

The Agreement should provide that the States concerned shall make suitable arrangements to determine the point at which the transfer of responsibility will take place. No State shall be deemed to have such responsibility for *nuclear material* merely by reason of the fact that the *nuclear material* is in transit on or over its territory or territorial waters, or that it is being transported under its flag or in its aircraft.

Transfers out of the State

92.   The Agreement should provide that any intended transfer out of the State of safeguarded *nuclear material* in an amount exceeding one *effective kilo gram*, or by successive shipments to the same State within a period of three months each of less than one *effective kilogram* but exceeding in total one *effective kilogram*, shall be notified to the Agency after the conclusion of the contractual arrangements leading to the transfer and normally at least two weeks before the *nuclear material* is to be prepared for shipping. The Agency and the State may agree on different procedures for advance notification. The notification shall specify:

(a)   The identification and, if possible, the expected quantity and composition of the *nuclear material* to be transferred, and the *material balance area* from which it will come;

(b)   The State for which the *nuclear material* is destined;

(c)   The dates on and locations at which the *nuclear material* is to be prepared for shipping;

(d)   The approximate dates of dispatch and arrival of the *nuclear material;* and

(e)   At what point of the transfer the recipient State will assume responsibility for the *nuclear material,* and the probable date on which this point will be reached.

93.   The Agreement should further provide that the purpose of this notification shall be to enable the Agency if necessary to identify, and if possible verify the quantity and composition of, *nuclear material* subject to safeguards under the Agreement before it is transferred out of the State and, if the Agency so wishes or the State so requests, to affix seals to the *nuclear material* when it has been prepared for shipping. However, the transfer of the *nuclear material* shall not be delayed in any way by any action taken or contemplated by the Agency pursuant to this notification.

94.   The Agreement should provide that, if the *nuclear material* will not be subject to Agency safeguards in the recipient State, the exporting State shall make

arrangements for the Agency to receive, within three months of the time when the recipient State accepts responsibility for the *nuclear material* from the exporting State, confirmation by the recipient State of the transfer.

Transfers into the State

95. The Agreement should provide that the expected transfer into the State of *nuclear material* required to be subject to safeguards in an amount greater than one *effective kilogram*, or by successive shipments from the same State within a period of three months each of less than one *effective kilogram* but exceeding in total one *effective kilogram*, shall be notified to the Agency as much in advance as possible of the expected arrival of the *nuclear material*, and in any case not later than the date on which the recipient State assumes responsibility therefor. The Agency and the State may agree on different procedures for advance notification. The notification shall specify:

   (a) The identification and, if possible, the expected quantity and composition of the *nuclear material;*

   (b) At what point of the transfer responsibility for the *nuclear material* will be assumed by the State for the purposes of the Agreement, and the probable date on which this point will be reached ; and

   (c) The expected date of arrival, the location to which the *nuclear material* is to be delivered and the date on which it is intended that the *nuclear material* should be unpacked.

96. The Agreement should provide that the purpose of this notification shall be to enable the Agency if necessary to identify, and if possible verify the quantity and composition of, *nuclear material* subject to safeguards which has been transferred into the State, by means of inspection of the consignment at the time it is unpacked. However, unpacking shall not be delayed by any action taken or contemplated by the Agency pursuant to this notification.

Special reports

97. The Agreement should provide that in the case of international transfers a special report as envisaged in paragraph 68 above shall be made if any unusual incident or circumstances lead the State to believe that there is or may have been loss of *nuclear material*, including the occurrence of significant delay during the transfer.

DEFINITIONS

98. "Adjustment" means an entry into an accounting record or a report showing a *shipper/ receiver difference* or *material unaccounted for.*

99. "Annual throughput" means, for the purposes of paragraphs 79 and 80 above, the amount of *nuclear material* transferred annually out of a *facility* working at nominal capacity.

100. "Batch" means a portion of *nuclear material* handled as a unit for accounting purposes at a *key measurement point* and for which the composition and quantity are defined by a single set of specifications or measurements. The *nuclear material* may be in bulk form or contained in a number of separate items.

101. "Batch data" means the total weight of each element of *nuclear material* and, in the case of plutonium and uranium, the isotopic composition when appropriate. The units of account shall be as follows:

    (a) Grams of contained plutonium;
    (b) Grams of total uranium and grams of contained uranium-235 plus uranium-233 for uranium enriched in these isotopes; and
    (c) Kilograms of contained thorium, natural uranium or depleted uranium. For reporting purposes the weights of individual items in the *batch* shall be added together before rounding to the nearest unit.

102. "Book inventory" of a *material balance area* means the algebraic sum of the most recent *physical inventory* of that *material balance area* and of all *inventory changes* that have occurred since that *physical inventory* was taken.

103. "Correction" means an entry into an accounting record or a report to rectify an identified mistake or to reflect an improved measurement of a quantity previously entered into the record or report. Each correction must identify the entry to which it pertains.

104. "Effective kilogram" means a special unit used in safeguarding *nuclear material*. The quantity in "effective kilograms" is obtained by taking:

    (a) For plutonium, its weight in kilograms;
    (b) For uranium with an *enrichment* of 0.01 (1%) and above, its weight in kilograms multiplied by the· square of its *enrichment;*
    (c) For uranium with an *enrichment* below 0.01 (1%) and above 0.005 (0.5 %), its weight in kilograms multiplied by 0.0001; and
    (d) For depleted uranium with an *enrichment* of 0.005 (0.5%) or below, and for thorium, its weight in kilograms multiplied by 0.00005.

105. "Enrichment" means the ratio of the combined weight of the isotopes uranium-233 and uranium-235 to that of the total uranium in question.

106. "Facility" means:

(a) A reactor, a critical facility, a conversion plant, a fabrication plant, a repro-cessing plant, an isotope separation plant or a separate storage installa-tion; or

(b) Any location where *nuclear material* in amounts greater than one *effective kilogram* is customarily used.

107. "Inventory change" means an increase or decrease, in terms of *batches,* of *nuclear material* in a *material balance area;* such a change shall involve one of the following:

(a) Increases:
   (i) Import;
   (ii) Domestic receipt: receipts from other *material balance areas,* receipts from a non-safeguarded (non-peaceful) activity or receipts at the starting point of safeguards;
   (ill) Nuclear production: production of special fissionable material in a reactor; and
   (iv) De-exemption: reapplication of safeguards on *nuclear material* previ-ously exempted therefrom on account of its use or quantity.

(b) Decreases:
   (i) Export;
   (ii) Domestic shipment: shipments to other material balance areas or shipments for a non-safeguarded (non-peaceful) activity;
   (iii) Nuclear loss: loss of nuclear material due to its transformation into other element(s) or isotope(s) as a result of nuclear reactions; (iv) Measured discard: nuclear material which has been measured, or estimated on the basis of measurements, and disposed of in such a way that it is not suitable for further nuclear use;
   (v) Retained waste: nuclear material generated from processing or from an operational accident, which is deemed to be unrecoverable for the time being but which is stored;
   (vi) Exemption: exemption of nuclear material from safeguards on account of its use or quantity; and
   (vii) Other loss: for example, accidental loss (that is, irretrievable and inadvertent loss of nuclear material as the result of an operational accident) or theft.

108. "Key measurement point" means a location where nuclear material appears in such a form that it may be measured to determine material flow or inventory. "Key measurement points" thus include, but are not limited to, the inputs and outputs (including measured discards) and storages in material balance areas.

109. "Man-year of inspection" means, for the purposes of paragraph 80 above, 300 man-days of inspection, a man-day being a day during which a single inspector has access to a facility at any time for a total of not more than eight hours.

110. "Material balance area" means an area in or outside of a facility such that:

(a) The quantity of nuclear material in each transfer into or out of each "material balance area" can be determined; and

(b) The physical inventory of nuclear material in each "material balance area" can be determined when necessary, in accordance with specified procedures, in order that the material balance for Agency safeguards purposes can be established.

111. "Material unaccounted for" means the difference between book inventory and physical inventory.

112. "Nuclear material" means any source or any special fissionable material as defined in Article XX of the Statute. The term source material shall not be interpreted as applying to ore or ore residue. Any determination by the Board under Article XX of the Statute after the entry into force of this Agreement which adds to the materials considered to be source material or special fission able material shall have effect under this Agreement only upon acceptance by the State.

113. "Physical inventory" means the sum of all the measured or derived estimates of batch quantities of nuclear material on hand at a given time within a material balance area, obtained in accordance with specified procedures.

114. "Shipper/receiver difference" means the difference between the quantity of nuclear material in a batch as stated by the shipping material balance area and as measured at the receiving material balance area.

115. "Source data" means those data, recorded during measurement or calibration or used to derive empirical relationships, which identify nuclear material and provide batch data. "Source data" may include, for example, weight of compounds, conversion factors to determine weight of element, specific gravity, element concentration, isotopic ratios, relationship between volume and manometer readings and relationship between plutonium produced and power generated.

116. "Strategic point" means a location selected during examination of design information where, under normal conditions and when combined with the information from all "strategic points" taken together, the information necessary and sufficient for the implementation of safeguards measures is obtained and verified; a "strategic point" may include any location where key measurements related to material balance accountancy are made and where containment and surveillance measures are executed.

Status of NPT Safeguards Agreements in Non-nuclear-weapon States

The 185 NPT non-nuclear-weapon states are obligated by the Treaty to bring into force NPT comprehensive (INFCIRC/153) safeguards agreements.

One hundred and seventy-three have done so.

As of 31 December 2013, twelve States had not, as listed below, together with the status of their agreements:[26]

- Benin   Agreement signed but not in force
- Cabo Verde   Agreement signed but not in force
- Djibouti   Agreement signed but not in force
- Guinea   Agreement signed but not in force
- Guinea-Bissau   Agreement signed but not in force
- Timor-Leste   Agreement signed but not in force
- Equatorial Guinea   Agreement approved by IAEA Board but not signed
- Eritrea   First step, submission to Board, not taken
- Liberia   First step, submission to Board, not taken
- Micronesia   First step, submission to Board, not taken
- São Tome and Principé   First step, submission to Board, not taken
- Somalia   First step, submission to Board, not taken

---

26   Data from the IAEA, http://www.iaea.org/Publications/Factsheets/English/nptstatus_overview.html (March 5, 2014).

C. Evolution and Strengthening of the NPT Safeguards System

Background

Implementation of safeguards under INFCIRC/153 required the development and deployment of new concepts, new technologies, and new techniques. In the initial phase, the primary focus of safeguards was on the diversion of nuclear material from declared inventories. However, in the late 1970s, the IAEA began to plan for the application of safeguards at uranium enrichment plants that would soon be coming on line in Germany and the Netherlands.

The IAEA needed to address the possibility that such plants could produce weapon-grade high-enriched uranium[27] using either declared or undeclared nuclear material. As a result, the IAEA focus of safeguards was broadened to include the production of undeclared nuclear material at declared enrichment plants, reactors, and reprocessing plants.

After the first Gulf War in 1991, Iraq's clandestine nuclear-weapon program was revealed. Iraq had pursued this program at undeclared locations using undeclared nuclear material, sometimes nearby to where the IAEA was conducting inspections. This discovery triggered an intensive review of the IAEA's NPT safeguards system. A major objective of the review was to identify ways to strengthen the IAEA's capabilities to address undeclared nuclear activities.

The review focused both on steps that could be taken within the IAEA's existing authorities under NPT safeguards agreements; and on measures that would require additional authorities. This section describes the former. The need for additional authorities led to the adoption of the Model Protocol in 1997, which is addressed in the next section.

Four significant steps were taken to strengthen the implementation of safeguards under NPT safeguards agreements on the basis of the authorities already contained in INFCIRC/153.

1. Special Inspections

INFCIRC/153 provides for three types of inspections:

- Ad hoc inspections to verify the nuclear material reported by a state when its safeguards agreement first enters into force;
- Routine inspections that replace ad hoc inspections when the IAEA and a State agree on all of the modalities for inspections and these are codified in subsidiary arrangements;
- Special inspections if the Agency "considers that the information made available by the State, including explanations from the State and information obtained

---

27 Weapon-grade uranium consists of uranium where the isotope U-235 is about 90% of the total uranium.

from routine inspections, is not adequate for the IAEA to fulfill is responsibilities under the Agreement." (INFCIRC/153, para. 73)

Special inspections are of "special" interest for addressing undeclared nuclear activities for two reasons:

- Indicators of undeclared nuclear material are indicators that the IAEA is not able to apply safeguards to all nuclear material in all peaceful nuclear activities, which is its fundamental responsibility; and
- Special inspections provide the basis for the IAEA to seek access to information and to locations in addition to that which is otherwise available.

In light of this potentially important role, the Board affirmed the role of special inspections in its meeting of 25 February 1992 as follows:[28]

The Board urged the full exercise of all Agency rights and obligations as provided under the Statute and in all comprehensive safeguards agreements (i.e. those which are based on the guidelines set forth in INFCIRC/153 (Corrected), as well as others which provide for the application of Agency safeguards to all nuclear materials in all peaceful nuclear activities within a State). The Board reaffirmed the Agency's right to undertake special inspections, when necessary and appropriate as described in the above-mentioned agreements and to ensure that all nuclear materials in peaceful nuclear activities are under safeguards. The Board anticipates that these special inspections should only occur on rare occasions. The Board further reaffirmed the Agency's rights to obtain and to have access to additional information and locations in accordance with the Agency's Statute and all comprehensive safeguards agreements.

2. Environmental sampling

Environmental sampling takes advantage of the ability of modern analytical techniques to detect and measure extremely small quantities of nuclear material. Precise measurements can be made of particles too small to be seen that might be picked up by swiping a surface with a cotton cloth.

The IAEA used this measure to good effect in detecting anomalies in the declarations of the Democratic Republic of Korea in 1992. Field trials demonstrated that the technique was both effective and efficient. As a result of the field trials, the Board agreed that IAEA inspectors could use environmental sampling at all locations to which they had access: where they conduct ad hoc inspections, routine inspections, special inspections or conduct visits to verify design information.

---

28 IAEA document GOV/OR/776.

3. Correctness and completeness of States' declarations; assurance of the absence of undeclared nuclear material and activities

In a report to the Board of Governors in 1995 (GOV/2784), the Director General requested that the Board confirm a set of key principles:

i) The purpose of comprehensive safeguards agreements is the continuing verification of the correctness and completeness of State's declarations of nuclear material in order to provide maximum assurance of the non-diversion of nuclear material from declared activities and of the absence of undeclared nuclear activities;

ii) The safeguards system of the IAEA should be so designed as to give effect to that purpose. The IAEA should be enabled to fulfill its mandate under such agreements, either on the basis of existing authority provided for under such agreements or on the basis of complementary authority to be conferred.

iii) An increased access to safeguards-relevant information and safeguards-relevant sites is of key importance to the realization of a more effective and efficient safeguards system;

iv) Under comprehensive safeguards agreements, the States parties and the Agency have an obligation to co-operate fully to achieve effective implementation of the agreements. The Agency must fully perform its part of the cooperation. Similarly, the States Parties must take administrative and other measures to enable the Agency to fulfill its responsibilities under these agreements.

In March 1995, the Board endorsed points i) and ii) in the following statement (GOV/OR/864 March 1995):

The Board reiterates that the purpose of comprehensive safeguards agreements, where safeguards are applied to all nuclear material in all nuclear activities within the territory of a State party to such an agreement, under its jurisdiction or carried out under its control anywhere, is to verify that such material is not diverted to nuclear weapons or other nuclear explosive devices. To this end, the safeguards system for implementing comprehensive safeguards agreements should be designed to provide for verification by the Agency of the correctness and completeness of States' declarations, so that there is credible assurance of the non-diversion of nuclear material from declared activities and of the absence of undeclared nuclear activities.

4. Early provision of design information

NPT comprehensive safeguards agreements require that information concerning a new facility be provided as early as possible before nuclear material is introduced into a new facility (paragraph 42). "As early as possible" lacks any prescriptive value, so as a practical matter, the IAEA asked states to provide it with completed Agency Design Information Questionnaires for new facilities "normally not later than 180 days before the facilities are scheduled to receive nuclear material for the first time."

But design information is needed much earlier. Nuclear facilities often take many years to design and build, and only with early provision of design information is it possible to incorporate features into the facility design that would make safeguards easier to implement. In addition, safeguards research and development work may be necessary; the Agency needs sound information for budget planning purposes; the installation of safeguards equipment during construction of the facility is much easier and less costly than retrofitting; and verification of information on the design of the facility may not be possible when the facility has been completed.

In order to met these needs the IAEA Board of Governors agreed that parties to comprehensive safeguards agreements should provide design information as follows:[29]

(a)   inform the Agency of their programmes for new nuclear facilities and activities and for any modifications to existing facilities through the provision of preliminary design information as soon as the decision to construct, to authorize construction or to modify has been taken; and

(b)   provide the Agency with further information on designs as they are developed. The information should be provided early in the project definition, preliminary design, construction and commissioning phases; and

(c)   provide the Agency with completed Design Information Questionnaires for new facilities based on preliminary construction plans as early as possible, and in any event not later than 180 days prior to the start of construction. Design Information Questionnaires based on "as-built" designs should be provided as early as possible, and in any event not later than 180 days before the first receipt of nuclear material at the facility.

The Board called on all parties to comprehensive safeguards agreement to provide this information and to make necessary changes to the Subsidiary Arrangements.[30]

---

29   Strengthening of Agency Safeguards: The Provision and use of Design Information, GOV/2554/Atachment 2/Rev.2/, April 1, 1992

30   The relevant section of the subsidiary arrangements is known as Code 3.1. It is this section that Iran agreed to and then asserted that it was not bound by.

D. INFCIRC/540 – The Model Protocol

Model Protocol Additional to the Agreement(s) between State(s) and the International Atomic Energy Agency for the Application of Safeguards

INFCIRC/540
(Corrected)

Foreword

This document is a model Additional Protocol designed for States having a Safeguards Agreement with the Agency, in order to strengthen the effectiveness and improve the efficiency of the safeguards system as a contribution to global nuclear non-proliferation objectives.

The Board of Governors has requested the Director General to use this Model Protocol as the standard for additional protocols that are to be concluded by States and other parties to comprehensive safeguards agreements with the Agency. Such protocols shall contain all of the measures in this Model Protocol.

The Board of Governors has also requested the Director General to negotiate additional protocols or other legally binding agreements with nuclear-weapon States incorporating those measures provided for in the Model Protocol that each nuclear-weapon State has identified as capable of contributing to the non-proliferation and efficiency aims of the Protocol, when implemented with regard to that State, and as consistent with that State's obligations under Article I of the NPT.

The Board of Governors has further requested the Director General to negotiate additional protocols with other States that are prepared to accept measures provided for in the Model Protocol in pursuance of safeguards effectiveness and efficiency objectives.

In conformity with the requirements of the Statute, each individual Protocol or other legally binding agreement will require the approval of the Board and its authorization to the Director General to conclude and subsequently implement the Protocol so approved.

NUCLEARPEDIA

CONTENTS

MODEL PROTOCOL ADDITIONAL TO THE AGREEMENT(S) BETWEEN .... AND THE INTERNATIONAL ATOMIC ENERGY AGENCY FOR THE APPLICATION OF SAFEGUARDS

Preamble

WHEREAS .... (hereinafter referred to as "..........") is a party to (an) Agreement(s) between .... and the International Atomic Energy Agency (hereinafter referred to as the "Agency") for the application of safeguards [full title of the Agreement(s) to be inserted] (hereinafter referred to as the "Safeguards Agreement(s)"), which entered into force on ....;

AWARE OF the desire of the international community to further enhance nuclear non-proliferation by strengthening the effectiveness and improving the efficiency of the Agency's safeguards system;

RECALLING that the Agency must take into account in the implementation of safeguards the need to: avoid hampering the economic and technological development of .... or international co-operation in the field of peaceful nuclear activities; respect health, safety, physical protection and other security provisions in force and the rights of individuals; and take every precaution to protect commercial, technological and industrial secrets as well as other confidential information coming to its knowledge;

WHEREAS the frequency and intensity of activities described in this Protocol shall be kept to the minimum consistent with the objective of strengthening the effectiveness and improving the efficiency of Agency safeguards;

NOW THEREFORE .... and the Agency have agreed as follows:

RELATIONSHIP BETWEEN THE PROTOCOL AND THE SAFEGUARDS AGREEMENT

Article 1

The provisions of the Safeguards Agreement shall apply to this Protocol to the extent that they are relevant to and compatible with the provisions of this Protocol. In case of conflict between the provisions of the Safeguards Agreement and those of this Protocol, the provisions of this Protocol shall apply.

PROVISION OF INFORMATION

Article 2

a.   .... shall provide the Agency with a declaration containing:

(i)   A general description of and information specifying the location of *nuclear fuel cycle-related research and development activities** not involving *nuclear material* carried out anywhere that are funded, specifically authorized or controlled by, or carried out on behalf of, ...

(ii)   Information identified by the Agency on the basis of expected gains in effectiveness or efficiency, and agreed to by .... on operational activities of safeguards relevance at *facilities* and at *locations outside facilities* where *nuclear material* is customarily used.

(iii)   A general description of each building on each *site*, including its use and, if not apparent from that description, its contents. The description shall include a map of the *site*.

(iv)   A description of the scale of operations for each location engaged in the activities specified in Annex I to this Protocol.

(v)   Information specifying the location, operational status and the estimated annual production capacity of uranium mines and concentration plants and thorium concentration plants, and the current annual production of such mines and concentration plants for .... as a whole. .... shall provide, upon request by the Agency, the current annual production of an individual mine or concentration plant. The provision of this information does not require detailed *nuclear material* accountancy.

(vi)   Information regarding source material which has not reached the composition and purity suitable for fuel fabrication or for being isotopically enriched, as follows:

(a)   The quantities, the chemical composition, the use or intended use of such material, whether in nuclear or non-nuclear use, for each location in .... at which the material is present in quantities exceeding ten metric tons of uranium and/or twenty metric tons of thorium, and for other locations with quantities of more than one metric ton, the aggregate for .... as a whole if the aggregate exceeds ten metric tons of uranium or twenty metric tons of thorium. The provision of this information does not require detailed *nuclear material* accountancy;

---

* Terms in italics have specialized meanings, which are defined in Article 18 below.

(b) The quantities, the chemical composition and the destination of each export out of .... of such material for specifically non-nuclear purposes in quantities exceeding:

(1) Ten metric tons of uranium, or for successive exports of uranium from .... to the same State, each of less than ten metric tons, but exceeding a total of ten metric tons for the year;

(2) Twenty metric tons of thorium, or for successive exports of thorium from .... to the same State, each of less than twenty metric tons, but exceeding a total of twenty metric tons for the year;

(c) The quantities, chemical composition, current location and use or intended use of each import into .... of such material for specifically non-nuclear purposes in quantities exceeding:

(1) Ten metric tons of uranium, or for successive imports of uranium into .... each of less than ten metric tons, but exceeding a total of ten metric tons for the year;

(2) Twenty metric tons of thorium, or for successive imports of thorium into .... each of less than twenty metric tons, but exceeding a total of twenty metric tons for the year;

it being understood that there is no requirement to provide information on such material intended for a non-nuclear use once it is in its non-nuclear end-use form.

(vii) (a) Information regarding the quantities, uses and locations of nuclear material exempted from safeguards pursuant to [paragraph 37 of INFCIRC/153]
(b) Information regarding the quantities (which may be in the form of estimates) and uses at each location, of nuclear material exempted from safeguards pursuant to [paragraph 36(b) of INFCIRC/153] but not yet in a non-nuclear end-use form, in quantities exceeding those set out in [paragraph 37 of INFCIRC/153].** The provision of this information does not require detailed *nuclear material* accountancy.

(viii) Information regarding the location or further processing of intermediate or high-level waste containing plutonium, *high enriched uranium* or uranium-233 on which safeguards have been terminated pursuant to [paragraph 11 of INFCIRC/153]. For the purpose of this paragraph,

---

** The reference to the corresponding provision of the relevant Safeguards Agreement should be inserted where bracketed references to INFCIRC/153 are made.

"further processing" does not include repackaging of the waste or its further conditioning not involving the separation of elements, for storage or disposal.

(ix) The following information regarding specified equipment and non-nuclear material listed in Annex II:

    (a) For each export out of .... of such equipment and material: the identity, quantity, location of intended use in the receiving State and date or, as appropriate, expected date, of export;

    (b) Upon specific request by the Agency, confirmation by ...., as importing State, of information provided to the Agency by another State concerning the export of such equipment and material to ....

(x) General plans for the succeeding ten-year period relevant to the development of the nuclear fuel cycle (including planned *nuclear fuel cycle-related research and development activities*) when approved by the appropriate authorities in ....

b.   .... shall make every reasonable effort to provide the Agency with the following information:

(i) A general description of and information specifying the location of *nuclear fuel cycle-related research and development activities* not involving *nuclear material* which are specifically related to enrichment, reprocessing of nuclear fuel or the processing of intermediate or high-level waste containing plutonium, *high enriched uranium* or uranium-233 that are carried out anywhere in .... but which are not funded, specifically authorized or controlled by, or carried out on behalf of, ... For the purpose of this paragraph, "processing" of intermediate or high-level waste does not include repackaging of the waste or its conditioning not involving the separation of elements, for storage or disposal.

(ii) A general description of activities and the identity of the person or entity carrying out such activities, at locations identified by the Agency outside a *site* which the Agency considers might be functionally related to the activities of that *site*. The provision of this information is subject to a specific request by the Agency. It shall be provided in consultation with the Agency and in a timely fashion.

c.   Upon request by the Agency, ... shall provide amplifications or clarifications of any information it has provided under this Article, in so far as relevant for the purpose of safeguards.

Article 3

a. .... shall provide to the Agency the information identified in Article 2.a.(i), (iii), (iv), (v), (vi)(a), (vii) and (x) and Article 2.b.(i) within 180 days of the entry into force of this Protocol.

b. .... shall provide to the Agency, by 15 May of each year, updates of the information referred to in paragraph a. above for the period covering the previous calendar year. If there has been no change to the information previously provided, ... shall so indicate.

c. .... shall provide to the Agency, by 15 May of each year, the information identified in Article 2.a.(vi)(b) and (c) for the period covering the previous calendar year.

d. .... shall provide to the Agency on a quarterly basis the information identified in Article 2.a.(ix)(a). This information shall be provided within sixty days of the end of each quarter.

e. .... shall provide to the Agency the information identified in Article 2.a.(viii) 180 days before further processing is carried out and, by 15 May of each year, information on changes in location for the period covering the previous calendar year.

f. .... and the Agency shall agree on the timing and frequency of the provision of the information identified in Article 2.a.(ii).

g. .... shall provide to the Agency the information in Article 2.a.(ix)(b) within sixty days of the Agency's request.

COMPLEMENTARY ACCESS

Article 4

The following shall apply in connection with the implementation of complementary access under Article 5 of this Protocol:

a. The Agency shall not mechanistically or systematically seek to verify the information referred to in Article 2; however, the Agency shall have access to:
    (i)   Any location referred to in Article 5.a.(i) or (ii) on a selective basis in order to assure the absence of undeclared *nuclear material* and activities;
    (ii) Any location referred to in Article 5.b. or c. to resolve a question relating to the correctness and completeness of the information provided pursuant to Article 2 or to resolve an inconsistency relating to that information;

(iii) Any location referred to in Article 5.a.(iii) to the extent necessary for the Agency to confirm, for safeguards purposes, ...'s declaration of the decommissioned status of a *facility* or of a *location outside facilities* where *nuclear material* was customarily used.

b. (i) Except as provided in paragraph (ii) below, the Agency shall give .... advance notice of at least 24 hours;

(ii) For access to any place on a *site* that is sought in conjunction with design information verification visits or ad hoc or routine inspections on that *site*, the period of advance notice shall, if the Agency so requests, be at least two hours but, in exceptional circumstances, it may be less than two hours.

c. Advance notice shall be in writing and shall specify the reasons for access and the activities to be carried out during such access.

d. In the case of a question or inconsistency, the Agency shall provide .... with an opportunity to clarify and facilitate the resolution of the question or inconsistency. Such an opportunity will be provided before a request for access, unless the Agency considers that delay in access would prejudice the purpose for which the access is sought. In any event, the Agency shall not draw any conclusions about the question or inconsistency until .... has been provided with such an opportunity.

e. Unless otherwise agreed to by .... access shall only take place during regular working hours.

f. .... shall have the right to have Agency inspectors accompanied during their access by representatives of ...., provided that the inspectors shall not thereby be delayed or otherwise impeded in the exercise of their functions.

Article 5

.... shall provide the Agency with access to:

a. (i) Any place on a *site*;
(ii) Any location identified by .... under Article 2.a.(v)-(viii);
(iii) Any *decommissioned facility* or *decommissioned location outside facilities* where *nuclear material* was customarily used.

b. Any location identified by .... under Article 2.a.(i), Article 2.a.(iv), Article 2.a.(ix)(b) or Article 2.b, other than those referred to in paragraph a.(i) above, provided that if .... is unable to provide such access, ... shall make every reasonable effort to satisfy Agency requirements, without delay, through other means.

c.   Any location specified by the Agency, other than locations referred to in paragraphs a. and b. above, to carry out *location-specific environmental sampling*, provided that if .... is unable to provide such access, ... shall make every reasonable effort to satisfy Agency requirements, without delay, at adjacent locations or through other means.

Article 6

When implementing Article 5, the Agency may carry out the following activities:

a.   For access in accordance with Article 5.a.(i) or (iii): visual observation; collection of environmental samples; utilization of radiation detection and measurement devices; application of seals and other identifying and tamper indicating devices specified in Subsidiary Arrangements; and other objective measures which have been demonstrated to be technically feasible and the use of which has been agreed by the Board of Governors (hereinafter referred to as the "Board") and following consultations between the Agency and ....

b.   For access in accordance with Article 5.a.(ii): visual observation; item counting of nuclear material; non-destructive measurements and sampling; utilization of radiation detection and measurement devices; examination of records relevant to the quantities, origin and disposition of the material; collection of environmental samples; and other objective measures which have been demonstrated to be technically feasible and the use of which has been agreed by the Board and following consultations between the Agency and ....

c.   For access in accordance with Article 5.b.: visual observation; collection of environmental samples; utilization of radiation detection and measurement devices; examination of safeguards relevant production and shipping records; and other objective measures which have been demonstrated to be technically feasible and the use of which has been agreed by the Board and following consultations between the Agency and ....

d.   For access in accordance with Article 5.c.: collection of environmental samples and, in the event the results do not resolve the question or inconsistency at the location specified by the Agency pursuant to Article 5.c., utilization at that location of visual observation, radiation detection and measurement devices, and, as agreed by .... and the Agency, other objective measures.

Article 7

a.   Upon request by .... the Agency and .... shall make arrangements for managed access under this Protocol in order to prevent the dissemination of proliferation sensitive information, to meet safety or physical protection requirements, or to protect proprietary or commercially sensitive information. Such arrangements shall not preclude the Agency from conducting activities necessary to provide credible assurance of the absence of undeclared *nuclear material* and activities at the location in question, including the resolution of a question relating to the correctness and completeness of the information referred to in Article 2 or of an inconsistency relating to that information.

b. .... may, when providing the information referred to in Article 2, inform the Agency of the places at a *site* or location at which managed access may be applicable.

c. Pending the entry into force of any necessary Subsidiary Arrangements, ... may have recourse to managed access consistent with the provisions of paragraph a. above.

Article 8

Nothing in this Protocol shall preclude .... from offering the Agency access to locations in addition to those referred to in Articles 5 and 9 or from requesting the Agency to conduct verification activities at a particular location. The Agency shall, without delay, make every reasonable effort to act upon such a request.

Article 9

.... shall provide the Agency with access to locations specified by the Agency to carry out *wide-area environmental sampling*, provided that if .... is unable to provide such access it shall make every reasonable effort to satisfy Agency requirements at alternative locations. The Agency shall not seek such access until the use of *wide-area environmental sampling* and the procedural arrangements therefor have been approved by the Board and following consultations between the Agency and ....

Article 10

The Agency shall inform .... of:
a. The activities carried out under this Protocol, including those in respect of any questions or inconsistencies the Agency had brought to the attention of ...., within sixty days of the activities being carried out by the Agency.
b. The results of activities in respect of any questions or inconsistencies the Agency had brought to the attention of ...., as soon as possible but in any case within thirty days of the results being established by the Agency.
c. The conclusions it has drawn from its activities under this Protocol. The conclusions shall be provided annually.

DESIGNATION OF AGENCY INSPECTORS

Article 11

a. (i)   The Director General shall notify .... of the Board's approval of any Agency official as a safeguards inspector. Unless .... advises the Director General of its rejection of such an official as an inspector for .... within three months of receipt of notification of the Board's approval, the inspector so notified to .... shall be considered designated to .... ;
(ii)   The Director General, acting in response to a request by .... or on his own initiative, shall immediately inform .... of the withdrawal of the designation of any official as an inspector for ....

b. A notification referred to in paragraph a. above shall be deemed to be received by .... seven days after the date of the transmission by registered mail of the notification by the Agency to ....

VISAS

Article 12

.... shall, within one month of the receipt of a request therefor, provide the designated inspector specified in the request with appropriate multiple entry/exit and/or transit visas, where required, to enable the inspector to enter and remain on the territory of .... for the purpose of carrying out his/her functions. Any visas required shall be valid for at least one year and shall be renewed, as required, to cover the duration of the inspector's designation to ....

SUBSIDIARY ARRANGEMENTS

Article 13

a. Where .... or the Agency indicates that it is necessary to specify in Subsidiary Arrangements how measures laid down in this Protocol are to be applied, ... and the Agency shall agree on such Subsidiary Arrangements within ninety days of the entry into force of this Protocol or, where the indication of the need for such Subsidiary Arrangements is made after the entry into force of this Protocol, within ninety days of the date of such indication.

b. Pending the entry into force of any necessary Subsidiary Arrangements, the Agency shall be entitled to apply the measures laid down in this Protocol.

COMMUNICATIONS SYSTEMS

Article 14

a.   .... shall permit and protect free communications by the Agency for official purposes between Agency inspectors in .... and Agency Headquarters and/or Regional Offices, including attended and unattended transmission of information generated by Agency containment and/or surveillance or measurement devices. The Agency shall have, in consultation with ...., the right to make use of internationally established systems of direct communications, including satellite systems and other forms of telecommunication, not in use in .... At the request of .... or the Agency, details of the implementation of this paragraph with respect to the attended or unattended transmission of information generated by Agency containment and/or surveillance or measurement devices shall be specified in the Subsidiary Arrangements.

b.   Communication and transmission of information as provided for in paragraph a. above shall take due account of the need to protect proprietary or commercially sensitive information or design information which .... regards as being of particular sensitivity.

PROTECTION OF CONFIDENTIAL INFORMATION

Article 15

a.   The Agency shall maintain a stringent regime to ensure effective protection against disclosure of commercial, technological and industrial secrets and other confidential information coming to its knowledge, including such information coming to the Agency's knowledge in the implementation of this Protocol.

b.   The regime referred to in paragraph a. above shall include, among others, provisions relating to:

(i)   General principles and associated measures for the handling of confidential information;
(ii)   Conditions of staff employment relating to the protection of confidential information;
(iii) Procedures in cases of breaches or alleged breaches of confidentiality.

c.   The regime referred to in paragraph a. above shall be approved and periodically reviewed by the Board.

ANNEXES

Article 16

a.   The Annexes to this Protocol shall be an integral part thereof. Except for the purposes of amendment of the Annexes, the term "Protocol" as used in this instrument means the Protocol and the Annexes together.

b.   The list of activities specified in Annex I, and the list of equipment and material specified in Annex II, may be amended by the Board upon the advice of an open-ended working group of experts established by the Board. Any such amendment shall take effect four months after its adoption by the Board.

ENTRY INTO FORCE

Article 17

a.   This Protocol shall enter into force on the date on which the Agency receives from .... written notification that ....'s statutory and/or constitutional requirements for entry into force have been met.

OR[***]

upon signature by the representatives of .... and the Agency.

b.   .... may, at any date before this Protocol enters into force, declare that it will apply this Protocol provisionally.

c.   The Director General shall promptly inform all Member States of the Agency of any declaration of provisional application of, and of the entry into force of, this Protocol.

[***] The choice of alternative depends on the preference of the State concerned according to its internal legal requirements

DEFINITIONS

Article 18

For the purpose of this Protocol:

a.   *Nuclear fuel cycle-related research and development activities* means those activities which are specifically related to any process or system development aspect of any of the following:

- conversion of *nuclear material,*
- enrichment of *nuclear material,*
- nuclear fuel fabrication,
- reactors,
- critical facilities,
- reprocessing of nuclear fuel,
- processing (not including repackaging or conditioning not involving the separation of elements, for storage or disposal) of intermediate or high-level waste containing plutonium, *high enriched uranium* or uranium-233,

but do not include activities related to theoretical or basic scientific research or to research and development on industrial radioisotope applications, medical, hydrological and agricultural applications, health and environmental effects and improved maintenance.

b.   *Site* means that area delimited by .... in the relevant design information for a *facility,* including a *closed-down facility,* and in the relevant information on a *location outside facilities* where *nuclear material* is customarily used, including a *closed-down location outside facilities* where *nuclear material* was customarily used (this is limited to locations with hot cells or where activities related to conversion, enrichment, fuel fabrication or reprocessing were carried out). It shall also include all installations, co-located with the *facility* or location, for the provision or use of essential services, including: hot cells for processing irradiated materials not containing *nuclear material;* installations for the treatment, storage and disposal of waste; and buildings associated with specified activities identified by .... under Article 2.a.(iv) above.

c.   *Decommissioned facility* or *decommissioned location outside facilities* means an installation or location at which residual structures and equipment essential for its use have been removed or rendered inoperable so that it is not used to store and can no longer be used to handle, process or utilize *nuclear material.*

d.   *Closed-down facility* or *closed-down location outside facilities* means an installation or location where operations have been stopped and the *nuclear material* removed but which has not been decommissioned.

e. *High enriched uranium* means uranium containing 20 percent or more of the isotope uranium-235.

f. *Location-specific environmental sampling* means the collection of environmental samples (e.g., air, water, vegetation, soil, smears) at, and in the immediate vicinity of, a location specified by the Agency for the purpose of assisting the Agency to draw conclusions about the absence of undeclared *nuclear material* or nuclear activities at the specified location.

g. *Wide-area environmental sampling* means the collection of environmental samples (e.g., air, water, vegetation, soil, smears) at a set of locations specified by the Agency for the purpose of assisting the Agency to draw conclusions about the absence of undeclared *nuclear material* or nuclear activities over a wide area.

h. *Nuclear material* means any source or any special fissionable material as defined in Article XX of the Statute. The term source material shall not be interpreted as applying to ore or ore residue. Any determination by the Board under Article XX of the Statute of the Agency after the entry into force of this Protocol which adds to the materials considered to be source material or special fissionable material shall have effect under this Protocol only upon acceptance by ....

i. *Facility* means:

(i) A reactor, a critical facility, a conversion plant, a fabrication plant, a reprocessing plant, an isotope separation plant or a separate storage installation; or

(ii) Any location where *nuclear material* in amounts greater than one effective kilogram is customarily used.

j. *Location outside facilities* means any installation or location, which is not a *facility*, where *nuclear material* is customarily used in amounts of one effective kilogram or less.

ANNEX I

LIST OF ACTIVITIES REFERRED TO IN ARTICLE 2.a.(iv) OF THE PROTOCOL

(i)   The manufacture of *centrifuge rotor tubes* or the assembly of *gas centrifuges*.

       Centrifuge rotor tubes means thin-walled cylinders as described in entry 5.1.1(b) of Annex II.

       Gas centrifuges means centrifuges as described in the Introductory Note to entry 5.1 of Annex II.

(ii)   The manufacture of *diffusion barriers*.

       Diffusion barriers means thin, porous filters as described in entry 5.3.1(a) of Annex II.

(iii)   The manufacture or assembly of *laser-based systems*.

       Laser-based systems means systems incorporating those items as described in entry 5.7 of Annex II.

(iv)   The manufacture or assembly of *electromagnetic isotope separators*.

       Electromagnetic isotope separators means those items referred to in entry 5.9.1 of Annex II containing ion sources as described in 5.9.1(a) of Annex II.

(v)   The manufacture or assembly of *columns* or *extraction equipment*.

       Columns or *extraction equipment* means those items as described in entries 5.6.1, 5.6.2, 5.6.3, 5.6.5, 5.6.6, 5.6.7 and 5.6.8 of Annex II.

(vi)   The manufacture of *aerodynamic separation nozzles* or *vortex tubes*.

       Aerodynamic separation nozzles or *vortex tubes* means separation nozzles and vortex tubes as described respectively in entries 5.5.1 and 5.5.2 of Annex II.

(vii) The manufacture or assembly of *uranium plasma generation systems*.

       Uranium plasma generation systems means systems for the generation of uranium plasma as described in entry 5.8.3 of Annex II.

(viii) The manufacture of *zirconium tubes*.

       Zirconium tubes means tubes as described in entry 1.6 of Annex II.

(ix)   The manufacture or upgrading of *heavy water or deuterium.*

Heavy water or deuterium means deuterium, heavy water (deuterium oxide) and any other deuterium compound in which the ratio of deuterium to hydrogen atoms exceeds 1:5000.

(x)   The manufacture of *nuclear grade graphite.*

Nuclear grade graphite means graphite having a purity level better than 5 parts per million boron equivalent and with a density greater than 1.50 g/cm3 .

(xi)   The manufacture of *flasks for irradiated fuel.*

A *flask for irradiated fuel* means a vessel for the transportation and/or storage of irradiated fuel which provides chemical, thermal and radiological protection, and dissipates decay heat during handling, transportation and storage.

(xii)   The manufacture of *reactor control rods.*

Reactor control rods means rods as described in entry 1.4 of Annex II.

(xiii)   The manufacture of *criticality safe tanks and vessels.*

Criticality safe tanks and vessels means those items as described in entries 3.2 and 3.4 of Annex II.

(xiv)   The manufacture of *irradiated fuel element chopping machines.*

Irradiated fuel element chopping machines means equipment as described in entry 3.1 of Annex II.

(xv)   The construction of *hot cells.*

Hot cells means a cell or interconnected cells totalling at least 6 m3 in volume with shielding equal to or greater than the equivalent of 0.5 m of concrete, with a density of 3.2 g/cm3 or greater, outfitted with equipment for remote operations.

ANNEX II

LIST OF SPECIFIED EQUIPMENT AND NON-NUCLEAR MATERIAL FOR THE
REPORTING OF EXPORTS AND IMPORTS
ACCORDING TO ARTICLE 2.a.(ix)*/

[NOTE TO READER: Annex II is not included here. Few if any readers will find the level of detail of interest. Annex II in the Model Protocol was taken as a whole from the 1992 NSG trigger list. Since then, the NSG list has been updated many times. Readers interested in the most recent version of the Nuclear Suppliers Guidelines should turn to iaea.org to see the most recent version of INFCIRC/254. END NOTE]

E. Small Quantities Protocol

Background

Many non-nuclear-weapon states parties to the NPT have minimal or no nuclear programs. As a result, conclusion and implementation of an NPT safeguards agreement may result in costs - both to the State and to the IAEA - that have no corresponding safeguards benefits.

In order to encourage states to bring the safeguards agreements required by the NPT into force without incurring unnecessary costs, the Secretariat of the IAEA prepared a protocol to NPT safeguards agreements to ameliorate unnecessary burdens. So-called "small quantities protocols" (SQP) suspend implementation of many requirements of INFCIRC/153.[31]

A State was eligible for an SQP if it had only small quantities of nuclear material (less than the amount that could be exempted from safeguards under the terms of INFCIRC/153)[32] and no nuclear material in a nuclear facility (as facility is defined by the IAEA). (The exemption limits are complicated, but, for example, a state is allowed to exempt up to one kilogram of plutonium.) The SQP did not suspend the obligation to establish a State System of Accounting for and Control of nuclear material or the obligation to report imports and exports of nuclear material.

Under the 1974 SQP, eligible states did not have to report these small quantities or give the IAEA advance notice of plans to build nuclear facilities. The SQP also suspended the IAEA rights of inspection, even special inspections. Thus, even if the Secretariat became aware that a state with an SQP might no longer eligible for it, the IAEA's rights to pursue this issue formally were limited.

As the emphasis on detecting undeclared nuclear material and activities grew in the early 1990s, the contrast between imitations of the SQP became increasingly at odds with the safeguards strengthening measures that had been put in place to improve the IAEA's ability to address undeclared activities. As a result, in 2005 the Secretariat launched an initiative to revise the SQP, and later that year, the Board agreed on a modification that corrected the defects described above. [33]

The eligibility requirements were changed. To be eligible a State would need both little nuclear material and no existing or <u>planned</u> nuclear facilities. The modified version of the SQP:

---

31 The Small Quantities Protocol appears to have been drafted by the Secretariat and not approved by the Board prior to its use. The text of the Small Quantities Protocol used from 1971 to 2005, together with the text of INFCIRC/153 was published in GOV/INF/276 in 1974.

32 See Paragraphs 36-38 of INFCIRC/153.

33 Small Quantities Protocol (SQP), Standard Text of the IAEA Small Quantities Protocol as revised in 2005, GOV/INF/276/Mod.1, 21 February 2006.

- reinstates the requirement to provide initial reports to the IAEA on all nuclear material;
- gives the IAEA access to verify the initial report;
- requires early information on a decision to build a nuclear facility and early provision of design information for any planned nuclear facilities; and
- reinstates the Agency's right to conduct ad hoc and special inspections.

The Board also decided to approve in the future only the modified text, and it called on each state with the original version of the SQP to modify it or to rescind it. As of the end of 2010, 99 states had an SQP in force, of which 58 used the original text and 41 used the modified text.

Revised Small Quantities Protocol

...... (hereinafter referred to as "......") and the International Atomic Energy Agency (hereinafter referred to as "the Agency") have agreed as follows:

I.   (1)   Until such time as ......

        (a)   has, in peaceful nuclear activities within its territory or under its jurisdiction or control anywhere, nuclear material in quantities exceeding the limits stated, for the type of material in question, in Article 36 of the Agreement between ...... and the Agency for the Application of Safeguards in Connection with the Treaty on the Non-Proliferation of Nuclear Weapons (hereinafter referred to as "the Agreement"), or

        (b)   has taken the decision to construct or authorize construction of a facility, as defined in the Definitions, the implementation of the provisions of Part II of the Agreement shall be held in abeyance, with the exception of Articles 32–38, 40, 48, 49, 59, 61, 67, 68, 70, 72–76, 82, 84–90, 94 and 95.

    (2)   The information to be reported pursuant to paragraphs (a) and (b) of Article 33 of the Agreement may be consolidated and submitted in an annual report; similarly, an annual report shall be submitted, if applicable, with respect to the import and export of nuclear material described in paragraph (c) of Article 33.

    (3)   In order to enable the timely conclusion of the Subsidiary Arrangements provided for in Article 38 of the Agreement, Vanuatu shall:

        (a)   notify the Agency sufficiently in advance of its having nuclear material in peaceful nuclear activities within its territory or under its jurisdiction or control anywhere in quantities that exceed the limits, as referred to in section (1) hereof, or

        (b)   notify the Agency as soon as the decision to construct or to authorize construction of a facility has been taken, whichever occurs first.

II.   This Protocol shall be signed by the representative of ...... and the Agency and shall enter into force on the same date as the Agreement.

F. Implementation of IAEA safeguards in China, France, Russia, the United Kingdom, and the United States

Background

The NPT requires the application of IAEA safeguards only in non-nuclear-weapon states, not in nuclear-weapon states. This differentiation troubled non-nuclear-weapon states even during the negotiation of the NPT. Germany and Japan anticipated having large nuclear fuel cycles and feared that they would be put at a competitive disadvantage with the nuclear-weapon states both from the cost of applying safeguards and from the potential loss to international inspectors of commercially sensitive information. It was clear that the Treaty would need to include Germany and Japan to be successful. In addition, this view was widely held among non-nuclear-weapon states. The pressure from them led the United Kingdom and the United States to make commitments to accept safeguards.

In the case of the United States, President Lyndon Johnson made this commitment in 1967 when he said that, "I want to make clear to the world that we in the United States are not asking any country to accept safeguards that we are not willing to accept ourselves." He went on to state that when safeguards were applied under the Treaty, the IAEA would be permitted to apply safeguards to all nuclear activities in the US, "excluding only those with direct national security significance."[34]

In 1977, the United States also addressed the fears of non-nuclear weapon states when it stated that, "By submitting itself to the same safeguards others are subject to, it is the United States' intention to demonstrate that adherence to the Treaty does not place other countries at a commercial disadvantage, either because of the increased costs associated with safeguards or because of risk of exposure or proprietary information. President Johnson first enunciated this policy in 1967."[35]

In the Letter of Submittal of the Treaty to President Carter in 1978, the purposes of the Offer were explained as:

- [Demonstrating] that adherence to the Treaty does not place other countries at a commercial disadvantage, either because of the increased costs associated with safeguards or because of risk of exposure or proprietary information;
- [Encouraging] adherence to the Treaty; and
- [Helping] to improve safeguards by permitting Agency inspectors to "combine their experience and collaborate [with DOE and NRC personnel] in making the safeguards system more efficient and effective.

In time, China, France and the Soviet Union made similar commitments, and today, each has brought into force a safeguards agreement with the IAEA that permits, but does

---

34 Letter of Transmittal to Senate by President Carter, February 1978. Although President Johnson's offer was made in 1967, the United States chose to implement it in 1977 when the safeguards agreements of Germany and Japan entered into force. (See http://www.presidency.ucsb.edu/ws/index.php?pid=30304.)

35 Letter of Submittal to President Carter from Secretary Christopher. December 14, 1977.

not require, the application of IAEA safeguards. (Because they are not required by the NPT, these are often called "voluntary offer agreements" or VOA).

F.1. Purposes of the Voluntary Offer Agreements

Broadly speaking, the voluntary offer agreements in nuclear-weapon states could serve a number of purposes:

- encourage adherence to the NPT;[36]
- demonstrate that adherence to the NPT does not place non-nuclear-weapon states at a commercial disadvantage;
- satisfy requirements of non-nuclear-weapon states that supply uranium to nuclear-weapon states of peaceful use assurances and/or safeguards as a condition of supply;
- provide test beds for new safeguards equipment and techniques or for training IAEA inspectors in cooperative environments;
- allow for continuing insight by the inspected nuclear-weapon state into IAEA safeguards implementation policies, procedures, and practices; and
- reinforce the message that the application of IAEA safeguards is the norm for international nuclear cooperation.

In general, of these objectives, only the first two are contained in the agreements in their preambles as follows:

China: WHEREAS China has made this offer and entered into this Agreement for the purpose of promoting the peaceful application of nuclear energy throughout the world for the benefit of mankind and supporting the objectives set forth in the Statute of the Agency (hereinafter referred to as the "Statute")

France: WHEREAS with a view to *encouraging the acceptance of such safeguards by an ever greater number of States*, France is prepared to afford the Agency the opportunity to apply its safeguards on French territory by concluding with it an agreement for that purpose;[37]

Russia: WHEREAS the Soviet Union has made this offer and has entered into this agreement for the *purpose of promoting widespread adherence to the Treaty, further development of Agency safeguards* and *encouraging their acceptance by an even greater number of States.*

United States: WHEREAS the United States has made this offer and has entered into this agreement for the purpose of *encouraging widespread adherence to the Treaty* by *demonstrating to non-nuclear-weapon states that they would not be placed at a commercial disadvantage by reason of the application of safeguards pursuant to the Treaty;*

---

36 This motivation is no longer significant because adherence to the NPT is almost universal.

37 INFCIRC/290: The French voluntary offer was concluded before France had joined the NPT. As a result, its preamble does not refer to the NPT.

United Kingdom: WHEREAS the United Kingdom, as a nuclear-weapon state within the meaning of the Treaty, has throughout desired to encourage *widespread adherence to the Treaty by demonstrating to non-nuclear-weapon states that they would not be placed at a commercial disadvantage by reason of the application of safeguards pursuant to the Treaty.*

F.2. Scope of the five Voluntary Offer Safeguards agreements

Each of the five NPT nuclear-weapon states has a voluntary offer safeguards agreement in place. However, they differ from those in non-nuclear-weapon states in two important ways.

One is that the IAEA is obligated to apply safeguards under INFCIRC/153 agreements. On the contrary, this is not the case for the nuclear-weapon states. There, the IAEA may elect to apply safeguards. It is optional. For example, the United States lists over 200 facilities as eligible for safeguards. The IAEA could select all of them for the application of safeguards if it chose to.

As an obligation of the IAEA, safeguards implementation in non-nuclear-weapon states is funded out of the regular budget of the IAEA. However, there is no such obligation in nuclear-weapon states, and no funding for it in the regular budget. A major budget increase might be required (depending on coverage), and there is little or no propensity within the IAEA to make funds available for this purpose.

Not all states consider the implementation of safeguards in nuclear-weapon states to be important or even to make sense. Mexico, for example, observed in 1989 that:

> With regard to the voluntary submission offers made by nuclear-weapon states, it should not be forgotten that the object of safeguards was to ensure that nuclear material was not used for nuclear weapons. In that context, there seemed little sense in applying them in such countries. His delegation's main concern was that if civilian nuclear facilities in nuclear-weapon states were placed under safeguards, the cost of safeguards would greatly increase. Hence the question was whether that would really contribute to non-proliferation. Obviously, the answer was no.[8]

In general, the IAEA applies safeguards in nuclear-weapon states only when they agree to cover the costs.[38]

A second significant difference is the scope of coverage of the agreements with nuclear-weapon states. They are necessarily not comprehensive because the IAEA cannot apply safeguards to nuclear weapons or to nuclear weapon related activities.

---

38 A nuclear weapon-state or a non-NPT party may accept safeguards implementation as obligatory as a condition of supply or otherwise.

In addition, the nuclear weapon states made different choices about the civil facilities that would be eligible for safeguards, that is, those to which the IAEA could apply safeguards if it elected to.

The following shows how the five agreements differ in scope.

China: INFCIRC/369 1989: China shall accept the application of safeguards by the Agency, in accordance with the terms of this Agreement, on all source or special fissionable material in peaceful nuclear facilities to be designated by China within its territory with a view to enabling the Agency to verify that such material is not withdrawn, except as provided for in this Agreement, from those facilities while such material is subject to safeguards under this Agreement.

France: INFCIRC/290 1981: France shall accept the application of safeguards, in accordance with the terms of this Agreement, on source or special fissionable material to be designated by France, in facilities or parts thereof within France, with a view to enabling the Agency to verify that such material is not withdrawn from civil activities, except as provided for in this Agreement.

Russia: INFCIRC/237 1985: The Soviet Union shall accept the application of safeguards by the Agency, in accordance with the terms of this Agreement, on all source or special fissionable material in peaceful nuclear facilities to be designated by the Soviet Union within its territory with a view to enabling the Agency to verify that such material is not withdrawn, except as provided for in this Agreement, from those facilities while such material is subject to safeguards under this Agreement.

United Kingdom: INFCIRC/263 1978: The United Kingdom shall accept the application of safeguards, in accordance with the terms of this Agreement on all source or special fissionable material in facilities or parts thereof within the United Kingdom, subject to exclusions for national security reasons only, with a view to enabling the Agency to verify that such material is not, except as provided for in this Agreement, withdrawn from civil activities.

United States: INFCIRC/288 1980: The United States undertakes to permit the Agency to apply safeguards, in accordance with the terms of this Agreement, on all source or special fissionable material in all facilities within the United States, excluding only those facilities associated with activities with direct national security significance to the United States, with a view to enabling the Agency to verify that such material is not withdrawn, except as provided for in this Agreement, from activities in facilities while such material is being safeguarded under this Agreement.

As can be seen, the United States and the United Kingdom chose to make their agreements "comprehensive" in applying to all facilities – except where the national security exclusion applies – but the other NWS agreements permit the application of safeguards only to facilities designated by them.[39]

F.3. Application of the Model Protocol in China, France, Russia, the United Kingdom, and the United States

During the negotiation of the NPT also took place during the negotiation of the Model Additional Protocol. It became clear during the negotiation of the Model Protocol, non-nuclear-weapon states also pressed for a non-discriminatory outcome where the Model Protocol would be accepted by all states. It became clear that the negotiating committee would not agree to send a draft Model Protocol to the Board of Governors without commitments by the nuclear-weapon states to conclude Additional Protocols themselves.

This interest was reflected in the Foreword to the Model Protocol. It notes that the Board of Governors considered that the Model Protocol as a whole was to be the standard for Additional Protocols with NPT non-nuclear-weapon states, but that it expected that Additional Protocols would be negotiated with NPT nuclear-weapon states that would "incorporat[e] those measures provided for in the Model Protocol that each nuclear-weapon State has identified as capable of contributing to the non-proliferation and efficiency aims of the Protocol, when implemented with regard to that State, and as consistent with that State's obligations under Article I of the NPT."

When the IAEA Board of Governors met to consider the Model Protocol, each NPT nuclear weapon-state made a statement to the Board that it intended to conclude an Additional Protocol with the IAEA in accordance with the Foreword.

The Board approved the Model Protocol. But it is clear that it would not have done so without these commitments.

These commitments have been fulfilled. As with the voluntary offer safeguards agreements, the scope of coverage of the five varies widely. The texts of the five nuclear-weapon state Additional Protocols have been published by the IAEA as additions to the Information Circulars noted above.

F.4. IAEA inspections in China, France, Russia, the United Kingdom, and the United States

According to the IAEA 2012 Annual Report, the IAEA applied safeguards in each of the five NPT NWS at a total of 13 facilities: a research reactor, power reactor, and uranium enrichment plant in China; an enrichment plant, reprocessing plants, and a fuel fabrication plant in France; a storage facility in Russia; a uranium enrichment plant and storage facilities in the United Kingdom; and a storage facility in the United States.

---

39   The five NPT NWS have also made voluntary commitments to notify the IAEA of exports and imports of nuclear material. These notifications allow the IAEA to reconcile its nuclear material accounting records. The commitments are found in IAEA INFCIRC/207 (1974) for Russia, the United Kingdom, and the United States; INFCIRC/207/Add.1 (1984) for France; and INFCIRC/207/Add.2 (1991) for China.

F.5. Implementation of Safeguards in India, Israel, and Pakistan

The IAEA safeguards system was established before the NPT was adopted. The first ad hoc application of safeguards by the IAEA was in Japan in 1959, and that year, the IAEA concluded its first safeguards agreement in connection with the supply of natural uranium from Canada to Japan for a small research reactor.

Japan's 1963 safeguards agreement was based on safeguards principles and procedures agreed by the Board of Governors and published in 1961 in INFCIRC/26. They covered small research, test, and power reactors. Over time, these safeguards principles and procedures were extended to cover additional nuclear facilities: first to large reactor facilities (INFCIRC/26/Add.1); in 1965 to all sizes of nuclear reactors (INFCIRC/66); in 1966 to cover reprocessing plants (INFCIRC/66/Rev.1); and in 1968 to cover fuel fabrication plants (INFCIRC/66/Rev.2). These safeguards agreements are known as INFCIRC/66 agreements.

The number of INFCIRC/66 safeguards agreements grew as nuclear cooperation flourished. A key feature of these safeguards agreements was that safeguards were applied only to: (1) items that were supplied and listed in the safeguards agreement; (2) nuclear material produced as a result of the use of these items; and (3) facilities containing these items.

The last proviso meant that facilities not covered by a safeguards agreement under the first provision might become subject to safeguards only temporarily – i.e., while they contained nuclear material subject to safeguards, but not otherwise.

The adoption of NPT comprehensive safeguards agreements has had a major impact of the role of INFCIRC/66 safeguards agreements. NPT comprehensive safeguards agreements allow for the suspension of pre-existing INFCIRC/66 safeguards agreements (Paragraph 24 of INFCIRC/153).

As a result, INFCIRC/66 agreements are now relevant only to India, Israel, and Pakistan. According to the IAEA Annual Report for 2012, the "facilities under Agency safeguards or containing safeguarded nuclear material on 31 December 2012" in these states are:

Israel	Research Reactor	IRR-1
India	Power Reactors	KAPS 1 & 2
	KKNP	
	RAPS 1 & 2	
	RAPS 3 & 4	
	RAPS 5& 6	
	TAPS	
	Fuel Fabrication Plants	NFC
	NFC-NU	

	Separate Storage Facility	TAPS AFR
	Reprocessing Plant	PREFRE
Pakistan	Power Reactors	Chasnupp-1
	Chasnupp-2	
	Research Reactors	PARR-1
	PARR-2	

G. NON-COMPLIANCE WITH NON-PROLIFERATION OBLIGATIONS

United Security Council Resolution S/RES/1887: Maintenance of international peace and security: Nuclear non-proliferation and nuclear disarmament

Resolution 1887 (2009)

Adopted by the Security Council at its 6191st meeting, on 24 September 2009

The Security Council,

Resolving to seek a safer world for all and to create the conditions for a world without nuclear weapons, in accordance with the goals of the Treaty on the Non-Proliferation of Nuclear Weapons (NPT), in a way that promotes international stability, and based on the principle of undiminished security for all,

Reaffirming the Statement of its President adopted at the Council's meeting at the level of Heads of State and Government on 31 January 1992 (S/23500), including the need for all Member States to fulfil their obligations in relation to arms control and disarmament and to prevent proliferation in all its aspects of all weapons of mass destruction,

Recalling also that the above Statement (S/23500) underlined the need for all Member States to resolve peacefully in accordance with the Charter any problems in that context threatening or disrupting the maintenance of regional and global stability,

Reaffirming that proliferation of weapons of mass destruction, and their means of delivery, constitutes a threat to international peace and security,

Bearing in mind the responsibilities of other organs of the United Nations and relevant international organizations in the field of disarmament, arms control and non-proliferation, as well as the Conference on Disarmament, and supporting them to continue to play their due roles,

Underlining that the NPT remains the cornerstone of the nuclear non-proliferation regime and the essential foundation for the pursuit of nuclear disarmament and for the peaceful uses of nuclear energy,

Reaffirming its firm commitment to the NPT and its conviction that the international nuclear non-proliferation regime should be maintained and strengthened to ensure its effective implementation, and *recalling* in this regard the outcomes of past NPT Review Conferences, including the 1995 and 2000 final documents,

Calling for further progress on all aspects of disarmament to enhance global security,

Recalling the Statement by its President adopted at the Council's meeting held on 19 November 2008 (S/PRST/2008/43),

Welcoming the decisions of those non-nuclear-weapon States that have dismantled their nuclear weapons programs or renounced the possession of nuclear weapons,

Welcoming the nuclear arms reduction and disarmament efforts undertaken and accomplished by nuclear-weapon States, and *underlining* the need to pursue further efforts in the sphere of nuclear disarmament, in accordance with Article VI of the NPT,

Welcoming in this connection the decision of the Russian Federation and the United States of America to conduct negotiations to conclude a new comprehensive legally binding agreement to replace the Treaty on the Reduction and Limitation of Strategic Offensive Arms, which expires in December 2009,

Welcoming and *supporting* the steps taken to conclude nuclear-weapon-free zone treaties and *reaffirming* the conviction that the establishment of internationally recognized nuclear-weapon-free zones on the basis of arrangements freely arrived at among the States of the region concerned, and in accordance with the 1999 United Nations Disarmament Commission guidelines, enhances global and regional peace and security, strengthens the nuclear non-proliferation regime, and contributes toward realizing the objectives of nuclear disarmament,

Noting its support, in this context, for the convening of the Second Conference of States Parties and signatories of the Treaties that establish Nuclear-Weapon-Free Zones to be held in New York on 30 April 2010,

Reaffirming its resolutions 825 (1993), 1695 (2006), 1718 (2006), and 1874 (2009),

Reaffirming its resolutions 1696 (2006), 1737 (2006), 1747 (2007), 1803 (2008), and 1835 (2008),

Reaffirming all other relevant non-proliferation resolutions adopted by the Security Council,

Gravely concerned about the threat of nuclear terrorism, and *recognizing* the need for all States to take effective measures to prevent nuclear material or technical assistance becoming available to terrorists,

Noting with interest the initiative to convene, in coordination with the International Atomic Energy Agency (IAEA), an international conference on the peaceful uses of nuclear energy,

Expressing its support for the convening of the 2010 Global Summit on Nuclear Security,

Affirming its support for the Convention on the Physical Protection of Nuclear Material and its 2005 Amendment, and the Convention for the Suppression of Acts of Nuclear Terrorism,

Recognizing the progress made by the Global Initiative to Combat Nuclear Terrorism, and the G-8 Global Partnership,

Noting the contribution of civil society in promoting all the objectives of the NPT,

Reaffirming its resolution 1540 (2004) and the necessity for all States to implement fully the measures contained therein, and *calling upon* all Member States and international and regional organizations to cooperate actively with the Committee established pursuant to that resolution, including in the course of the comprehensive review as called for in resolution 1810 (2008),

1.   *Emphasizes* that a situation of non-compliance with non-proliferation obligations shall be brought to the attention of the Security Council, which will determine if that situation constitutes a threat to international peace and security, and *emphasizes* the Security Council's primary responsibility in addressing such threats;

2.   *Calls upon* States Parties to the NPT to comply fully with all their obligations and fulfil their commitments under the Treaty,

3.   *Notes* that enjoyment of the benefits of the NPT by a State Party can be assured only by its compliance with the obligations thereunder;

4.   *Calls upon* all States that are not Parties to the NPT to accede to the Treaty as non-nuclear-weapon States so as to achieve its universality at an early date, and pending their accession to the Treaty, to adhere to its terms;

5.   *Calls upon* the Parties to the NPT, pursuant to Article VI of the Treaty, to undertake to pursue negotiations in good faith on effective measures relating to nuclear arms reduction and disarmament, and on a Treaty on general and complete disarmament under strict and effective international control, and *calls on* all other States to join in this endeavour;

6.   *Calls upon* all States Parties to the NPT to cooperate so that the 2010 NPT Review Conference can successfully strengthen the Treaty and set realistic and achievable goals in all the Treaty's three pillars: non-proliferation, the peaceful uses of nuclear energy, and disarmament;

7. *Calls upon* all States to refrain from conducting a nuclear test explosion and to sign and ratify the Comprehensive Nuclear Test Ban Treaty (CTBT), thereby bringing the treaty into force at an early date;

8. *Calls upon* the Conference on Disarmament to negotiate a Treaty banning the production of fissile material for nuclear weapons or other nuclear explosive devices as soon as possible, *welcomes* the Conference on Disarmament's adoption by consensus of its Program of Work in 2009, and *requests* all Member States to cooperate in guiding the Conference to an early commencement of substantive work;

9. *Recalls* the statements by each of the five nuclear-weapon States, noted by resolution 984 (1995), in which they give security assurances against the use of nuclear weapons to non-nuclear-weapon State Parties to the NPT, and *affirms* that such security assurances strengthen the nuclear non-proliferation regime;

10. *Expresses* particular concern at the current major challenges to the non-proliferation regime that the Security Council has acted upon, *demands* that the parties concerned comply fully with their obligations under the relevant Security Council resolutions, and *reaffirms* its call upon them to find an early negotiated solution to these issues;

11. *Encourages* efforts to ensure development of peaceful uses of nuclear energy by countries seeking to maintain or develop their capacities in this field in a framework that reduces proliferation risk and adheres to the highest international standards for safeguards, security, and safety;

12. *Underlines* that the NPT recognizes in Article IV the inalienable right of the Parties to the Treaty to develop research, production and use of nuclear energy for peaceful purposes without discrimination and in conformity with Articles I and II, and *recalls* in this context Article III of the NPT and Article II of the IAEA Statute;

13. *Calls upon* States to adopt stricter national controls for the export of sensitive goods and technologies of the nuclear fuel cycle;

14. *Encourages* the work of the IAEA on multilateral approaches to the nuclear fuel cycle, including assurances of nuclear fuel supply and related measures, as effective means of addressing the expanding need for nuclear fuel and nuclear fuel services and minimizing the risk of proliferation, and *urges* the IAEA Board of Governors to agree upon measures to this end as soon as possible;

15. *Affirms* that effective IAEA safeguards are essential to prevent nuclear proliferation and to facilitate cooperation in the field of peaceful uses of nuclear energy, and in that regard:

a.   *Calls upon* all non-nuclear-weapon States party to the NPT that have yet to bring into force a comprehensive safeguards agreement or a modified small quantities protocol to do so immediately,

b.   *Calls upon* all States to sign, ratify and implement an additional protocol, which together with comprehensive safeguards agreements constitute essential elements of the IAEA safeguards system,

c.   *Stresses* the importance for all Member States to ensure that the IAEA continue to have all the necessary resources and authority to verify the declared use of nuclear materials and facilities and the absence of undeclared activities, and for the IAEA to report to the Council accordingly as appropriate;

16. *Encourages* States to provide the IAEA with the cooperation necessary for it to verify whether a state is in compliance with its safeguards obligations, and *affirms* the Security Council's resolve to support the IAEA's efforts to that end, consistent with its authorities under the Charter;

17. *Undertakes* to address without delay any State's notice of withdrawal from the NPT, including the events described in the statement provided by the State pursuant to Article X of the Treaty, while noting ongoing discussions in the course of the NPT review on identifying modalities under which NPT States Parties could collectively respond to notification of withdrawal, and *affirms* that a State remains responsible under international law for violations of the NPT committed prior to its withdrawal;

18. *Encourages* States to require as a condition of nuclear exports that the recipient State agree that, in the event that it should terminate, withdraw from, or be found by the IAEA Board of Governors to be in non-compliance with its IAEA safeguards agreement, the supplier state would have a right to require the return of nuclear material and equipment provided prior to such termination, non-compliance or withdrawal, as well as any special nuclear material produced through the use of such material or equipment;

19. *Encourages* States to consider whether a recipient State has signed and ratified an additional protocol based on the model additional protocol in making nuclear export decisions;

20. *Urges* States to require as a condition of nuclear exports that the recipient State agree that, in the event that it should terminate its IAEA safeguards agreement, safeguards shall continue with respect to any nuclear material and equipment provided prior to such termination, as well as any special nuclear material produced through the use of such material or equipment;

21. *Calls for* universal adherence to the Convention on Physical Protection of Nuclear Materials and its 2005 Amendment, and the Convention for the Suppression of Acts of Nuclear Terrorism;

22. *Welcomes* the March 2009 recommendations of the Security Council Committee established pursuant to resolution 1540 (2004) to make more effective use of existing funding mechanisms, including the consideration of the establishment of a voluntary fund, and *affirms* its commitment to promote full implementation of resolution 1540 (2004) by Member States by ensuring effective and sustainable support for the activities of the 1540 Committee;

23. *Reaffirms* the need for full implementation of resolution 1540 (2004) by Member States and, with an aim of preventing access to, or assistance and financing for, weapons of mass destruction, related materials and their means of delivery by non-State actors, as defined in the resolution, *calls upon* Member States to cooperate actively with the Committee established pursuant to that resolution and the IAEA, including rendering assistance, at their request, for their implementation of resolution 1540 (2004) provisions, and in this context *welcomes* the forthcoming comprehensive review of the status of implementation of resolution 1540 (2004) with a view to increasing its effectiveness, and *calls upon* all States to participate actively in this review;

24. *Calls upon* Member States to share best practices with a view to improved safety standards and nuclear security practices and raise standards of nuclear security to reduce the risk of nuclear terrorism, with the aim of securing all vulnerable nuclear material from such risks within four years;

25. *Calls upon* all States to manage responsibly and minimize to the greatest extent that is technically and economically feasible the use of highly enriched uranium for civilian purposes, including by working to convert research reactors and radioisotope production processes to the use of low enriched uranium fuels and targets;

26. *Calls upon* all States to improve their national capabilities to detect, deter, and disrupt illicit trafficking in nuclear materials throughout their territories, and *calls upon* those States in a position to do so to work to enhance international partnerships and capacity building in this regard;

27. *Urges* all States to take all appropriate national measures in accordance with their national authorities and legislation, and consistent with international law, to prevent proliferation financing and shipments, to strengthen export controls, to secure sensitive materials, and to control access to intangible transfers of technology;

28. *Declares* its resolve to monitor closely any situations involving the proliferation of nuclear weapons, their means of delivery or related material, including to or by non-State actors as they are defined in resolution 1540 (2004), and, as appropriate, to take such measures as may be necessary to ensure the maintenance of international peace and security;

29. *Decides* to remain seized of the matter.

SECTION III

NUCLEAR COOPERATION

Background

If nuclear cooperation is a goal, then export controls offer the opportunity to cooperate selectively with partners where the risk of proliferation is perceived to be low and to deny export to countries where the risk is perceived to be too high. Even when cooperation is pursued, criteria for supply may be used to reduce the risks even further.

The concept of export controls is built into the NPT. It stipulates that nuclear material and especially designed equipment and material can only be exported when IAEA safeguards are applied in the recipient state. (Items that meet this NPT specification are called "trigger list" items, because they trigger the application of safeguards in the recipient country.) In order for export controls to be effective, all relevant suppliers need to use the same "trigger list" and apply the same ground rules. To allow buyers to shop for the weakest non-proliferation condition would undermine the control system.

In order to achieve common non-proliferation objectives and create a level playing field, likeminded states joined together to create multilateral organizations. The first of these was the NPT exporters' committee, called the Zangger Committee. It first convened in 1971 to agree on a trigger list and export guidelines that would satisfy NPT requirements.

Later, the Nuclear Suppliers Group (NSG) was created with a broader mandate. It covered topics not addressed in the NPT, physical protection for example, and it included France, a non-NPT party in 1978 when the Nuclear Suppliers Group guidelines were first published.[40]

The Nuclear Suppliers Group initially covered "trigger list items. However some states sought to evade these controls in order to pursue nuclear-weapon programs, by clandestine procurement of trigger list items and also to use dual-use items and technology. As a result, in 1992, multilateral export control arrangements were extended by the NSG to dual-use items and technology, including items related to nuclear weapons and to testing them. Because of their sensitivity, special controls have been placed on enrichment and reprocessing technologies and on materials and equipment related to them.

The Guidelines, themselves, are published by the IAEA in INFCIRC/254. They consist of two parts. Part 1 covers nuclear transfers of specialized equipment and materials, while Part 2 covers dual-use items and technology.

---

40 (For information about the Nuclear Suppliers Group, see "The Nuclear Suppliers Group: Its Origins, Role and Activities" in IAEA Document INFCIRC/539/Rev.4, November, 2009, at http://www.iaea.org/Publications/Documents/Infcircs/2009/infcirc539r4.pdf.)

A. Multilateral Export Control Arrangements

Zangger Committee

The Nuclear Non-proliferation Treaty, for the first time, established an obligatory export control regime. Specifically, according to Article III.2 of the Treaty,

Article III

...

2. Each State Party to the Treaty undertakes not to provide: (a) source or special fissionable material, or (b) equipment or material especially designed or prepared for the processing, use or production of special fissionable material, to any non-nuclear-weapon state for peaceful purposes, unless the source or special fissionable material[41] shall be subject to the safeguards required by this Article.

—

As can be seen, the NPT obligates each party to the Treaty to require safeguards in non-nuclear-weapon states both when it exports nuclear material directly and when it exports certain "especially designed or prepared" equipment or material.

In light of this obligation, nuclear suppliers were eager to ensure that there would be a "level playing field," i.e., a common understanding of how to interpret the export requirements of the NPT for all nuclear suppliers. To this end, fifteen States met informally in Vienna between 1971 and 1974. (The chairman of the group was Professor Claude Zangger of Switzerland, and, since then, the group, which has expanded to 39 members today, is known as the Zangger Committee.[42])

In order to harmonize implementation of the NPT requirements to apply International Atomic Energy Agency (IAEA) safeguards to nuclear exports, the Committee established three conditions of supply:

(a) For exports to non-nuclear-weapon states, source or special fissionable material either directly transferred, or produced, processed, or used in the facility for which the transferred item is intended, shall not be diverted to nuclear weapons or other nuclear explosive devices;

---

41 "Special fissionable material" means plutonium-239; uranium- 233; uranium enriched in the isotopes 235 or 233; any material containing one or more of the foregoing. The Board of Governors of the IAEA may determine that other materials should also be designated as special fissionable material, but it has not exercised this authority.

42 As of March, 2014, the 39 members are Argentina, Australia, Austria, Belarus, Belgium, Bulgaria, Canada, China, Croatia, Czech Republic, Denmark, Finland, France, Germany, Greece, Hungary, Ireland, Italy, Japan, Kazakhstan, Republic of Korea, Luxemburg, The Netherlands, New Zealand, Norway, Poland, Portugal, Romania, Russian Federation, Slovakia, Slovenia, South Africa, Spain, Sweden, Switzerland, Turkey, Ukraine, United Kingdom and United States of America.

(b) For exports to non-nuclear-weapon states, such source or special fissionable material, as well as transferred equipment and non-nuclear material, shall be subject to safeguards under an agreement with the International Atomic Energy Agency (IAEA);

(c) Source or special fissionable material, and equipment and non-nuclear material shall not be re-exported to a non-nuclear-weapon state unless the recipient State accepts safeguards on the re-exported item.

The Committee also maintains and updates a list of equipment and materials that may be exported only if safeguards are applied to the recipient facility (called the "Trigger List" because such exports trigger the requirement for safeguards).

The Trigger List is not reproduced here. It is long and complex and is now captured by the NSG Trigger List. In addition, the conditions of supply are included in he Nuclear Suppliers Group Guidelines.

Readers interested in more information about the Zangger Committee should turn to the working paper on "Multilateral nuclear supply principles of the Zangger Committee" that was submitted by Committee members to the NPT Review Conference held in 2010.[43]

---

43 http://www.un.org/ga/search/view_doc.asp?symbol=NPT/CONF.2010/WP.1 (March 22, 2014)

NSG Guidelines – Part 1: Export of Nuclear Material, Equipment and Technology

INFCIRC/254/Rev.11/Part 1
Date: 12 November 2012

GUIDELINES FOR NUCLEAR TRANSFERS

Export of Nuclear Material, Equipment and Technology

1.   The following fundamental principles for safeguards and export controls should apply to nuclear transfers for peaceful purposes to any non-nuclear-weapon State and, in the case of controls on retransfer, to transfers to any State. In this connection, suppliers have defined an export trigger list.

Prohibition on nuclear explosives

2.   Suppliers should authorize transfer of items or related technology identified in the trigger list only upon formal governmental assurances from recipients explicitly excluding uses which would result in any nuclear explosive device.

Physical protection

3.   (a)   All nuclear materials and facilities identified by the agreed trigger list should be placed under effective physical protection to prevent unauthorized use and handling. The levels of physical protection to be ensured in relation to the type of materials, equipment and facilities, have been agreed by the suppliers, taking account of international recommendations.

    (b)   The implementation of measures of physical protection in the recipient country is the responsibility of the Government of that country. However, in order to implement the terms agreed upon amongst suppliers, the levels of physical protection on which these measures have to be based should be the subject of an agreement between supplier and recipient.

    (c)   In each case special arrangements should be made for a clear definition of responsibilities for the transport of trigger list items.

Safeguards

4.   (a)   Suppliers should transfer trigger list items or related technology to a non-nuclear weapon State only when the receiving State has brought into force an agreement with the IAEA requiring the application of safeguards on all source and special fissionable material in its current and future peaceful activities. Suppliers should authorize such transfers only upon formal governmental assurances from the recipient that:

    – if the above-mentioned agreement should be terminated the recipient will bring into force an agreement with the IAEA based on existing IAEA model safeguards agreements requiring the application of safeguards on all trigger list items or related technology transferred by the supplier or processed, or produced or used in connection with such transfers; and

    – if the IAEA decides that the application of IAEA safeguards is no longer possible, the supplier and recipient should elaborate appropriate verification measures. If the recipient does not accept these measures, it should allow at the request of the supplier the restitution of transferred and derived trigger list items.

(b) Transfers covered by paragraph 4 (a) to a non-nuclear-weapon State without such a safeguards agreement should be authorized only in exceptional cases when they are deemed essential for the safe operation of existing facilities and if safeguards are applied to those facilities. Suppliers should inform and, if appropriate, consult in the event that they intend to authorize or to deny such transfers.

(c) The policy referred to in paragraph 4 (a) and 4 (b) does not apply to agreements or contracts drawn up on or prior to April 3, 1992. In case of countries that have adhered or will adhere to INFCIRC/254/Rev. 1/Part 1 later than April 3, 1992, the policy only applies to agreements (to be) drawn up after their date of adherence.

(d) Under agreements to which the policy referred to in paragraph 4 (a) does not apply (see paragraphs 4 (b) and (c)) suppliers should transfer trigger list items or related technology only when covered by IAEA safeguards with duration and coverage provisions in conformity with IAEA doc. GOV/1621. However, suppliers undertake to strive for the earliest possible implementation of the policy referred to in paragraph 4 (a) under such agreements.

(e) Suppliers reserve the right to apply additional conditions of supply as a matter of national policy.

5. Suppliers will jointly reconsider their common safeguards requirements, whenever appropriate.

Special controls on sensitive exports

6. Suppliers should exercise a policy of restraint in the transfer of sensitive facilities, equipment, technology and material usable for nuclear weapons or other nuclear explosive devices, especially in cases when a State has on its territory entities that are the object of active NSG Guidelines Part 2 denial notifications from more than one NSG Participating Government.

(a) In the context of this policy, suppliers should not authorize the transfer of enrichment and reprocessing facilities, and equipment and technology therefore if the recipient does not meet, at least, all of the following criteria:

(i) Is a Party to the Treaty on the Non-Proliferation of Nuclear Weapons and is in full compliance with its obligations under the Treaty;

(ii) Has not been identified in a report by the IAEA Secretariat which is under consideration by the IAEA Board of Governors, as being in breach of its obligations to comply with its safeguards agreement, nor continues to be the subject of Board of Governors decisions calling upon it to take additional steps to comply with its safeguards obligations or to build confidence in the peaceful nature of its nuclear programme, nor has been reported by the IAEA Secretariat as a state where the IAEA is currently unable to implement its safeguards agreement. This criterion would not apply in cases where the IAEA Board of Governors or the United Nations Security Council subsequently decides that adequate assurances exist as to the peaceful purposes of the recipient's nuclear programme and its compliance with its safeguards obligations. For the purposes of this paragraph, "breach" refers only to serious breaches of proliferation concern;

(iii) Is adhering to the NSG Guidelines and has reported to the Security Council of the United Nations that it is implementing effective export controls as identified by Security Council Resolution 1540;

(iv) Has concluded an inter-governmental agreement with the supplier including assurances regarding non-explosive use, effective safeguards in perpetuity, and retransfer;

(v) Has made a commitment to the supplier to apply mutually agreed standards of physical protection based on current international guidelines; and

(vi) Has committed to IAEA safety standards and adheres to accepted international safety conventions.

(b) In considering whether to authorize such transfers, suppliers, while taking into account paragraphs 4(e), 6(a), and 10, should consult with potential recipients to ensure that enrichment and reprocessing facilities, equipment and technology are intended for peaceful purposes only; also taking into account at their national discretion, any relevant factors as may be applicable.

(c) Suppliers will make special efforts in support of effective implementation of IAEA safeguards for enrichment or reprocessing facilities, equipment or technology and should, consistent with paragraphs 4 and 13 of the Guidelines, ensure their peaceful nature. In this regard suppliers should authorize transfers, pursuant to this paragraph, only when the recipient has brought into force a Comprehensive Safeguards Agreement, and an Additional Protocol based on the Model Additional Protocol or, pending this, is implementing appropriate safeguards agreements in cooperation with the IAEA, including a regional accounting and control arrangement for nuclear materials, as approved by the IAEA Board of Governors.

(d) In accordance with paragraph 16(b) of the Guidelines, prior to beginning transfers of enrichment or reprocessing facilities, equipment, or technology, suppliers should consult with Participating Governments regarding the nonproliferation related terms and conditions applicable to the transfer.

(e) If enrichment or reprocessing facilities, equipment, or technology are to be transferred, suppliers should encourage recipients to accept, as an alternative to national plants, supplier involvement and/or other appropriate multinational participation in resulting facilities. Suppliers should also promote international (including IAEA) activities concerned with multinational regional fuel cycle centres.

Special arrangements for export of enrichment facilities, equipment and technology

7. All States that meet the criteria in paragraph 6 above are eligible for transfers of enrichment facilities, equipment and technology. Suppliers recognize that the application of the Special Arrangements below must be consistent with NPT principles, in particular Article IV. Any application by the suppliers of the following Special Arrangements may not abrogate the rights of States meeting the criteria in paragraph 6.

(a) For a transfer of an enrichment facility, or equipment or technology therefor, suppliers should seek a legally-binding undertaking from the recipient state that neither the transferred facility, nor any facility incorporating such equipment or based on such technology, will be modified or operated for the production of greater than 20% enriched uranium. Suppliers should seek to design and construct such an enrichment facility or equipment therefor so as to preclude, to the greatest extent practicable, the possibility of production of greater than 20% enriched uranium.

(b) For a transfer of an enrichment facility or equipment based on a particular enrichment technology which has been demonstrated to produce enriched uranium on a significant scale as of 31 December 2008, suppliers should:

(1) Avoid, as far as practicable, the transfer of enabling design and manufacturing technology associated with such items; and

(2) Seek from recipients an appropriate agreement to accept sensitive enrichment equipment, and enabling technologies, or an operable enrichment facility under conditions that do not permit or enable replication of the facilities.

Information required for regulatory purposes or to ensure safe installation and operation of a facility should be shared to the extent necessary without divulging enabling technology.

(c) Cooperative enrichment enterprises based on a particular enrichment technology which has not been demonstrated to produce enriched uranium on a significant scale as of 31 December 2008, may be developed by participants individually or jointly; and any transfer of the resulting facilities and equipment will become subject to paragraph 7(b) no later than prior to the deployment of a prototype. For the purposes of paragraph 7(c) of the Guidelines, a prototype is a system or facility which is operated to generate technical information to confirm the technical potential or viability of the separation process for large-scale separation of uranium isotopes.

Suppliers may propose alternative arrangements relating to control of transfers of new enrichment technology to facilitate cooperation on enrichment technology. Such arrangements should be equivalent to those in Paragraph 7(b), and the NSG should be consulted on these arrangements. Participating Governments will review the arrangements for export of enrichment facilities, equipment and technology every five years beginning in 2013 for the purpose of addressing changes in enrichment technology and commercial practices.

(d) Suppliers recognize that when implementing the arrangements envisaged by Paragraph 7 in relation to existing and new cooperative enrichment enterprises, enabling technology may be held by, shared among, and transferred between partners of such enterprises, if partners agree to do so on the basis of their established decision making processes. Suppliers recognize that uranium enrichment may involve supply chains for the production and transfer of equipment for enrichment facilities and such transfers can be made, subject to the relevant provisions of these Guidelines.

(e) Suppliers should make special efforts to ensure effective implementation of IAEA safeguards at supplied enrichment facilities, consistent with paragraphs 13 and 14 of the Guidelines. For a transfer of an enrichment facility, the supplier and recipient state should work together to ensure that the design and construction of the transferred facility is implemented in such a way so as to facilitate IAEA safeguards. The supplier and recipient state should consult with the IAEA about such design and construction features at the earliest possible time during the facility design phase, and in any event before construction of the enrichment facility is started. The supplier and recipient state should also work together to assist the recipient state in developing effective nuclear material and facilities protection measures, consistent with paragraphs 12 and 14 of the Guidelines.

(f) Suppliers should satisfy themselves that recipients have security arrangements in place that are equivalent or superior to their own to protect the facilities and technology from use or transfer inconsistent with the national laws of the receiving state.

Definitions Section:

For the purpose of implementing Paragraph 7 of the Guidelines "Cooperative Enrichment Enterprise" means a multi-country or multi-company (where at least two of the companies are incorporated in different countries) joint development or production effort. It could be a consortium of states or companies or a multinational corporation.

Controls on supplied or derived material usable for nuclear weapons or other nuclear explosive devices

8. Suppliers should, in order to advance the objectives of these guidelines and to provide opportunities further to reduce the risks of proliferation, include, whenever appropriate and practicable, in agreements on supply of nuclear materials or of facilities which produce material usable for nuclear weapons or other nuclear explosive devices, provisions calling for mutual agreement between the supplier and the recipient on arrangements for reprocessing, storage, alteration, use, transfer or retransfer of any material usable for nuclear weapons or other nuclear explosive devices involved.

Controls on retransfer

9. (a) Suppliers should transfer trigger list items or related technology only upon the recipient's assurance that in the case of:

   (1) retransfer of such items or related technology, or
   (2) transfer of trigger list items derived from facilities originally transferred by the supplier, or with the help of equipment or technology originally transferred by the supplier the recipient of the retransfer or transfer will have provided the same assurances as those required by the supplier for the original transfer.

(b) In addition the supplier's consent should be required for:

   (1) any retransfer of trigger list items or related technology and any transfer referred to under paragraph 9(a) (2) from any State which

does not require full scope safeguards, in accordance with paragraph 4(a) of these Guidelines, as a condition of supply;

(2) any retransfer of enrichment, reprocessing or heavy water production facilities, equipment or related technology, and for any transfer of facilities or equipment of the same type derived from items originally transferred by the supplier;

(3) any retransfer of heavy water or material usable for nuclear weapons or other nuclear explosive devices.

(c) To ensure the consent right as defined under paragraph 9(b), government to government assurances will be required for any relevant original transfer.

(d) Suppliers should consider restraint in the transfer of items and related technology identified in the trigger list if there is a risk of retransfers contrary to the assurances given under paragraph 9(a) and (c) as a result of a failure by the recipient to develop and maintain appropriate, effective national export and transshipment controls, as identified by UNSC Resolution 1540.

Non-proliferation Principle

10. Notwithstanding other provisions of these Guidelines, suppliers should authorize transfer of items or related technology identified in the trigger list only when they are satisfied that the transfers would not contribute to the proliferation of nuclear weapons or other nuclear explosive devices or be diverted to acts of nuclear terrorism.

Implementation

11. Suppliers should have in place legal measures to ensure the effective implementation of the Guidelines, including export licensing regulations, enforcement measures, and penalties for violations.

SUPPORTING ACTIVITIES

Support for access to nuclear material for peaceful uses

12. Suppliers should, in accordance with the objectives of these guidelines, facilitate access to nuclear material for the peaceful uses of nuclear energy, and encourage, within the scope of Article IV of the NPT, recipients to take the fullest possible advantage of the international commercial market and other

available international mechanisms for nuclear fuel services while not undermining the global fuel market.

Physical security

13. Suppliers should promote international co-operation in the areas of physical security through the exchange of physical security information, protection of nuclear materials in transit, and recovery of stolen nuclear materials and equipment. Suppliers should promote broadest adherence to the respective international instruments, inter alia, to the Convention on the Physical Protection of Nuclear Material, as well as implementation of INFCIRC/225, as amended from time to time. Suppliers recognize the importance of these activities and other relevant IAEA activities in preventing the proliferation of nuclear weapons and countering the threat of nuclear terrorism.

Support for effective IAEA safeguards

14. Suppliers should make special efforts in support of effective implementation of IAEA safeguards. Suppliers should also support the Agency's efforts to assist Member States in the improvement of their national systems of accounting and control of nuclear material and to increase the technical effectiveness of safeguards.

    Similarly, they should make every effort to support the IAEA in increasing further the adequacy of safeguards in the light of technical developments and the rapidly growing number of nuclear facilities, and to support appropriate initiatives aimed at improving the effectiveness of IAEA safeguards.

Trigger list plant design features

15. Suppliers should encourage the designers and makers of trigger list facilities to construct them in such a way as to facilitate the application of safeguards and to enhance physical protection, taking also into consideration the risk of terrorist attacks. Suppliers should promote protection of information on the design of trigger list installations, and stress to recipients the necessity of doing so. Suppliers also recognize the importance of including safety and non-proliferation features in designing and construction of trigger list facilities.

Export Controls

16. Suppliers should, where appropriate, stress to recipients the need to subject transferred trigger list items and related technology and trigger list items derived from facilities originally transferred by the supplier or with the help of equipment or technology originally transferred by the supplier to export controls as outlined in UNSC Resolution 1540. Suppliers are encouraged to

offer assistance to recipients to fulfil their respective obligations under UNSC Resolution 1540 where appropriate and feasible.

Consultations

17. (a) Suppliers should maintain contact and consult through regular channels on matters connected with the implementation of these Guidelines.

    (b) Suppliers should consult, as each deems appropriate, with other governments concerned on specific sensitive cases, to ensure that any transfer does not contribute to risks of conflict or instability.

    (c) Without prejudice to sub-paragraphs (d) to (f) below:

        – In the event that one or more suppliers believe that there has been a violation of supplier/recipient understanding resulting from these Guidelines, particularly in the case of an explosion of a nuclear device, or illegal termination or violation of IAEA safeguards by a recipient, suppliers should consult promptly through diplomatic channels in order to determine and assess the reality and extent of the alleged violation. Suppliers are also encouraged to consult where nuclear material or nuclear fuel cycles activity undeclared to the IAEA or a nuclear explosive activity is revealed.

        – Pending the early outcome of such consultations, suppliers will not act in a manner that could prejudice any measure that may be adopted by other suppliers concerning their current contacts with that recipient. Each supplier should also consider suspending transfers of Trigger List items while consultations under 16(c) are ongoing, pending supplier agreement on an appropriate response.

        – Upon the findings of such consultations, the suppliers, bearing in mind Article XII of the IAEA Statute, should agree on an appropriate response and possible action, which could include the termination of nuclear transfers to that recipient.

    (d) If a recipient is reported by the IAEA to be in breach of its obligation to comply with its safeguards agreement, suppliers should consider the suspension of the transfer of Trigger List items to that State whilst it is under investigation by the IAEA. For the purposes of this paragraph, "breach" refers only to serious breaches of proliferation concern;

    (e) Suppliers support the suspension of transfers of Trigger List items to States that violate their nuclear non-proliferation and safeguards obligations, recognising that the responsibility and authority for such decisions rests with national governments or the United Nations Security Council.

In particular, this is applicable in situations where the IAEA Board of Governors takes any of the following actions:

- finds, under Article XII.C of the Statute, that there has been non-compliance in the recipient, or requires a recipient to take specific actions to bring itself into compliance with its safeguards obligations;

- Decides that the Agency is not able to verify that there has been no diversion of nuclear material required to be safeguarded, including situations where actions taken by a recipient have made the IAEA unable to carry out its safeguards mission in that State.

  An extraordinary Plenary meeting will take place within one month of the Board of Governors' action, at which suppliers will review the situation, compare national policies and decide on an appropriate response.

(f) The provisions of subparagraph (e) above do not apply to transfers under paragraph 4 (b) of the Guidelines.

18. Unanimous consent is required for any changes in these Guidelines, including any which might result from the reconsideration mentioned in paragraph 5.

ANNEX A

TRIGGER LIST REFERRED TO IN GUIDELINES

ANNEX A

TRIGGER LIST REFERRED TO IN GUIDELINES MATERIAL AND EQUIPMENT

1. Source and special fissionable material

1.1. "Source material"

1.2. "Special fissionable material"

2. Equipment and Non-nuclear Materials

2.1. Nuclear reactors and especially designed or prepared equipment and components therefor (see Annex B, section 1.);

2.2. Non-nuclear materials for reactors (see Annex B, section 2.);

2.3. Plants for the reprocessing of irradiated fuel elements, and equipment especially designed or prepared therefor (see Annex B, section 3.);

2.4. Plants for the fabrication of nuclear reactor fuel elements, and equipment especially designed or prepared therefor (see Annex B, section 4.);

2.5. Plants for the separation of isotopes of natural uranium, depleted uranium or special fissionable material and equipment, other than analytical instruments, especially designed or prepared therefor (see Annex B, section 5.);

2.6. Plants for the production or concentration of heavy water, deuterium and deuterium compounds and equipment especially designed or prepared therefor (see Annex B, section 6.);

2.7. Plants for the conversion of uranium and plutonium for use in the fabrication of fuel elements and the separation of uranium isotopes as defined in sections 4 and 5 respectively, and equipment especially designed or prepared therefor (See Annex B, section 7.).

[NOTE TO READER: The full trigger list is omitted. The NSG Trigger List consists of the categories of nuclear material and facilities, as well as associated technology, in the list above.

Each item is elaborated in considerable detail in the trigger list in order to identify the characteristics of what makes it especially suited for nuclear use.

For example, the description of rotor tubes that are controlled for centrifuge enrichment plants is:

(b) Rotor tubes:

Especially designed or prepared thin-walled cylinders with thickness of 12 mm (0.5 in) or less, a diameter of between 75 mm (3 in) and 400 mm (16 in), and manufactured from one or more of the high strength to density ratio materials described in the EXPLANATORY NOTE to this Section.

EXPLANATORY NOTE

The materials used for centrifuge rotating components are:

(a) Maraging steel capable of an ultimate tensile strength of 2.05×10^9 N/m2 (300,000 psi) or more;

(b) Aluminium alloys capable of an ultimate tensile strength of 0.46×10^9 N/m2 (67,000 psi) or more;

(c) Filamentary materials suitable for use in composite structures and having a specific modulus of 3.18×10^6 m or greater and a specific ultimate tensile strength of 7.62×10^4 m or greater ('Specific Modulus' is the Young's Modulus in N/m2 divided by the specific weight in N/m3; 'Specific Ultimate Tensile Strength' is the ultimate tensile strength in N/ m2 divided by the specific weight in N/ m3).

Few, if any readers will need this level of detail. Those who do should refer to the most recent version of INFCIRC/254, Part 1, which is available at iaea.org. END NOTE]

NSG Guidelines – Part 2: Dual-Use Transfers

INFCIRC/254/Rev.8/Part 2
June 2010

GUIDELINES FOR TRANSFERS OF NUCLEAR-RELATED DUAL-USE EQUIPMENT, MATERIALS, SOFTWARE, AND RELATED TECHNOLOGY

OBJECTIVE

1. With the objective of averting the proliferation of nuclear weapons and preventing acts of nuclear terrorism, suppliers have had under consideration procedures in relation to the transfer of certain equipment, materials, software, and related technology that could make a major contribution to a "nuclear explosive activity," an "unsafeguarded nuclear fuel-cycle activity" or acts of nuclear terrorism. In this connection, suppliers have agreed on the following principles, common definitions, and an export control list of equipment, materials, software, and related technology. The Guidelines are not designed to impede international co-operation as long as such co-operation will not contribute to a nuclear explosive activity, an unsafeguarded nuclear fuel-cycle activity or acts of nuclear terrorism. Suppliers intend to implement the Guidelines in accordance with national legislation and relevant international commitments.

BASIC PRINCIPLE

2. Suppliers should not authorize transfers of equipment, materials, software, or related technology identified in the Annex:

    -   for use in a non-nuclear-weapon state in a nuclear explosive activity or an unsafeguarded nuclear fuel-cycle activity, or

    -   in general, when there is an unacceptable risk of diversion to such an activity, or when the transfers are contrary to the objective of averting the proliferation of nuclear weapons, or

    -   when there is an unacceptable risk of diversion to acts of nuclear terrorism.

EXPLANATION OF TERMS

3. (a) "Nuclear explosive activity" includes research on or development, design, manufacture, construction, testing or maintenance of any nuclear explosive device or components or subsystems of such a device.

(b) "Unsafeguarded nuclear fuel-cycle activity" includes research on or development, design, manufacture, construction, operation or maintenance of any reactor, critical facility, conversion plant, fabrication plant, reprocessing plant, plant for the separation of isotopes of source or special fissionable material, or separate storage installation, where there is no obligation to accept International Atomic Energy Agency (IAEA) safeguards at the relevant facility or installation, existing or future, when it contains any source or special fissionable material; or of any heavy water production plant where there is no obligation to accept IAEA safeguards on any nuclear material produced by or used in connection with any heavy water produced therefrom; or where any such obligation is not met.

ESTABLISHMENT OF EXPORT LICENSING PROCEDURES

4. Suppliers should have in place legal measures to ensure the effective implementation of the Guidelines, including export licensing regulations, enforcement measures, and penalties for violations. In considering whether to authorize transfers, suppliers should exercise prudence in order to carry out the Basic Principle and should take relevant factors into account, including:

(a) Whether the recipient state is a party to the Nuclear Non-Proliferation Treaty (NPT) or to the Treaty for the Prohibition of Nuclear Weapons in Latin America (Treaty of Tlatelolco), or to a similar international legally-binding nuclear non-proliferation agreement, and has an IAEA safeguards agreement in force applicable to all its peaceful nuclear activities;

(b) Whether any recipient state that is not party to the NPT, Treaty of Tlatelolco, or a similar international legally-binding nuclear non-proliferation agreement has any facilities or installations listed in paragraph 3(b) above that are operational or being designed or constructed that are not, or will not be, subject to IAEA safeguards;

(c) Whether the equipment, materials, software, or related technology to be transferred is appropriate for the stated end-use and whether that stated end-use is appropriate for the end-user;

(d) Whether the equipment, materials, software, or related technology to be transferred is to be used in research on or development, design, manufacture, construction, operation, or maintenance of any reprocessing or enrichment facility;

(e) Whether governmental actions, statements, and policies of the recipient state are supportive of nuclear non-proliferation and whether the recipient state is in compliance with its international obligations in the field of non-proliferation;

(f) Whether the recipients have been engaged in clandestine or illegal procurement activities; and

(g) Whether a transfer has not been authorized to the end-user or whether the end-user has diverted for purposes inconsistent with the Guidelines any transfer previously authorized.

(h) Whether there is reason to believe that there is a risk of diversion to acts of nuclear terrorism;

(i) Whether there is a risk of retransfers of equipment, material, software, or related technology identified in the Annex or of transfers of any replica thereof contrary to the Basic Principle, as a result of a failure by the recipient State to develop and maintain appropriate, effective national export and transshipment controls, as identified by UNSC Resolution 1540.

5. Suppliers should ensure that their national legislation requires an authorisation for the transfer of items not listed in the Annex if the items in question are or may be intended, in their entirety or in part, for use in connection with a "nuclear explosive activity."

Suppliers will implement such an authorisation requirement in accordance with their domestic licensing practices.

Suppliers are encouraged to share information on "catch all" denials.

CONDITIONS FOR TRANSFERS

6. In the process of determining that the transfer will not pose any unacceptable risk of diversion, in accordance with the Basic Principle and to meet the objectives of the Guidelines, the supplier should obtain, before authorizing the transfer and in a manner consistent with its national law and practices, the following:

(a) a statement from the end-user specifying the uses and end-use locations of the proposed transfers; and

(b) an assurance explicitly stating that the proposed transfer or any replica thereof will not be used in any nuclear explosive activity or unsafeguarded nuclear fuel-cycle activity.

CONSENT RIGHTS OVER RETRANSFERS

7. Before authorizing the transfer of equipment, materials, software, or related technology identified in the Annex to a country not adhering to the Guidelines, suppliers should obtain assurances that their consent will be secured, in a manner consistent with their national law and practices, prior to any retransfer to a

third country of the equipment, materials, software, or related technology, or any replica thereof.

CONCLUDING PROVISIONS

8.   The supplier reserves to itself discretion as to the application of the Guidelines to other items of significance in addition to those identified in the Annex, and as to the application of other conditions for transfer that it may consider necessary in addition to those provided for in paragraph 5 of the Guidelines.

9.   In furtherance of the effective implementation of the Guidelines, suppliers should, as necessary and appropriate, exchange relevant information and consult with other states adhering to the Guidelines.

10.   In the interest of international peace and security, the adherence of all states to the Guidelines would be welcome.

ANNEX CONTENTS

LIST OF NUCLEAR-RELATED DUAL-USE EQUIPMENT, MATERIALS, SOFTWARE, AND RELATED TECHNOLOGY

[NOTE TO READER: The dual use list is not included here. It has a level of detail that few if any readers will need. If needed, the full list can be found in the most recent version of INFCIRC/254, Part 2 at iaea.org.

The differences between the trigger list and the dual use list are that items in the trigger are all specialized for nuclear fuel cycle use, but items on the dual use list are not, even where they are related to the nuclear fuel cycle. They are items that are used to manufacture specialized items for nuclear fuel cycle use or materials used in the manufacture of specialized items. For example the list contains high strength metals that could be used to manufacture specialized centrifuge rotors, but not the rotors, which are on the trigger list.

The categories of controlled items on the dual use list include specified industrial equipment, such as remote manipulators and machine tools; many materials relevant to nuclear weapon production or the manufacture of nuclear fuel cycle items; test and measurement equipment for the development of nuclear explosive devices, and components for nuclear explosive devices. END NOTE]

B. United States Nuclear Cooperation

Nuclear cooperation between the United States and other countries is governed by a complex set of legal and institutional requirements. The Department of Commerce, the Department of Energy, the Department of State, or the Nuclear Regulatory Commission may be the licensing or authorizing agency. In some instances, more than one of them is involved.

The system is too complex to be covered in one place. As a result, this section provides only an overview of U.S. legal requirements for nuclear cooperation.

In broad terms, the Nuclear Regulatory Commission licenses "trigger list" items (Part 1 of the Nuclear Suppliers' Guidelines), the Department of Commerce licenses nuclear-related dual use items (Part 2 of the Nuclear Suppliers' Guidelines), and authorization must be obtained from the Department of Energy in certain instances where assistance would lead to the production of special nuclear material overseas.

The U.S. export control system has been streamlined to facilitate nuclear cooperation with states of little or no proliferation concern. In these instances, many exports may be made, but not all, without a specific licensing review. In other instances, a case-by-case review is always needed.

States that wish to proliferate do not necessarily confine themselves to seeking assistance from others in commodities that are specifically identified in export control lists. In order to avoid assisting such efforts, the United States adopted so-called catch-all controls, i.e., controls that require a license for all items if the supplier knows that the end-use is "risky."

B.1. Agreements for Nuclear Cooperation ("123 Agreements")

In Section 123, the Atomic Energy Act of 1954 authorized the conclusion of Agreements for Cooperation with other countries and made them a prerequisite for the most important kinds of U.S. international cooperation in peaceful uses of nuclear energy. An Agreement for Cooperation is mandatory for U.S. supply of nuclear reactors and other major facilities, including enrichment and reprocessing plants, and special nuclear material (that is, enriched uranium, plutonium and uranium-233).

Many other forms of cooperation, such as exchange of unclassified technology and export of materials such as heavy water can take place without an Agreement for Cooperation, but they may still require export licenses or authorizations from the Departments of Commerce or Energy or the Nuclear Regulatory Commission. As of June

2011 there were 25 agreements for cooperation in force in force, with several additional under negotiation.[44]

The conditions of supply in early agreements for cooperation were relatively modest – a peaceful use assurance and acceptance of safeguards. (Note that: 1) a "peaceful use assurance" does not explicitly preclude development of a nuclear explosive device for peaceful purposes; and 2) at that time safeguards could only be bilateral since the IAEA had not yet been created.)

The establishment of the IAEA safeguards system, the entry into force of the NPT, and the perceived risk of nuclear proliferation in more than a few countries in the 1970s gave impetus in the United States to efforts to improve the clarity of controls, to increase their scope, and to reduce the risk that safeguarded cooperation might be used to support unsafeguarded nuclear activities. The new approach was contained in the Nuclear Non-proliferation Act of 1978 (NNPA). The NNPA provided for strict and detailed controls over significant nuclear cooperation.

In particular, Section 123a of the Atomic Energy Act lists nine criteria that a nuclear cooperation agreement must meet unless the President determines an exemption is necessary. These include guarantees that:

- safeguards on transferred nuclear material and equipment continue in perpetuity;
- full-scope IAEA safeguards are applied in non-nuclear-weapon states;
- nothing transferred under the Agreement for Cooperation may be used for any nuclear explosive device or for any other military purpose; except in the case of military cooperation agreements with nuclear-weapon states;
- the US has the right to demand the return of transferred nuclear material and equipment, as well as any special nuclear material produced through their use, if the cooperating state detonates a nuclear explosive device or terminates or abrogates an IAEA safeguards agreement;
- there is no retransfer of material, equipment or components or classified data without US consent;
- physical security on nuclear material is maintained;
- there is no enrichment or reprocessing by the recipient state of transferred nuclear material or nuclear material produced with materials or facilities transferred pursuant to the agreement without prior approval of the US;
- storage for plutonium and HEU subject to the agreement is approved in advance by the US and

---

44 A list of the Agreements for Cooperation that were in force as of June 2011 can be found in Nuclear Energy Cooperation with Foreign Countries: Issues for Congress; Paul K. Kerr, Mark Holt, Mary Beth Nikitin; Congressional Research Service, July 11, 2011.
http://www.hsdl.org/?search&collection=crs&so=date&submitted=Search&creatormore=true&page=1&creator=Nikitin%2C+Mary+Beth+Dunham&fct.

- any material or facility produced or constructed through use of sensitive nuclear technology transferred under the cooperation agreement is subject to all of the above requirements. [45] [46]

The major change made in the NNPA was the requirement that significant nuclear cooperation could take place only if safeguards were being applied to all nuclear activities in a non-nuclear-weapon state at the time of the transfer. This requirement is met for non-nuclear-weapon states with NPT safeguards agreements in force. (A non-NPT party could also meet it if all of its nuclear activities were subject to safeguards under INFCIRC/66 agreements. Such a situation was called "de facto" rather than "de jure" full-scope safeguards because safeguards coverage was complete but it was not required in the non-NPT state.)

The NNPA added other requirements as conditions of supply under Agreements for Cooperation. For example, it tightened the ground-rules for U.S. approval of any reprocessing of U.S.-provided nuclear fuel.[47]

In recent years, strong U.S. interest in restraining the spread of enrichment and reprocessing capabilities has encouraged support for making U.S. nuclear cooperation contingent on a commitment to eschew the right to develop enrichment or reprocessing facilities. While not required by U.S. law, one state, United Arab Emirates, has done so on a voluntary basis.[48]

B.2. Assistance to Foreign Atomic Energy Activities (Technology) – Part 810

In addition to the requirements for Agreements for Cooperation for major nuclear cooperation, another provision of the Atomic energy Act, Section 57.b, is of particular importance. It makes it "unlawful for any person to engage *directly or indirectly* in the development or production of any [fissionable] material outside of the United States" [emphasis added] unless authorized either by an Agreement for Cooperation or by the Department of Energy.

---

45 From Nuclear Cooperation with Other Countries: A Primer, Paul K. Kerr, Mary Beth Nikitin, Congressional Research Service, August 11, 2011. http://www.fas.org/sgp/crs/nuke/RS22937.pdf.
This is a generally useful reference for background information on Agreements for Cooperation. Also useful is "Nuclear Energy Cooperation with Foreign Countries: Issues for Congress; Paul K. Kerr, Mark Holt, Mary Beth Nikitin; Congressional Research Service, July 11, 2011. http://www.hsdl.org/?search&collection=crs&so=date&submitted=Search&creatormore=true&page=1&creator=Nikitin%2C+Mary+Beth+Dunham&fct.

46 Although an Agreement for Cooperation is required for significant nuclear cooperation, the Atomic Energy Act requires export licenses or authorizations for many, but by no means all, forms of nuclear cooperation. U.S. nuclear export controls are complex and may require export licenses from the Nuclear Regulatory Commission, the Department of Energy, the Department of State, or the Department of Commerce. The Department of Commerce, "Nuclear Exporter's Guide," May, 2009, provides a brief overview of these controls. http://ita.doc.gov/td/energy/Civil%20Nuclear%20Exporters%20Guide%20(FINAL).pdf.

47 LOOKING BACK: The 1978 Nuclear Nonproliferation Act, Sharon Squassoni, Arms Control Today, December 2008. http://www.armscontrol.org/act/2008_12/lookingback_NPT (March 15, 2010).

48 The commitment was made to the United States in the U.S.-UAE Agreement for Cooperation as described in testimony of Ellen Tauscher, Under Secretary for Arms Control and International Security before the House Foreign Affairs Committee, Washington, DC, July 8, 2009. http://www.state.gov/t/us/125782.htm. (January 16, 2013).

This extremely broad language – directly or indirectly – can be the source of great difficulty in interpreting the scope of coverage. For example, is teaching nuclear physics to foreign students unlawful without authorization. To focus the implementation of Section 57.b on significant non-proliferation concerns and reduce unnecessary burden on nuclear cooperation, the Department of Energy has clarified the implementation requirements of Section 57.b. For example, there are general authorizations and country specific rules. Nonetheless, some activities always require specific authorization - transfer of enrichment, reprocessing, and plutonium bearing fuel technologies – as does assistance to countries on a restricted list, for example, countries that are embargoed or not parties to the NPT.

Part 810—Assistance to Foreign Atomic Energy Activities[49]

Contents

---

49   From http://www.ecfr.gov/cgi-bin/text-idx?rgn=div5&node=10:4.0.2.5.23 (March 3, 2014) Electronic Code of Federal Regulations, e-CFR Data is current as of February 27, 2014

50   The sections crossed out are omitted from this text.

§810.1 Purpose.

These regulations implement section 57b of the Atomic Energy Act which empowers the Secretary of Energy to authorize U.S. persons to engage directly or indirectly in the production of special nuclear material outside the United States. Their purpose is to:

(a) Indicate activities which have been generally authorized by the Secretary of Energy and thus require no further authorization;

(b) Indicate activities which require specific authorization by the Secretary and explain how to request authorization; and

(c) Explain reporting requirements for various activities.

810.2 Scope.
10 CFR Part 810:

(a) Applies to all persons subject to the jurisdiction of the United States who engage directly or indirectly in the production of special nuclear material outside the United States.

(b) Applies to activities conducted either in the United States or abroad by such persons or by licensees, contractors or subsidiaries under their direction, supervision, responsibility or control.

(c) Applies, but is not limited to, activities involving nuclear reactors and other nuclear fuel cycle facilities for the following: fluoride or nitrate conversion; isotope separation (enrichment); the chemical, physical or metallurgical processing, fabricating, or alloying of special nuclear material; production of heavy water, zirconium (hafnium-free or low-hafnium), nuclear-grade graphite, or reactor-grade beryllium; production of reactor-grade uranium dioxide from yellowcake; and certain uranium milling activities.

(d) Does not apply to exports licensed by the Nuclear Regulatory Commission.

§810.3 Definitions.
As used in part 810:

Accelerator-driven subcritical assembly system is a system comprising a "subcritical assembly" and a "production accelerator" and which is designed or used for the purpose of producing or processing special nuclear material (SNM) or which a U.S. provider of assistance knows or has reason to know will be used for the production or processing of SNM. In such a system, the "production accelerator" provides a source of neutrons used to effect SNM production in the "subcritical assembly."

Agreement for cooperation means an agreement with another nation or group of nations concluded under sections 123 or 124 of the Atomic Energy Act.

Atomic Energy Act means the Atomic Energy Act of 1954, as amended.

Classified information means National Security Information classified under Executive Order 12356 or any superseding order, or Restricted Data classified under the Atomic Energy Act.

General authorization means an authorization granted by the Secretary of Energy under section 57b(2) of the Atomic Energy Act to provide certain assistance to foreign atomic energy activities and which is effective without a specific request to the Secretary or the issuance of an authorization to a particular person.

IAEA means the International Atomic Energy Agency.

Non-nuclear-weapon state is a country not recognized as a nuclear-weapon state by the NPT (i.e., states other than the United States, Russia, the United Kingdom, France, and China).

NNPA means the Nuclear Non-Proliferation Act of 1978.

NPT means the Treaty on the Non-Proliferation of Nuclear Weapons.

Nuclear reactor means an apparatus, other than a nuclear explosive device, designed or used to sustain nuclear fission in a self-supporting chain reaction.

Open meeting means a conference, seminar, trade show or other gathering that all technically qualified members of the public may attend and at which they may make written or other personal record of the proceedings, notwithstanding that (1) a reasonable registration fee may be charged, or (2) a reasonable numerical limit exists on actual attendance.

Operational safety means the capability of a reactor to be operated in a manner that prevents uncontrolled or inadvertent criticality, prevents or mitigates uncontrolled release of radioactivity to the environment, monitors and limits staff exposure to radiation and radioactivity, and protects off-site population from exposure to radiation or radioactivity. Operational safety may be enhanced by providing expert advice, equipment, instrumentation, technology, software, services, analyses, procedures, training, or other assistance that improves the capability of the reactor to be operated in such a manner.

Person means (1) any individual, corporation, partnership, firm, association, trust, estate, public or private institution, group, Government agency other than the Department of Energy, any State or political entity within a State; and (2) any legal successor, representative, agent or agency of the foregoing. Persons under U.S. jurisdiction are responsible for their foreign licensees, contractors or subsidiaries to the extent that the former have control over the activities of the latter.

Production accelerator is a particle accelerator designed and/or intended to be used, with a subcritical assembly, for the production or processing of SNM or which a U.S.

provider of assistance knows or has reason to know will be used for the production or processing of SNM.

Production reactor means a nuclear reactor specially designed or used primarily for the production of plutonium or uranium-233.

Public information means: (1) Information available in periodicals, books or other print or electronic media for distribution to any member of the public, or to a community of persons such as those in a scientific, engineering, or educational discipline or in a particular commercial activity who are interested in a subject matter; (2) Information available in public libraries, public reading rooms, public document rooms, public archives, or public data banks, or in university courses; (3) Information that has been presented at an open meeting (see definition of "open meeting"); (4) Information that has been made available internationally without restriction on its further dissemination; or (5) Information contained in an application which has been filed with the U.S. Patent Office and eligible for foreign filing under 35 U.S.C. 184 or which has been made available under 5 U.S.C. 552, the Freedom of Information Act. Public information must be available to the public prior to or at the same time as it is transmitted to a foreign recipient. It does not include any technical embellishment, enhancement, explanation or interpretation which in itself is not public information, or information subject to sections 147 and 148 of the Atomic Energy Act.

Restricted Data means all data concerning (1) design, manufacture or utilization of atomic weapons; (2) the production of special nuclear material; or (3) the use of special nuclear material in the production of energy, but shall not include data declassified or removed from the Restricted Data category pursuant to section 142 of the Atomic Energy Act.

Sensitive nuclear technology means any information (including information incorporated in a production or utilization facility or important component part thereof) which is not available to the public [see definition of "public information"] which is important to the design, construction, fabrication, operation, or maintenance of a uranium enrichment or nuclear fuel reprocessing facility or a facility for the production of heavy water, but shall not include Restricted Data controlled pursuant to Chapter 12 of the Atomic Energy Act. The information may take a tangible form such as a model, prototype, blueprint, or operation manual or an intangible form such as technical services.

Source Material means: (1) Uranium or thorium, other than special nuclear material or (2) ores which contain by weight 0.05 percent or more of uranium or thorium, or any combination of these.

Special nuclear material means (1) plutonium, (2) uranium-233, or (3) uranium enriched above 0.711 percent by weight in the isotope uranium-235.

Specific authorization means an authorization granted by the Secretary of Energy under section 57b(2) of the Atomic Energy Act to a person to provide specified assistance to a foreign atomic energy activity in response to an application filed under 10 CFR part 810.

Subcritical assembly is an apparatus containing source material or SNM designed or used to produce a nuclear fission chain reaction that is not self-sustaining.

United States, when used in a geographical sense, includes all territories and possessions of the United States.

§810.6 Authorization requirement.

Section 57b of the Atomic Energy Act in pertinent part provides that:

It shall be unlawful for any person to directly or indirectly engage in the production of any special nuclear material outside of the United States except (1) as specifically authorized under an agreement for cooperation made pursuant to section 123, including a specific authorization in a subsequent arrangement under section 131 of this Act, or (2) upon authorization by the Secretary of Energy after a determination that such activity will not be inimical to the interest of the United States: Provided, That any such determination by the Secretary of Energy shall be made only with the concurrence of the Department of State and after consultation with the Arms Control and Disarmament Agency, the Nuclear Regulatory Commission, the Department of Commerce, and the Department of Defense.

§810.7 Generally authorized activities.
In accordance with section 57b(2) of the Atomic Energy Act, the Secretary of Energy has determined that the following activities are generally authorized, provided no sensitive nuclear technology is transferred:

(a)   Furnishing public information as defined in §810.3;

(b)   Furnishing information or assistance to prevent or correct a current or imminent radiological emergency posing a significant danger to the health and safety of the off-site population, provided the Department of Energy is notified in advance and does not object;

(c)   Furnishing information or assistance, including through continuing programs, to enhance the operational safety of an existing civilian nuclear power plant in a country listed in §810.8(a) or to prevent, reduce, or correct a danger to the health and safety of the off-site population posed by a civilian nuclear power plant in such a country; provided the Department of Energy is notified in advance by certified mail, return receipt requested, and approves the use of the authorization in writing; the Department will notify the applicant of the status of the request within 30 days from the date of receipt of the notification.

(d)   Implementing the Agreement between the United States of America and the International Atomic Energy Agency for the Application of Safeguards in the United States;

(e)   Participation in exchange programs approved by the Department of State in consultation with the Department of Energy;

(f)   Participation approved by a U.S. Government agency in IAEA programs, and activities of IAEA employees whose employment was approved by the U.S. Government;

(g)   Participation in open meetings as defined in §810.3 that are sponsored by educational, scientific, or technical organizations or institutions;

(h)   Otherwise engaging directly or indirectly in the production of SNM outside the United States in ways that:

        (1)   Do not involve any of the countries listed in §810.8(a); and

        (2)   Do not involve production reactors, accelerator-driven subcritical assembly systems, enrichment, reprocessing, fabrication of nuclear fuel containing plutonium, production of heavy water, or research reactors, or test reactors, as described in §810.8 (c)(1) through (6).

§810.8 Activities requiring specific authorization.

Unless generally authorized by §810.7, a person requires specific authorization by the Secretary of Energy before:

(a)   Engaging directly or indirectly in the production of special nuclear material in any of the following countries. Countries marked with an asterisk (*) are non-nuclear-weapon states that do not have full-scope IAEA safeguards agreements in force.

Afghanistan	Kyrgyzstan*
Albania	Laos*
Algeria	Liberia*
Andorra*	Libya
Angola*	Macedonia
Armenia	Mali*
Azerbaijan*	Marshall Islands*
Bahrain*	Mauritania*
Belarus	Micronesia*
Benin*	Moldova*
Botswana*	Mongolia
Burkina Faso*	Mozambique*
Burma (Myanmar)	Niger*
Burundi*	Oman*
Cambodia*	Pakistan*
Cameroon*	Palau*

Cape Verde*

Central African Republic*

Chad*

China, People's Republic of

Comoros*

Congo* (Zaire)

Cuba*

Djibouti*

Equatorial Guinea*

Eritrea*

Gabon*

Georgia*

Guinea*

Guinea-Bissau*

Haiti*

India*

Iran

Iraq*

Israel*

Kazakhstan

Kenya*

Korea, People's Democratic Republic of*

Kuwait*

Qatar*

Russia

Rwanda*

Sao Tome and Principe*

Saudi Arabia*

Seychelles*

Sierra Leone*

Somalia*

Sudan

Syria

Tajikistan*

Tanzania*

Togo*

Turkmenistan*

Uganda*

Ukraine

United Arab Emirates*

Uzbekistan

Vanuatu*

Vietnam

Yemen*

Yugoslavia

(b) Providing sensitive nuclear technology for an activity in any foreign country.

(c) Engaging in or providing assistance or training in any of the following activities with respect to any foreign country.

   (1) Designing production reactors, accelerator-driven subcritical assembly systems, or facilities for the separation of isotopes of source or SNM (enrichment), chemical processing of irradiated SNM (reprocessing), fabrication of nuclear fuel containing plutonium, or the production of heavy water;

   (2) Constructing, fabricating, operating, or maintaining such reactors, accelerator-driven subcritical assembly systems, or facilities;

   (3) Designing, constructing, fabricating, operating or maintaining components especially designed, modified or adapted for use in such reactors, accelerator-driven subcritical assembly systems, or facilities;

   (4) Designing, constructing, fabricating, operating or maintaining major critical components for use in such reactors, accelerator-driven subcritical assembly systems, or production-scale facilities; or

(5) Designing, constructing, fabricating, operating, or maintaining research reactors, test reactors or subcritical assemblies capable of continuous operation above five megawatts thermal.

(6) Training in the activities of paragraphs (c)(1) through (5) of this section.

§810.9 Restrictions on general and specific authorization.

A general or specific authorization granted by the Secretary of Energy under these regulations:

(a) Is limited to activities involving only unclassified information and does not permit furnishing Restricted Data or other classified information.

(b) Does not relieve a person from complying with relevant laws or the regulations of other Government agencies applicable to exports;

(c) Does not authorize a person to engage in any activity when the person knows or has reason to know that the activity is intended to provide assistance in designing, developing, fabricating or testing a nuclear explosive device.

§810.10 Grant of specific authorization.

(a) Any person proposing to provide assistance for which §810.8 indicates specific authorization is required may apply for the authorization to the U.S. Department of Energy, National Nuclear Security Administration, Washington, DC 20585, Attention: Director, Nuclear Transfer and Supplier Policy Division, NN-43, Office of Arms Control and Nonproliferation.

(b) The Secretary of Energy will approve an application for specific authorization if he determines, with the concurrence of the Department of State and after consultation with the Arms Control and Disarmament Agency, the Nuclear Regulatory Commission, the Department of Commerce, and the Department of Defense, that the activity will not be inimical to the interest of the United States. In making this determination, the Secretary will take into account:

(1) Whether the United States has an agreement for nuclear cooperation with the nation or group of nations involved;

(2) Whether the country involved is a party to the NPT, or a country for which the Treaty for the Prohibition of Nuclear Weapons in Latin America (Treaty of Tlatelolco) is in force;

(3) Whether the country involved has entered into an agreement with the IAEA for the application of safeguards on all its peaceful nuclear activities;

(4)   Whether the country involved, if it has not entered into such an agreement, has agreed to accept IAEA safeguards when applicable to the proposed activity;

(5)   Other nonproliferation controls or conditions applicable to the proposed activity;

(6)   The relative significance of the proposed activity;

(7)   The availability of comparable assistance from other sources;

(8)   Any other factors that may bear upon the political, economic, or security interests of the United States, including U.S. obligations under international agreements or treaties.

(c)   If the proposed assistance involves the export of "sensitive nuclear technology" as defined in §810.3, the requirements of sections 127 and 128 of the Atomic Energy Act and of any applicable U.S. international commitments must also be met.

(d)   Approximately 30 days after the Secretary's grant of a specific authorization, a copy of the Secretary's determination may be provided to any person requesting it at the Department's Public Reading Room, unless the applicant submits information showing that public disclosure will cause substantial harm to its competitive position. This provision does not affect any other authority provided by law for the Department not to disclose information.

§810.11 Revocation, suspension, or modification of authorization.
The Secretary may revoke, suspend, or modify a general or specific authorization:

(a)   For any material false statement in an application for specific authorization or in any additional information submitted in its support;

(b)   For failing to provide a report or for any material false statement in a report submitted pursuant to §810.13;

(c)   If any authorized assistance is subsequently determined to be inimical to the interest of the United States or otherwise no longer meets the legal criteria for approval; or

(d)   Pursuant to section 129 of the Atomic Energy Act.

B.3. Dual use controls and catchall provisions.

The Department of Commerce licenses the items on the NSG dual-use list as well as many items related to nuclear power plants, for example:
- turbines, generators, switching gear, and pipes and valves
- health and safety equipment for radiation detection and monitoring, fire safety, and facility security; and
- general infrastructure, telecommunications, tools and maintenance equipment.

The Department of Commerce is also responsible for implementing the catchall controls noted above. These are focused on sensitive nuclear activities, including nuclear explosive activities, reprocessing and enrichment, and heavy water production. They also take into account the location of the end-user and the safeguards status of the use.

See below for more detail.

3. *Catchall Controls - Title 15: Commerce and Foreign Trade*

Title 15: Commerce and Foreign Trade
PART 744—CONTROL POLICY: END-USER AND END-USE BASED[51]

§744.2 Restrictions on certain nuclear end-uses.

(a) General prohibition. In addition to the license requirements for items specified on the CCL, you may not export, reexport, or transfer (in-country) to any destination, other than countries in Supplement No. 3 to this part, an item subject to the EAR without a license if, at the time of export, reexport, or transfer (in-country) you know[52] that the item will be used directly or indirectly in any one or more of the following activities described in paragraphs (a)(1), (a)(2), and (a)(3) of this section:

   (1) *Nuclear explosive activities.* Nuclear explosive activities, including research on or development, design, manufacture, construction, testing or maintenance of any nuclear explosive device, or components or subsystems of such a device.[53] [54]

   (2) *Unsafeguarded nuclear activities.* Activities including research on, or development, design, manufacture, construction, operation, or maintenance of any nuclear reactor, critical facility, facility for the fabrication of nuclear fuel, facility for the conversion of nuclear material from one chemical form to another, or separate storage installation, where there is no obligation to accept International Atomic Energy Agency (IAEA) safeguards at the relevant facility or installation when it contains any source or special fissionable material (regardless of whether or not it contains such material at the time of export), or where any such obligation is not met.

   (3) *Safeguarded and unsafeguarded nuclear activities.* Safeguarded and unsafeguarded nuclear fuel cycle activities, including research on or

---

51 From http://www.ecfr.gov/cgi-bin/text-idx?c=ecfr&sid=0b553a6807d4a1cff1582d8f38f031a9&rgn=div8&view=text&node=15:2.1.3.4.28.0.1.2&idno=15 (March 3, 2014)

52 Part 772 of the EAR defines "knowledge" for all of the EAR except part 760, Restrictive Trade Practices and Boycotts. The definition, which includes variants such as "know" and "reason to know", encompasses more than positive knowledge. Thus, the use of "know" in this section in place of the former wording "know or have reason to know" does not lessen or otherwise change the responsibilities of persons subject to the EAR.

53 Nuclear explosive devices and any article, material, equipment, or device specifically designed or specially modified for use in the design, development, or fabrication of nuclear weapons or nuclear explosive devices are subject to export licensing or other requirements of the Directorate of Defense Trade Controls, U.S. Department of State, or the licensing or other restrictions specified in the Atomic Energy Act of 1954, as amended. Similarly, items specifically designed or specifically modified for use in devising, carrying out, or evaluating nuclear weapons tests or nuclear explosions (except such items as are in normal commercial use for other purposes) are subject to the same requirements.

54 Also see §§744.5 and 748.4 of the EAR for special provisions relating to technical data for maritime nuclear propulsion plants and other commodities.

development, design, manufacture, construction, operation or maintenance of any of the following facilities, or components for such facilities:[55]

(i) Facilities for the chemical processing of irradiated special nuclear or source material;

(ii) Facilities for the production of heavy water;

(iii) Facilities for the separation of isotopes of source and special nuclear material; or

(iv) Facilities for the fabrication of nuclear reactor fuel containing plutonium.

(b) *Additional prohibition on persons informed by BIS.* BIS may inform persons, either individually by specific notice or through amendment to the EAR, that a license is required for a specific export, reexport, or transfer (in-country), or for the export, reexport, or transfer (in-country) of specified items to a certain end-user, because there is an unacceptable risk of use in, or diversion to, the activities specified in paragraph (a) of this section. Specific notice is to be given only by, or at the direction of, the Deputy Assistant Secretary for Export Administration. When such notice is provided orally, it will be followed by a written notice within two working days signed by the Deputy Assistant Secretary for Export Administration. However, the absence of any such notification does not excuse persons from compliance with the license requirements of paragraph (a) of this section.

(c) *Exceptions.* Despite the prohibitions described in paragraphs (a) and (b) of this section, you may export technology subject to the EAR under the operation technology and software or sales technology and software provisions of License Exception TSU (see §740.13(a) and (b)), but only to and for use in countries listed in Supplement No. 3 to Part 744 of the EAR (Countries Not Subject to Certain Nuclear End-Use Restrictions in §744.2(a)). Notwithstanding the provisions of Part 740 of the EAR, the provisions of §740.13(a) and (b) will only overcome General Prohibition Five for countries listed in Supplement No. 3 to Part 744 of the EAR.

(d) *License review standards.* The following factors are among those used by the United States to determine whether to grant or deny license applications required under this section:

---

[55] Such activities may also require a specific authorization from the Secretary of Energy pursuant to §57.b.(2) of the Atomic Energy Act of 1954, as amended, as implemented by the Department of Energy's regulations published in 10 CFR 810.

(1) Whether the commodities, software, or technology to be transferred are appropriate for the stated end-use and whether that stated end-use is appropriate for the end-user;

(2) The significance for nuclear purposes of the particular commodity, software, or technology;

(3) Whether the commodities, software, or technology to be exported are to be used in research on or for the development, design, manufacture, construction, operation, or maintenance of any reprocessing or enrichment facility;

(4) The types of assurances or guarantees given against use for nuclear explosive purposes or proliferation in the particular case;

(5) Whether the end-user has been engaged in clandestine or illegal procurement activities;

(6) Whether an application for a license to export to the end-user has previously been denied, or whether the end-use has previously diverted items received under a license, License Exception, or NLR to unauthorized activities;

(7) Whether the export would present an unacceptable risk of diversion to a nuclear explosive activity or unsafeguarded nuclear fuel-cycle activity described in §744.2 of this part; and

(8) The nonproliferation credentials of the importing country, based on consideration of the following factors:

> (i) Whether the importing country is a party to the Nuclear Non-Proliferation Treaty (NPT) or to the Treaty for the Prohibition of Nuclear Weapons in Latin America (Treaty of Tlatelolco) (see Supplement No. 2 to part 742 of the EAR), or to a similar international legally-binding nuclear nonproliferation agreement;

> (ii) Whether the importing country has all of its nuclear activities, facilities or installations that are operational, being designed, or under construction, under International Atomic Energy Agency (IAEA) safeguards or equivalent full scope safeguards;

> (iii) Whether there is an agreement for cooperation in the civil uses of atomic energy between the U.S. and the importing country;

> (iv) Whether the actions, statements, and policies of the government of the importing country are in support of nuclear nonproliferation

and whether that government is in compliance with its international obligations in the field of nonproliferation;

(v) The degree to which the government of the importing country cooperates in nonproliferation policy generally (e.g., willingness to consult on international nonproliferation issues);

(vi) Intelligence data on the importing country's nuclear intentions and activities.

NUCLEAR SECURITY

Background

Nuclear security focuses on efforts to reduce the risks that terrorists or others could acquire and use nuclear-weapon-useable or radiological material maliciously. This must be pursued through all possible means, including multinational and regional efforts, through international, legally binding conventions, and through national efforts. International organizations, especially the United Nations and the Intentional Atomic Energy agency are deeply involved.

This section contains the texts of the three most relevant legally binding conventions. One is the Convention on the Physical Protection of Nuclear Material, which establishes internationally legally binding obligations that cover nuclear material during international transport. It entered into force in 1987. An amendment to the Convention was agreed in 2005, and, when it enters into force, the Convention will also cover nuclear material in domestic use.

Another Convention of importance is the International Convention for the Suppression of Acts of Nuclear Terrorism. It addresses steps that States can take to improve their ability to deter and prevent nuclear terrorism as well as establishing modes of cooperation.

The United Nations Security Council adopted Resolution 1540 under Chapter VII of the United Nations Charter. It obligates states to take a wide range of steps to ensure that the risks of all forms of WMD terrorism are reduced. In addition, it created a Committee to monitor implantation of the Convention by members of the United Nations. But the role of the Committee goes beyond monitoring. It also established means through which states can seek assistance.

The importance of nuclear security led President Obama to convene a nuclear security summit in 2010. Since then, two additional summit meetings have been held. The next will be held in the United States in 2016.

It is difficult to understate the important role played by the International Atomic Energy Agency. Its role includes, for example, establishing guidelines on physical protection and other nuclear security requirements and providing assistance to its Member States. Its publications are too many to include here but are readily found on iaea.org.

A. International Conventions and United Nations Security Council Resolutions

The Convention on the Physical Protection of Nuclear Material
(entered into force on February 8, 1986)[56]

THE STATES PARTIES TO THIS CONVENTION,

RECOGNIZING the right of all States to develop and apply nuclear energy for peaceful purposes and their legitimate interests in the potential benefits to be derived from the peaceful application of nuclear energy,

CONVINCED of the need for facilitating international co-operation in the peaceful application of nuclear energy,

DESIRING to avert the potential dangers posed by the unlawful taking and use of nuclear material,

CONVINCED that offences relating to nuclear material are a matter of grave concern and that there is an urgent need to adopt appropriate and effective measures to ensure the prevention, detection and punishment of such offences,

AWARE OF THE NEED FOR international co-operation to establish, in conformity with the national law of each State Party and with this Convention, effective measures for the physical protection of nuclear material,

CONVINCED that this Convention should facilitate the safe transfer of nuclear material,

STRESSING also the importance of the physical protection of nuclear material in domestic use, storage and transport,

RECOGNIZING the importance of effective physical protection of nuclear material used for military purposes, and understanding that such material is and will continue to be accorded stringent physical protection,

HAVE AGREED as follows:

Article 1

For the purposes of this Convention:

a. "nuclear material" means plutonium except that with isotopic concentration exceeding 80% in plutonium-238; uranium-233; uranium enriched in the

---

[56] As of March 22, 2014, the Convention had 149 parties according to the IAEA.

isotope 235 or 233; uranium containing the mixture of isotopes as occurring in nature other than in the form of ore or ore-residue; any material containing one or more of the foregoing;

b.   "uranium enriched in the isotope 235 or 233" means uranium containing the isotope 235 or 233 or both in an amount such that the abundance ratio of the sum of these isotopes to the isotope 238 is greater than the ratio of the isotope 235 to the isotope 238 occurring in nature;

c.   "international nuclear transport" means the carriage of a consignment of nuclear material by any means of transportation intended to go beyond the territory of the State where the shipment originates beginning with the departure from a facility of the shipper in that State and ending with the arrival at a facility of the receiver within the State of ultimate destination.

Article 2

1.   This Convention shall apply to nuclear material used for peaceful purposes while in international nuclear transport.

2.   With the exception of articles 3 and 4 and paragraph 3 of article 5, this Convention shall also apply to nuclear material used for peaceful purposes while in domestic use, storage and transport.

3.   Apart from the commitments expressly undertaken by States Parties in the articles covered by paragraph 2 with respect to nuclear material used for peaceful purposes while in domestic use, storage and transport, nothing in this Convention shall be interpreted as affecting the sovereign rights of a State regarding the domestic use, storage and transport of such nuclear material.

Article 3

Each State Party shall take appropriate steps within the framework of its national law and consistent with international law to ensure as far as practicable that, during international nuclear transport, nuclear material within its territory, or on board a ship or aircraft under its jurisdiction insofar as such ship or aircraft is engaged in the transport to or from that State, is protected at the levels described in Annex I.

Article 4

1.   Each State Party shall not export or authorize the export of nuclear material unless the State Party has received assurances that such material will be protected during the international nuclear transport at the levels described in Annex I.

2.   Each State Party shall not import or authorize the import of nuclear material from a State not party to this Convention unless the State Party has received

assurances that such material will during the international nuclear transport be protected at the levels described in Annex I.

3.   A State Party shall not allow the transit of its territory by land or internal waterways or through its airports or seaports of nuclear material between States that are not parties to this Convention unless the State Party has received assurances as far as practicable that this nuclear material will be protected during international nuclear transport at the levels described in Annex I.

4.   Each State Party shall apply within the framework of its national law the levels of physical protection described in Annex I to nuclear material being transported from a part of that State to another part of the same State through international waters or airspace.

5.   The State Party responsible for receiving assurances that the nuclear material will be protected at the levels described in Annex I according to paragraphs 1 to 3 shall identify and inform in advance States which the nuclear material is expected to transit by land or internal waterways, or whose airports or seaports it is expected to enter.

6.   The responsibility for obtaining assurances referred to in paragraph 1 may be transferred, by mutual agreement, to the State Party involved in the transport as the importing State.

7.   Nothing in this article shall be interpreted as in any way affecting the territorial sovereignty and jurisdiction of a State, including that over its airspace and territorial sea.

Article 5

1.   States Parties shall identify and make known to each other directly or through the International Atomic Energy Agency their central authority and point of contact having responsibility for physical protection of nuclear material and for coordinating recovery and response operations in the event of any unauthorized removal, use or alteration of nuclear material or in the event of credible threat thereof.

2.   In the case of theft, robbery or any other unlawful taking of nuclear material or of credible threat thereof, States Parties shall, in accordance with their national law, provide co-operation and assistance to the maximum feasible extent in the recovery and protection of such material to any State that so requests. In particular:

    a.   a State Party shall take appropriate steps to inform as soon as possible other States, which appear to it to be concerned, of any theft, robbery or other unlawful taking of nuclear material or credible threat thereof and to inform, where appropriate, international organizations;

b.   as appropriate, the States Parties concerned shall exchange information with each other or international organizations with a view to protecting threatened nuclear material, verifying the integrity of the shipping container, or recovering unlawfully taken nuclear material and shall:

  i.   co-ordinate their efforts through diplomatic and other agreed channels;

  ii.   render assistance; if requested;

  iii.   ensure the return of nuclear material stolen or missing as a consequence of the above-mentioned events.

The means of implementation of this co-operation shall be determined by the States Parties concerned.

States Parties shall co-operate and consult as appropriate, with each other directly or through international organizations, with a view to obtaining guidance on the design, maintenance and improvement of systems of physical protection of nuclear material in international transport.

Article 6

1.   States Parties shall take appropriate measures consistent with their national law to protect the confidentiality of any information which they receive in confidence by virtue of the provisions of this Convention form another State Party or through participation in an activity carried out for the implementation of this Convention. If States Parties provide information to international organizations in confidence, steps shall be taken to ensure that the confidentiality of such information is protected.

2.   States Parties shall not be required by this Convention to provide any information which they are not permitted to communicate pursuant to national law or which would jeopardize the security of the State concerned or the physical protection of nuclear material.

Article 7

1.   The intentional commission of:

a.   an act without lawful authority which constitutes the receipt, possession, use, transfer, alteration, disposal or dispersal of nuclear material and which causes or is likely to cause death or serious injury to any person or substantial damage to property;

b.   a theft or robbery of nuclear material;

    c.   an embezzlement or fraudulent obtaining of nuclear material;

    d.   an act constituting a demand for nuclear material by threat or use of force or by any other form of intimidation;

    e.   a threat:

        i.   to use nuclear material to cause death or serious injury to any person or substantial property damage, or

        ii.   to commit an offence described in sub-paragraph (b) in order to compel a natural or legal person, international organization or State to do or to refrain from doing any act;

    f.   an attempt to commit any offence described in paragraphs (a), (b) or (c); and

    g.   an act which constitutes participation in any offence described in paragraphs (a) to (f)

    h.   shall be made a punishable offence by each State Party under its national law.

2.   Each State Party shall make the offences described in this article punishable by appropriate penalties which take into account their grave nature.

Article 8

1.   Each State Party shall take such measures as may be necessary to establish its jurisdiction over the offences set forth in article 7 in the following cases;

    a.   when the offence is committed in the territory of that State or on board a ship or aircraft registered in that State;

    b.   when the alleged offender is a national of that State.

2.   Each State Party shall likewise take such measures as may be necessary to establish its jurisdiction over these offences in cases where the alleged offender is presented in its territory and it does not extradite him pursuant to article 11 to any of the States mentioned in paragraph 1.

3.   This Convention does not exclude any criminal jurisdiction exercised in accordance with national law.

4.   In addition to the States Parties mentioned in paragraphs 1 and 2, each State Party may, consistent with international law, establish its jurisdiction over the

offences set forth in article 7 when it is involved in international nuclear transport as the exporting or importing State.

Article 9

Upon being satisfied that the circumstances so warrant, the State Party in whose territory the alleged offender is present shall take appropriate measures, including detention, under its national law to ensure his presence for the purpose of prosecution or extradition. Measures taken according to this article shall be notified without delay to the States required to establish jurisdiction pursuant to article 8 and, where appropriate, all other States concerned.

Article 10

The State Party in whose territory the alleged offender is present shall, if it does not extradite him, submit, without exception whatsoever and without undue delay, the case to its competent authorities for the purpose of prosecution, through proceedings in accordance with the laws of that State.

Article 11

1. The offences in article 7 shall be deemed to be included as extraditable offences in any extradition treaty existing between States Parties. States Parties undertake to include those offences as extraditable offences in every future extradition treaty to be concluded between them.

2. If a State Party which makes extradition conditional on the existence of a treaty receives a request for extradition from another State Party with which it has no extradition treaty, it may at its option consider this Convention as the legal basis for extradition in respect of those offences. Extradition shall be subject to the other conditions provided by the law of the requested State.

3. States Parties which do not make extradition conditional on the existence of a treaty shall recognize those offences as extraditable offences between themselves subject to the conditions provided by the law of the requested State.

4. Each of the offences shall be treated, for the purpose of extradition between States Parties, as if it had been committed not only in the place in which it occurred but also in the territories of the States Parties required to establish their jurisdiction in accordance with paragraph 1 of article 8.

Article 12

Any person regarding whom proceedings are being carried out in connection with any of the offences set forth in article 7 shall be guaranteed fair treatment at all stages of the proceedings.

Article 13

1. States Parties shall afford one another the greatest measure of assistance in connection with criminal proceedings brought in respect of the offences set forth in article 7, including the supply of evidence at their disposal necessary for the proceedings. The law of the State requested shall apply in all cases.

2. The provisions of paragraph 1 shall not affect obligations under any other treaty, bilateral or multilateral, which governs or will govern, in whole or in part, mutual assistance in criminal matters.

Article 14

1. Each State Party shall inform the depositary of its laws and regulations which give effect to this Convention. The depositary shall communicate such information periodically to all States Parties.

2. The State Party where an alleged offender is prosecuted shall, wherever practicable, first communicate the final outcome of the proceedings to the States directly concerned. The State Party shall also communicate the final outcome to the depositary who shall inform all States.

3. Where an offence involves nuclear material used for peaceful purposes in domestic use, storage or transport, and both the alleged offender and the nuclear material remain in the territory of the State Party in which the offence was committed, nothing in this Convention shall be interpreted as requiring that State Party to provide information concerning criminal proceedings arising out of such an offence.

Article 15

The Annexes constitute an integral part of this Convention.

Article 16

1. A conference of States Parties shall be convened by the depositary of five years after the entry into force of this Convention to review the implementation of the Convention and its adequacy as concerns the preamble, the whole of the operative part and the annexes in the light of the then prevailing situation.

2. At intervals of not less than five years thereafter, the majority of States Parties may obtain, by submitting a proposal to this effect to the depositary, the convening of further conferences with the same objective.

Article 17

1. In the event of a dispute between two or more States Parties concerning the interpretation or application of this Convention, such States Parties shall consult with a view to the settlement of the dispute by negotiation, or by any other peaceful means of settling disputes acceptable to all parties to the dispute.

2. Any dispute of this character which cannot be settled in the manner prescribed in paragraph 1 shall, at the request of any party to such dispute, be submitted to arbitration or referred to the International Court of Justice for decision. Where a dispute is submitted to arbitration, if, within six months from the date of the request, the parties to the dispute are unable to agree on the organization of the arbitration, a party may request the President of the International Court of Justice or the Secretary-General of the United Nations to appoint one or more arbitrators. In case of conflicting requests by the parties to the dispute, the request to the Secretary-General of the United Nations shall have priority.

3. Each State Party may at the time of signature, ratification, acceptance or approval of this Convention or accession thereto declare that it does not consider itself bound by either or both of the dispute settlement procedures provided for in paragraph 2. The other States Parties shall not be bound by a dispute settlement procedure provided for in paragraph 2, with respect to a State Party which has made a reservation to that procedure.

4. Any State Party which has made a reservation in accordance with paragraph 3 may at any time withdraw that reservation by notification to the depositary.

Article 18

1. This Convention shall be open for signature by all States at the Headquarters of the International Atomic Energy Agency in Vienna and at the Headquarters of the United Nations in New York from 3 March 1980 until its entry into force.

2. This Convention is subject to ratification, acceptance or approval by the signatory States.

3. After its entry into force, this Convention will be open for accession by all States.

4. a. This Convention shall be open for signature or accession by international organizations and regional organizations of an integration or other nature, provided that any such organization is constituted by sovereign States and has competence in respect of the negotiation, conclusion and application of international agreements in matters covered by this Convention.

b.   In matters within their competence, such organizations shall, on their own behalf, exercise the rights and fulfil the responsibilities which this Convention attributes to States Parties.

c.   When becoming party to this Convention such an organization shall communicate to the depository a declaration indicating which States are members thereof and which articles of this Convention do not apply to it.

d.   Such an organization shall not hold any vote additional to those of its Member States.

Instruments of ratification, acceptance, approval or accession shall be deposited with depositary.

Article 19

1.   This Convention shall enter into force on the thirtieth day following the date of deposit of the twenty-first instrument of ratification, acceptance or approval with the depositary.

2.   For each State ratifying, accepting, approving or acceding to the Convention after the date of deposit of the twenty-first instrument of ratification, acceptance or approval, the Convention shall enter into force on the thirtieth day after the deposit by such State of its instrument of ratification, acceptance, approval or accession.

Article 20

1.   Without prejudice to article 16 a State Party may propose amendments to this Convention. The proposed amendment shall be submitted to the depositary who shall circulate it immediately to all States Parties. If a majority of States Parties request the depositary to convene a conference to consider the proposed amendments, the depositary shall invite all States Parties to attend such a conference to being not sooner than thirty days after the invitations are issued. Any amendment adopted at the conference by a two-thirds majority of all States Parties shall be promptly circulated by the depositary to all States Parties.

2.   The amendment shall enter into force for each State Party that deposits its instrument of ratification, acceptance or approval of the amendment on the thirtieth day after the date on which two thirds of the States Parties have deposited their instruments of ratification, acceptance or approval with the depositary. Thereafter, the amendment shall enter into force for any other State Party on the day on which that State Party deposits its instrument of ratification, acceptance or approval of the amendment.

Article 21

1. Any State Party any denounce this Convention by written notification to the depositary.

2. Denunciation shall take effect one hundred and eighty days following the date on which notification is received by the depositary.

Article 22

The depositary shall promptly notify all States of:

a. each signature of this Convention;

b. each deposit of an instrument of ratification, acceptance, approval or accession;

c. any reservation or withdrawal in accordance with article 17;

d. any communication made by an organization in accordance with paragraph 4(c) of article 18;

e. the entry into force of this Convention;

f. the entry into force of any amendment to this Convention; and

g. any denunciation made under article 21.

Article 23

The original of this Convention, of which the Arabic, Chinese, English, French, Russian and Spanish texts are equally authentic, shall be deposited with the Director General of the International Atomic Energy Agency who shall send certified copies thereof to all States.

IN WITNESS WHEREOF, the undersigned, being duly authorized, have signed this Convention, opened for signature at Vienna and at New York on 3 March 1980.

Annex I

Levels of Physical Protection to be applied in International Transport of Nuclear Materials as Categorized in Annex II

1. Levels of physical protection for nuclear material during storage incidental to international nuclear transport include:

    a. For Category III materials, storage within an area to which access is controlled;

    b. For Category II materials, storage within an area under constant surveillance by guards or electronic devices, surrounded by a physical barrier with a limited number of points of entry under appropriate control or any area with an equivalent level of physical protection;

    c. For Category I material, storage within a protected area as defined for Category II above, to which, in addition, access is restricted to persons whose trustworthiness has been determined, and which is under surveillance by guards who are in close communication with appropriate response forces. Specific measures taken in this context should have as their object the detection and prevention of any assault, unauthorized access or unauthorized removal of material.

2. Levels of physical protection for nuclear material during international transport include:

    a. For Category II and III materials, transportation shall take place under special precautions including prior arrangements among sender, receiver, and carrier, and prior agreement between natural or legal persons subject to the jurisdiction and regulation of exporting and importing States, specifying time, place and procedures for transferring transport responsibility;

    b. For Category I materials, transportation shall take place under special precautions identified above for transportation of Category II and III materials, and in addition, under constant surveillance by escorts and under conditions which assure close communication with appropriate response forces;

    c. For natural uranium other than in the form of ore or ore-residue; transportation protection for quantities exceeding 500 kilograms uranium shall include advance notification of shipment specifying mode of transport, expected time of arrival and confirmation of receipt of shipment.

Annex II
Table: Categorization of Nuclear Material

Material	Form	Category		
		I	II	III[c]
1. Plutonium[a]	Unirradiated[b]	2 kg or more	Less than 2 kg but more than 500 g	500 g or less but more than 15 g
2. Uranium-235	Unirradiated[b] • uranium enriched to 20% ^{235}U or more • uranium enriched to 10% ^{235}U but less than 20% • uranium enriched above natural, but less than 10% ^{235}U	5 kg or more	Less than 5 kg but more than 1 kg 10 kg or more	1 kg or less but more than 15 g Less than 10 kg but more than 1 kg 10 kg or more
3. Uranium-233	Unirradiated[b]	2 kg or more	Less than 2 kg but more than 500 g	500 g or less but more than 15 g
4. Irradiated fuel			Depleted or natural uranium, thorium or low-enriched fuel (less than 10% fissile content)[d/e]	

[a] All plutonium except that with isotopic concentration exceeding 80% in plutonium-238.
[b] Material not irradiated in a reactor or material irradiated in a reactor but with a radiation level equal to or less than 100 rads/hour at one metre unshielded.
[c] Quantities not falling in Category III and natural uranium should be protected in accordance with prudent management practice.

d/ Although this level of protection is recommended, it would be open to States, upon evaluation of the specific circumstances, to assign a different category of physical protection.
e/ Other fuel which by virtue of its original fissile material content is classified as Category I and II before irradiation may be reduced one category level while the radiation level from the fuel exceeds 100 rads/hour at one metre unshielded.

Amendment to the Convention on the Physical Protection of Nuclear Material

1. The Title of the Convention on the Physical Protection of Nuclear Material adopted on 26 October 1979 (hereinafter referred to as "the Convention") is replaced by the following title:

   CONVENTION ON THE PHYSICAL PROTECTION OF NUCLEAR MATERIAL AND NUCLEAR FACILITIES

2. The Preamble of the Convention is replaced by the following text: THE STATES PARTIES TO THIS CONVENTION,

RECOGNIZING the right of all States to develop and apply nuclear energy for peaceful purposes and their legitimate interests in the potential benefits to be derived from the peaceful application of nuclear energy,

CONVINCED of the need to facilitate international co-operation and the transfer of nuclear technology for the peaceful application of nuclear energy,

BEARING IN MIND that physical protection is of vital importance for the protection of public health, safety, the environment and national and international security,

HAVING IN MIND the purposes and principles of the Charter of the United Nations concerning the maintenance of international peace and security and the promotion of good-neighbourliness and friendly relations and co-operation among States,

CONSIDERING that under the terms of paragraph 4 of Article 2 of the Charter of the United Nations, "All members shall refrain in their international relations from the threat or use of force against the territorial integrity or political independence of any state, or in any other manner inconsistent with the Purposes of the United Nations,"

RECALLING the Declaration on Measures to Eliminate International Terrorism, annexed to General Assembly resolution 49/60 of 9 December 1994,

DESIRING to avert the potential dangers posed by illicit trafficking, the unlawful taking and use of nuclear material and the sabotage of nuclear material and nuclear facilities, and noting that physical protection against such acts has become a matter of increased national and international concern,

DEEPLY CONCERNED by the worldwide escalation of acts of terrorism in all its forms and manifestations, and by the threats posed by international terrorism and organized crime,

BELIEVING that physical protection plays an important role in supporting nuclear non-proliferation and counter-terrorism objectives,

DESIRING through this Convention to contribute to strengthening worldwide the physical protection of nuclear material and nuclear facilities used for peaceful purposes,

CONVINCED that offences relating to nuclear material and nuclear facilities are a matter of grave concern and that there is an urgent need to adopt appropriate and effective measures, or to strengthen existing measures, to ensure the prevention, detection and punishment of such offences,

DESIRING to strengthen further international co-operation to establish, in conformity with the national law of each State Party and with this Convention, effective measures for the physical protection of nuclear material and nuclear facilities,

CONVINCED that this Convention should complement the safe use, storage and transport of nuclear material and the safe operation of nuclear facilities,

RECOGNIZING that there are internationally formulated physical protection recommendations that are updated from time to time which can provide guidance on contemporary means of achieving effective levels of physical protection,

RECOGNIZING also that effective physical protection of nuclear material and nuclear facilities used for military purposes is a responsibility of the State possessing such nuclear material and nuclear facilities, and understanding that such material and facilities are and will continue to be accorded stringent physical protection,

HAVE AGREED as follows:

3.   In Article 1 of the Convention, after paragraph (c), two new paragraphs are added as follows:

(d)   "nuclear facility" means a facility (including associated buildings and equipment) in which nuclear material is produced, processed, used, handled, stored or disposed of, if damage to or interference with such facility could lead to the release of significant amounts of radiation or radioactive material;

(e)   "sabotage" means any deliberate act directed against a nuclear facility or nuclear material in use, storage or transport which could directly or indirectly endanger the health and safety of personnel, the public or the environment by exposure to radiation or release of radioactive substances.

4.   After Article 1 of the Convention, a new Article 1A is added as follows:

Article 1A

The purposes of this Convention are to achieve and maintain worldwide effective physical protection of nuclear material used for peaceful purposes and of nuclear facilities used for peaceful purposes; to prevent and combat offences relating to such material and facilities worldwide; as well as to facilitate co-operation among States Parties to those ends.

5.   Article 2 of the Convention is replaced by the following text:

    1.   This Convention shall apply to nuclear material used for peaceful purposes in use, storage and transport and to nuclear facilities used for peaceful purposes, provided, however, that articles 3 and 4 and paragraph 4 of article 5 of this Convention shall only apply to such nuclear material while in international nuclear transport.

    2.   The responsibility for the establishment, implementation and maintenance of a physical protection regime within a State Party rests entirely with that State.

    3.   Apart from the commitments expressly undertaken by States Parties under this Convention, nothing in this Convention shall be interpreted as affecting the sovereign rights of a State.

    4.   (a)   Nothing in this Convention shall affect other rights, obligations and responsibilities of States Parties under international law, in particular the purposes and principles of the Charter of the United Nations and international humanitarian law.

        (b)   The activities of armed forces during an armed conflict, as those terms are understood under international humanitarian law, which are governed by that law, are not governed by this Convention, and the activities undertaken by the military forces of a State in the exercise of their official duties, inasmuch as they are governed by other rules of international law, are not governed by this Convention.

        (c)   Nothing in this Convention shall be construed as a lawful authorization to use or threaten to use force against nuclear material or nuclear facilities used for peaceful purposes.

        (d)   Nothing in this Convention condones or makes lawful otherwise unlawful acts, nor precludes prosecution under other laws.

    5.   This Convention shall not apply to nuclear material used or retained for military purposes or to a nuclear facility containing such material.

6.   After Article 2 of the Convention, a new Article 2A is added as follows:

Article 2A

1.   Each State Party shall establish, implement and maintain an appropriate physical protection regime applicable to nuclear material and nuclear facilities under its jurisdiction, with the aim of:

   (a)   protecting against theft and other unlawful taking of nuclear material in use, storage and transport;

   (b)   ensuring the implementation of rapid and comprehensive measures to locate and, where appropriate, recover missing or stolen nuclear material; when the material is located outside its territory, that State Party shall act in accordance with article 5;

   (c)   protecting nuclear material and nuclear facilities against sabotage; and

   (d)   mitigating or minimizing the radiological consequences of sabotage.

2.   In implementing paragraph 1, each State Party shall:

   (a)   establish and maintain a legislative and regulatory framework to govern physical protection;

   (b)   establish or designate a competent authority or authorities responsible for the implementation of the legislative and regulatory framework; and

   (c)   take other appropriate measures necessary for the physical protection of nuclear material and nuclear facilities.

3.   In implementing the obligations under paragraphs 1 and 2, each State Party shall, without prejudice to any other provisions of this Convention, apply insofar as is reasonable and practicable the following Fundamental Principles of Physical Protection of Nuclear Material and Nuclear Facilities.

FUNDAMENTAL PRINCIPLE A: *Responsibility of the State*

The responsibility for the establishment, implementation and maintenance of a physical protection regime within a State rests entirely with that State.

FUNDAMENTAL PRINCIPLE B: *Responsibilities During International Transport*

The responsibility of a State for ensuring that nuclear material is adequately protected extends to the international transport thereof, until that responsibility is properly transferred to another State, as appropriate.

FUNDAMENTAL PRINCIPLE C: *Legislative and Regulatory Framework*

The State is responsible for establishing and maintaining a legislative and regulatory framework to govern physical protection. This framework should provide for the establishment of applicable physical protection requirements and include a system of evaluation and licensing or other procedures to grant authorization. This framework should include a system of inspection of nuclear facilities and transport to verify compliance with applicable requirements and conditions of the license or other authorizing document, and to establish a means to enforce applicable requirements and conditions, including effective sanctions.

FUNDAMENTAL PRINCIPLE D: *Competent Authority*

The State should establish or designate a competent authority which is responsible for the implementation of the legislative and regulatory framework, and is provided with adequate authority, competence and financial and human resources to fulfill its assigned responsibilities. The State should take steps to ensure an effective independence between the functions of the State's competent authority and those of any other body in charge of the promotion or utilization of nuclear energy.

FUNDAMENTAL PRINCIPLE E: *Responsibility of the License Holders*

The responsibilities for implementing the various elements of physical protection within a State should be clearly identified. The State should ensure that the prime responsibility for the implementation of physical protection of nuclear material or of nuclear facilities rests with the holders of the relevant licenses or of other authorizing documents (e.g., operators or shippers).

FUNDAMENTAL PRINCIPLE F: *Security Culture*

All organizations involved in implementing physical protection should give due priority to the security culture, to its development and maintenance necessary to ensure its effective implementation in the entire organization.

FUNDAMENTAL PRINCIPLE G: *Threat*

The State's physical protection should be based on the State's current evaluation of the threat.

FUNDAMENTAL PRINCIPLE H: *Graded Approach*

Physical protection requirements should be based on a graded approach, taking into account the current evaluation of the threat, the relative attractiveness, the nature of the material and potential consequences associated with the unauthorized removal of nuclear material and with the sabotage against nuclear material or nuclear facilities.

FUNDAMENTAL PRINCIPLE I: *Defence in Depth*

The State's requirements for physical protection should reflect a concept of several layers and methods of protection (structural or other technical, personnel and organizational) that have to be overcome or circumvented by an adversary in order to achieve his objectives.

FUNDAMENTAL PRINCIPLE J: *Quality Assurance*

A quality assurance policy and quality assurance programmes should be established and implemented with a view to providing confidence that specified requirements for all activities important to physical protection are satisfied.

FUNDAMENTAL PRINCIPLE K: *Contingency Plans*

Contingency (emergency) plans to respond to unauthorized removal of nuclear material or sabotage of nuclear facilities or nuclear material, or attempts thereof, should be prepared and appropriately exercised by all license holders and authorities concerned.

FUNDAMENTAL PRINCIPLE L: *Confidentiality*

The State should establish requirements for protecting the confidentiality of information, the unauthorized disclosure of which could compromise the physical protection of nuclear material and nuclear facilities.

4.   (a)   The provisions of this article shall not apply to any nuclear material which the State Party reasonably decides does not need to be subject to the physical protection regime established pursuant to paragraph 1, taking into account the nature of the material, its quantity and relative attractiveness and the potential radiological and other consequences associated with any unauthorized act directed against it and the current evaluation of the threat against it.

       (b)   Nuclear material which is not subject to the provisions of this article pursuant to sub-paragraph (a) should be protected in accordance with prudent management practice.

7.   Article 5 of the Convention is replaced by the following text:

1.   States Parties shall identify and make known to each other directly or through the International Atomic Energy Agency their point of contact in relation to matters within the scope of this Convention.

2. In the case of theft, robbery or any other unlawful taking of nuclear material or credible threat thereof, States Parties shall, in accordance with their national law, provide co-operation and assistance to the maximum feasible extent in the recovery and protection of such material to any State that so requests. In particular:

   (a) a State Party shall take appropriate steps to inform as soon as possible other States, which appear to it to be concerned, of any theft, robbery or other unlawful taking of nuclear material or credible threat thereof, and to inform, where appropriate, the International Atomic Energy Agency and other relevant international organizations;

   (b) in doing so, as appropriate, the States Parties concerned shall exchange information with each other, the International Atomic Energy Agency and other relevant international organizations with a view to protecting threatened nuclear material, verifying the integrity of the shipping container or recovering unlawfully taken nuclear material and shall:

      (i) co-ordinate their efforts through diplomatic and other agreed channels;

      (ii) render assistance, if requested;

      (iii) ensure the return of recovered nuclear material stolen or missing as a consequence of the above-mentioned events.

The means of implementation of this co-operation shall be determined by the States Parties concerned.

3. In the case of a credible threat of sabotage of nuclear material or a nuclear facility or in the case of sabotage thereof, States Parties shall, to the maximum feasible extent, in accordance with their national law and consistent with their relevant obligations under international law, co-operate as follows:

   (a) if a State Party has knowledge of a credible threat of sabotage of nuclear material or a nuclear facility in another State, the former shall decide on appropriate steps to be taken in order to inform that State as soon as possible and, where appropriate, the International Atomic Energy Agency and other relevant international organizations of that threat, with a view to preventing the sabotage;

   (b) in the case of sabotage of nuclear material or a nuclear facility in a State Party and if in its view other States are likely to be radiologically affected, the former, without prejudice to its other obligations under international law, shall take appropriate steps to inform as soon as possible the State or the States which are likely to be radiologically affected and to inform, where appropriate, the International Atomic Energy Agency and other relevant international organizations, with a view to minimizing or mitigating the radiological consequences thereof;

(c)   if in the context of sub-paragraphs (a) and (b), a State Party requests assistance, each State Party to which a request for assistance is directed shall promptly decide and notify the requesting State Party, directly or through the International Atomic Energy Agencywhether it is in a position to render the assistance requested and the scope and terms of the assistance that may be rendered;

(d)   co-ordination of the co-operation under sub-paragraphs (a) to (c) shall be through diplomatic or other agreed channels. The means of implementation of this co-operation shall be determined bilaterally or multilaterally by the States Parties concerned.

4.   States Parties shall co-operate and consult, as appropriate, with each other directly or through the International Atomic Energy Agency and other relevant international organizations, with a view to obtaining guidance on the design, maintenance and improvement of systems of physical protection of nuclear material in international transport.

5.   A State Party may consult and co-operate, as appropriate, with other States Parties directly or through the International Atomic Energy Agency and other relevant international organizations, with a view to obtaining their guidance on the design, maintenance and improvement of its national system of physical protection of nuclear material in domestic use, storage and transport and of nuclear facilities.

8.   Article 6 of the Convention is replaced by the following text:

1.   States Parties shall take appropriate measures consistent with their national law to protect the confidentiality of any information which they receive in confidence by virtue of the provisions of this Convention from another State Party or through participation in an activity carried out for the implementation of this Convention. If States Parties provide information to international organizations or to States that are not parties to this Convention in confidence, steps shall be taken to ensure that the confidentiality of such information is protected. A State Party that has received information in confidence from another State Party may provide this information to third parties only with the consent of that other State Party.

2. States Parties shall not be required by this Convention to provide any information which they are not permitted to communicate pursuant to national law or which would jeopardize the security of the State concerned or the physical protection of nuclear material or nuclear facilities.

9. Paragraph 1 of Article 7 of the Convention is replaced by the following text:

1. The intentional commission of:

    (a) an act without lawful authority which constitutes the receipt, possession, use, transfer, alteration, disposal or dispersal of nuclear material and which causes or is likely to cause death or serious injury to any person or substantial damage to property or to the environment;

    (b) a theft or robbery of nuclear material;

    (c) an embezzlement or fraudulent obtaining of nuclear material;

    (d) an act which constitutes the carrying, sending, or moving of nuclear material into or out of a State without lawful authority;

    (e) an act directed against a nuclear facility, or an act interfering with the operation of a nuclear facility, where the offender intentionally causes, or where he knows that the act is likely to cause, death or serious injury to any person or substantial damage to property or to the environment by exposure to radiation or release of radioactive substances, unless the act is undertaken in conformity with the national law of the State Party in the territory of which the nuclear facility is situated;

    (f) an act constituting a demand for nuclear material by threat or use of force or by any other form of intimidation;

    (g) a threat:

        (i) to use nuclear material to cause death or serious injury to any person or substantial damage to property or to the environment or to commit the offence described in sub-paragraph (e), or

        (ii) to commit an offence described in sub-paragraphs (b) and (e) in order to compel a natural or legal person, international organization or State to do or to refrain from doing any act;

    (h) an attempt to commit any offence described in sub-paragraphs (a) to (e);

(i) an act which constitutes participation in any offence described in sub-paragraphs (a) to (h);

(j) an act of any person who organizes or directs others to commit an offence described in sub-paragraphs (a) to (h); and

(k) an act which contributes to the commission of any offence described in sub-paragraphs (a) to (h) by a group of persons acting with a common purpose; such act shall be intentional and shall either:

(i) be made with the aim of furthering the criminal activity or criminal purpose of the group, where such activity or purpose involves the commission of an offence described in sub-paragraphs (a) to (g), or

(ii) be made in the knowledge of the intention of the group to commit an offence described in sub-paragraphs (a) to (g) shall be made a punishable offence by each State Party under its national law.

10. After Article 11 of the Convention, two new articles, Article 11A and Article 11B, are added as follows:

Article 11A

None of the offences set forth in article 7 shall be regarded for the purposes of extradition or mutual legal assistance, as a political offence or as an offence connected with a political offence or as an offence inspired by political motives. Accordingly, a request for extradition or for mutual legal assistance based on such an offence may not be refused on the sole ground that it concerns a political offence or an offence connected with a political offence or an offence inspired by political motives.

Article 11B

Nothing in this Convention shall be interpreted as imposing an obligation to extradite or to afford mutual legal assistance, if the requested State Party has substantial grounds for believing that the request for extradition for offences set forth in article 7 or for mutual legal assistance with respect to such offences has been made for the purpose of prosecuting or punishing a person on account of that person's race, religion, nationality, ethnic origin or political opinion or that compliance with the request would cause prejudice to that person's position for any of these reasons.

11. After Article 13 of the Convention, a new Article 13A is added as follows:

Article 13A

Nothing in this Convention shall affect the transfer of nuclear technology for peaceful purposes that is undertaken to strengthen the physical protection of nuclear material and nuclear facilities.

12. Paragraph 3 of Article 14 of the Convention is replaced by the following text:

> 3. Where an offence involves nuclear material in domestic use, storage or transport, and both the alleged offender and the nuclear material remain in the territory of the State Party in which the offence was committed, or where an offence involves a nuclear facility and the alleged offender remains in the territory of the State Party in which the offence was committed, nothing in this Convention shall be interpreted as requiring that State Party to provide information concerning criminal proceedings arising out of such an offence.\

13. Article 16 of the Convention is replaced by the following text:

> 1. A conference of States Parties shall be convened by the depositary five years after the entry into force of the Amendment adopted on 8 July 2005 to review the implementation of this Convention and its adequacy as concerns the preamble, the whole of the operative part and the annexes in the light of the then prevailing situation.
>
> 2. At intervals of not less than five years thereafter, the majority of States Parties may obtain, by submitting a proposal to this effect to the depositary, the convening of further conferences with the same objective.

14. Footnote b/ of Annex II of the Convention is replaced by the following text:

> b/ Material not irradiated in a reactor or material irradiated in a reactor but with a radiation level equal to or less than 1 gray/hour (100 rads/hour) at one metre unshielded.

15. Footnote e/ of Annex II of the Convention is replaced by the following text:

> e/ Other fuel which by virtue of its original fissile material content is classified as Category I and II before irradiation may be reduced one category level while the radiation level from the fuel exceeds 1 gray/hour (100 rads/hour) at one metre unshielded.

International Convention for the Suppression of Acts of Nuclear Terrorism

INTERNATIONAL CONVENTION FOR THE SUPPRESSION OF ACTS OF NUCLEAR TERRORISM

Opened for Signature: 14 September 2005.
Entry into force: 7 July 2007

The States Parties to this Convention,

Having in mind the purposes and principles of the Charter of the United Nations concerning the maintenance of international peace and security and the promotion of good-neighbourliness and friendly relations and cooperation among States,

Recalling the Declaration on the Occasion of the Fiftieth Anniversary of the United Nations of 24 October 1995,

Recognizing the right of all States to develop and apply nuclear energy for peaceful purposes and their legitimate interests in the potential benefits to be derived from the peaceful application of nuclear energy,

Bearing in mind the Convention on the Physical Protection of Nuclear Material of 1980,

Deeply concerned about the worldwide escalation of acts of terrorism in all its forms and manifestations,

Recalling the Declaration on Measures to Eliminate International Terrorism annexed to General Assembly resolution 49/60 of 9 December 1994, in which, inter alia, the States Members of the United Nations solemnly reaffirm their unequivocal condemnation of all acts, methods and practices of terrorism as criminal and unjustifiable, wherever and by whomever committed, including those which jeopardize the friendly relations among States and peoples and threaten the territorial integrity and security of States, *Noting* that the Declaration also encouraged States to review urgently the scope of the existing international legal provisions on the prevention, repression and elimination of terrorism in all its forms and manifestations, with the aim of ensuring that there is a comprehensive legal framework covering all aspects of the matter,

Recalling General Assembly resolution 51/210 of 17 December 1996 and the Declaration to Supplement the 1994 Declaration on Measures to Eliminate International Terrorism annexed thereto,

Recalling also that, pursuant to General Assembly resolution 51/210, an ad hoc committee was established to elaborate, inter alia, an international convention for the suppression of acts of nuclear terrorism to supplement related existing international instruments,

Noting that acts of nuclear terrorism may result in the gravest consequences and may pose a threat to international peace and security,

Noting also that existing multilateral legal provisions do not adequately address those attacks,

Being convinced of the urgent need to enhance international cooperation between States in devising and adopting effective and practical measures for the prevention of such acts of terrorism and for the prosecution and punishment of their perpetrators,

Noting that the activities of military forces of States are governed by rules of international law outside of the framework of this Convention and that the exclusion of certain actions from the coverage of this Convention does not condone or make lawful otherwise unlawful acts, or preclude prosecution under other laws,

Have agreed as follows:

Article 1

For the purposes of this Convention:

1. "Radioactive material" means nuclear material and other radioactive substances which contain nuclides which undergo spontaneous disintegration (a process accompanied by emission of one or more types of ionizing radiation, such as alpha-, beta-, neutron particles and gamma rays) and which may, owing to their radiological or fissile properties, cause death, serious bodily injury or substantial damage to property or to the environment.

2. "Nuclear material" means plutonium, except that with isotopic concentration exceeding 80 per cent in plutonium-238; uranium-233; uranium enriched in the isotope 235 or 233; uranium containing the mixture of isotopes as occurring in nature other than in the form of ore or ore residue; or any material containing one or more of the foregoing;

    Whereby "uranium enriched in the isotope 235 or 233" means uranium containing the isotope 235 or 233 or both in an amount such that the abundance ratio of the sum of these isotopes to the isotope 238 is greater than the ratio of the isotope 235 to the isotope 238 occurring in nature.

3.　"Nuclear facility" means:

   (a)　Any nuclear reactor, including reactors installed on vessels, vehicles, aircraft or space objects for use as an energy source in order to propel such vessels, vehicles, aircraft or space objects or for any other purpose;

   (b)　Any plant or conveyance being used for the production, storage, processing or transport of radioactive material.

4.　"Device" means:

   (a)　Any nuclear explosive device; or

   (b)　Any radioactive material dispersal or radiation emitting device which may, owing to its radiological properties, cause death, serious bodily injury or substantial damage to property or to the environment.

5.　"State or government facility" includes any permanent or temporary facility or conveyance that is used or occupied by representatives of a State, members of a Government, the legislature or the judiciary or by officials or employees of a State or any other public authority or entity or by employees or officials of an intergovernmental organization in connection with their official duties.

6.　"Military forces of a State" means the armed forces of a State which are organized, trained and equipped under its internal law for the primary purpose of national defence or security and persons acting in support of those armed forces who are under their formal command, control and responsibility.

Article 2

1.　Any person commits an offence within the meaning of this Convention if that person unlawfully and intentionally:

   (a)　Possesses radioactive material or makes or possesses a device:

      (i)　With the intent to cause death or serious bodily injury; or

      (ii)　With the intent to cause substantial damage to property or to the environment;

   (b)　Uses in any way radioactive material or a device, or uses or damages a nuclear facility in a manner which releases or risks the release of radioactive material:

      (i)　With the intent to cause death or serious bodily injury; or

      (ii)　With the intent to cause substantial damage to property or to the environment; or

      (iii)　With the intent to compel a natural or legal person, an international organization or a State to do or refrain from doing an act.

2.　Any person also commits an offence if that person:

   (a)　Threatens, under circumstances which indicate the credibility of the threat, to commit an offence as set forth in paragraph 1 (*b*) of the present article; or

(b) Demands unlawfully and intentionally radioactive material, a device or a nuclear facility by threat, under circumstances which indicate the credibility of the threat, or by use of force.

3. Any person also commits an offence if that person attempts to commit an offence as set forth in paragraph 1 of the present article.

4. Any person also commits an offence if that person:
   (a) Participates as an accomplice in an offence as set forth in paragraph 1, 2 or 3 of the present article; or
   (b) Organizes or directs others to commit an offence as set forth in paragraph 1, 2 or 3 of the present article; or
   (c) In any other way contributes to the commission of one or more offences as set forth in paragraph 1, 2 or 3 of the present article by a group of persons acting with a common purpose; such contribution shall be intentional and either be made with the aim of furthering the general criminal activity or purpose of the group or be made in the knowledge of the intention of the group to commit the offence or offences concerned.

Article 3

This Convention shall not apply where the offence is committed within a single State, the alleged offender and the victims are nationals of that State, the alleged offender is found in the territory of that State and no other State has a basis under article 9, paragraph 1 or 2, to exercise jurisdiction, except that the provisions of articles 7, 12, 14, 15, 16 and 17 shall, as appropriate, apply in those cases.

Article 4

1. Nothing in this Convention shall affect other rights, obligations and responsibilities of States and individuals under international law, in particular the purposes and principles of the Charter of the United Nations and international humanitarian law.

2. The activities of armed forces during an armed conflict, as those terms are understood under international humanitarian law, which are governed by that law are not governed by this Convention, and the activities undertaken by military forces of a State in the exercise of their official duties, inasmuch as they are governed by other rules of international law, are not governed by this Convention.

3. The provisions of paragraph 2 of the present article shall not be interpreted as condoning or making lawful otherwise unlawful acts, or precluding prosecution under other laws.

4. This Convention does not address, nor can it be interpreted as addressing, in any way, the issue of the legality of the use or threat of use of nuclear weapons by States.

Article 5

Each State Party shall adopt such measures as may be necessary:
(a) To establish as criminal offences under its national law the offences set forth in article 2;
(b) To make those offences punishable by appropriate penalties which take into account the grave nature of these offences.

Article 6

Each State Party shall adopt such measures as may be necessary, including, where appropriate, domestic legislation, to ensure that criminal acts within the scope of this Convention, in particular where they are intended or calculated to provoke a state of terror in the general public or in a group of persons or particular persons, are under no circumstances justifiable by considerations of a political, philosophical, ideological, racial, ethnic, religious or other similar nature and are punished by penalties consistent with their grave nature.

Article 7

1. States Parties shall cooperate by:
(a)) Taking all practicable measures, including, if necessary, adapting their national law, to prevent and counter preparations in their respective territories for the commission within or outside their territories of the offences set forth in article 2, including measures to prohibit in their territories illegal activities of per sons, groups and organizations that encourage, instigate, organize, knowingly finance or knowingly provide technical assistance or information or engage in the perpetration of those offences;
(b) Exchanging accurate and verified information in accordance with their national law and in the manner and subject to the conditions specified herein, and coordinating administrative and other measures taken as appropriate to detect, prevent, suppress and investigate the offences set forth in article 2 and also in order to institute criminal proceedings against persons alleged to have committed those crimes. In particular, a State Party shall take appropriate measures in order to inform without delay the other States referred to in article 9 in respect of the commission of the offences set forth in article 2 as well as preparations to commit such offences about which it has learned, and also to inform, where appropriate, international organizations.

2.   States Parties shall take appropriate measures consistent with their national law to protect the confidentiality of any information which they receive in confidence by virtue of the provisions of this Convention from another State Party or through participation in an activity carried out for the implementation of this Convention. If States Parties provide information to international organizations in confidence, steps shall be taken to ensure that the confidentiality of such information is protected.

3.   States Parties shall not be required by this Convention to provide any information which they are not permitted to communicate pursuant to national law or which would jeopardize the security of the State concerned or the physical protection of nuclear material.

4.   States Parties shall inform the Secretary-General of the United Nations of their competent authorities and liaison points responsible for sending and receiving the information referred to in the present article. The Secretary-General of the United Nations shall communicate such information regarding competent authorities and liaison points to all States Parties and the International Atomic Energy Agency. Such authorities and liaison points must be accessible on a continuous basis.

Article 8

For purposes of preventing offences under this Convention, States Parties shall make every effort to adopt appropriate measures to ensure the protection of radioactive material, taking into account relevant recommendations and functions of the International Atomic Energy Agency.

Article 9

1.   Each State Party shall take such measures as may be necessary to establish its jurisdiction over the offences set forth in article 2 when:
      (a)   The offence is committed in the territory of that State; or
      (b)   The offence is committed on board a vessel flying the flag of that State or an aircraft which is registered under the laws of that State at the time the offence is committed; or
      (c)   The offence is committed by a national of that State.

2.   A State Party may also establish its jurisdiction over any such offence when:
      (a)   The offence is committed against a national of that State; or
      (b)   The offence is committed against a State or government facility of that State abroad, including an embassy or other diplomatic or consular premises of that State; or
      (c)   The offence is committed by a stateless person who has his or her habitual residence in the territory of that State; or

(d)   The offence is committed in an attempt to compel that State to do or abstain from doing any act; or

(e)   The offence is committed on board an aircraft which is operated by the Government of that State.

3.   Upon ratifying, accepting, approving or acceding to this Convention, each State Party shall notify the Secretary-General of the United Nations of the jurisdiction it has established under its national law in accordance with paragraph 2 of the present article. Should any change take place, the State Party concerned shall immediately notify the Secretary-General.

4.   Each State Party shall likewise take such measures as may be necessary to establish its jurisdiction over the offences set forth in article 2 in cases where the alleged offender is present in its territory and it does not extradite that person to any of the States Parties which have established their jurisdiction in accordance with paragraph 1 or 2 of the present article.

5.   This Convention does not exclude the exercise of any criminal jurisdiction established by a State Party in accordance with its national law.

Article 10

1.   Upon receiving information that an offence set forth in article 2 has been committed or is being committed in the territory of a State Party or that a person who has committed or who is alleged to have committed such an offence may be present in its territory, the State Party concerned shall take such measures as may be necessary under its national law to investigate the facts contained in the information.

2.   Upon being satisfied that the circumstances so warrant, the State Party in whose territory the offender or alleged offender is present shall take the appropriate measures under its national law so as to ensure that person's presence for the purpose of prosecution or extradition.

3.   Any person regarding whom the measures referred to in paragraph 2 of the present article are being taken shall be entitled:

(a)   To communicate without delay with the nearest appropriate representative of the State of which that person is a national or which is otherwise entitled to protect that person's rights or, if that person is a stateless person, the State in the territory of which that person habitually resides;

(b)   To be visited by a representative of that State;

(c)   To be informed of that person's rights under subparagraphs (*a*) and (*b*).

4.   The rights referred to in paragraph 3 of the present article shall be exercised in conformity with the laws and regulations of the State in the territory of which

the offender or alleged offender is present, subject to the provision that the said laws and regulations must enable full effect to be given to the purposes for which the rights accorded under paragraph 3 are intended.

5. The provisions of paragraphs 3 and 4 of the present article shall be without prejudice to the right of any State Party having a claim to jurisdiction in accordance with article 9, paragraph 1 (*c*) or 2 (*c*), to invite the International Committee of the Red Cross to communicate with and visit the alleged offender.

6. When a State Party, pursuant to the present article, has taken a person into custody, it shall immediately notify, directly or through the Secretary-General of the United Nations, the States Parties which have established jurisdiction in accordance with article 9, paragraphs 1 and 2, and, if it considers it advisable, any other interested States Parties, of the fact that that person is in custody and of the circumstances which warrant that person's detention. The State which makes the investigation contemplated in paragraph 1 of the present article shall promptly inform the said States Parties of its findings and shall indicate whether it intends to exercise jurisdiction.

Article 11

1. The State Party in the territory of which the alleged offender is present shall, in cases to which article 9 applies, if it does not extradite that person, be obliged, without exception whatsoever and whether or not the offence was committed in its territory, to submit the case without undue delay to its competent authorities for the purpose of prosecution, through proceedings in accordance with the laws of that State. Those authorities shall take their decision in the same manner as in the case of any other offence of a grave nature under the law of that State.

2. Whenever a State Party is permitted under its national law to extradite or otherwise surrender one of its nationals only upon the condition that the person will be returned to that State to serve the sentence imposed as a result of the trial or proceeding for which the extradition or surrender of the person was sought, and this State and the State seeking the extradition of the person agree with this option and other terms they may deem appropriate, such a conditional extradition or surrender shall be sufficient to discharge the obligation set forth in paragraph 1 of the present article.

Article 12

Any person who is taken into custody or regarding whom any other measures are taken or proceedings are carried out pursuant to this Convention shall be guaranteed fair treatment, including enjoyment of all rights and guarantees in conformity with the law of the State in the territory of which that person is present and applicable provisions of international law, including international law of human rights.

Article 13

1. The offences set forth in article 2 shall be deemed to be included as extraditable offences in any extradition treaty existing between any of the States Parties before the entry into force of this Convention. States Parties undertake to include such offences as extraditable offences in every extradition treaty to be subsequently concluded between them.

2. When a State Party which makes extradition conditional on the existence of a treaty receives a request for extradition from another State Party with which it has no extradition treaty, the requested State Party may, at its option, consider this Convention as a legal basis for extradition in respect of the offences set forth in article

3. Extradition shall be subject to the other conditions provided by the law of the requested State.

4. States Parties which do not make extradition conditional on the existence of a treaty shall recognize the offences set forth in article 2 as extraditable offences between themselves, subject to the conditions provided by the law of the requested State.

5. If necessary, the offences set forth in article 2 shall be treated, for the purposes of extradition between States Parties, as if they had been committed not only in the place in which they occurred but also in the territory of the States that have established jurisdiction in accordance with article 9, paragraphs 1 and 2.

6. The provisions of all extradition treaties and arrangements between States Parties with regard to offences set forth in article 2 shall be deemed to be modified as between States Parties to the extent that they are incompatible with this Convention.

Article 14

1. States Parties shall afford one another the greatest measure of assistance in connection with investigations or criminal or extradition proceedings brought in respect of the offences set forth in article 2, including assistance in obtaining evidence at their disposal necessary for the proceedings.

2. States Parties shall carry out their obligations under paragraph 1 of the present article in conformity with any treaties or other arrangements on mutual legal assistance that may exist between them. In the absence of such treaties or arrangements, States Parties shall afford one another assistance in accordance with their national law.

Article 15

None of the offences set forth in article 2 shall be regarded, for the purposes of extradition or mutual legal assistance, as a political offence or as an offence connected with a political offence or as an offence inspired by political motives. Accordingly, a request for extradition or for mutual legal assistance based on such an offence may not be refused on the sole ground that it concerns a political offence or an offence connected with a political offence or an offence inspired by political motives.

Article 16

Nothing in this Convention shall be interpreted as imposing an obligation to extradite or to afford mutual legal assistance if the requested State Party has substantial grounds for believing that the request for extradition for offences set forth in article 2 or for mutual legal assistance with respect to such offences has been made for the purpose of prosecuting or punishing a person on account of that person's race, religion, nationality, ethnic origin or political opinion or that compliance with the request would cause prejudice to that person's position for any of these reasons.

Article 17

1. A person who is being detained or is serving a sentence in the territory of one State Party whose presence in another State Party is requested for purposes of testimony, identification or otherwise providing assistance in obtaining evidence for the investigation or prosecution of offences under this Convention may be transferred if the following conditions are met:
   (a) The person freely gives his or her informed consent; and
   (b) The competent authorities of both States agree, subject to such conditions as those States may deem appropriate.

2. For the purposes of the present article:
   (a) The State to which the person is transferred shall have the authority and obligation to keep the person transferred in custody, unless otherwise requested or authorized by the State from which the person was transferred;
   (b) The State to which the person is transferred shall without delay implement its obligation to return the person to the custody of the State from which the person was transferred as agreed beforehand, or as otherwise agreed, by the competent authorities of both States;
   (c) The State to which the person is transferred shall not require the State from which the person was transferred to initiate extradition proceedings for the return of the person;
   (d) The person transferred shall receive credit for service of the sentence being served in the State from which he or she was transferred for time spent in the custody of the State to which he or she was transferred.

3.   Unless the State Party from which a person is to be transferred in accordance with the present article so agrees, that person, whatever his or her nationality, shall not be prosecuted or detained or subjected to any other restriction of his or her personal liberty in the territory of the State to which that person is transferred in respect of acts or convictions anterior to his or her departure from the territory of the State from which such person was transferred.

Article 18

1.   Upon seizing or otherwise taking control of radioactive material, devices or nuclear facilities, following the commission of an offence set forth in article 2, the State Party in possession of such items shall:

    (a)   Take steps to render harmless the radioactive material, device or nuclear facility;

    (b)   Ensure that any nuclear material is held in accordance with applicable International Atomic Energy Agency safeguards; and

    (c)   Have regard to physical protection recommendations and health and safety standards published by the International Atomic Energy Agency.

2.   Upon the completion of any proceedings connected with an offence set forth in article 2, or sooner if required by international law, any radioactive material, device or nuclear facility shall be returned, after consultations (in particular, regarding modalities of return and storage) with the States Parties concerned to the State Party to which it belongs, to the State Party of which the natural or legal person owning such radioactive material, device or facility is a national or resident, or to the State Party from whose territory it was stolen or otherwise unlawfully obtained.

3.   (*a*)   Where a State Party is prohibited by national or international law from returning or accepting such radioactive material, device or nuclear facility or where the States Parties concerned so agree, subject to paragraph 3 (*b*) of the present article, the State Party in possession of the radioactive material, devices or nuclear facilities shall continue to take the steps described in paragraph 1 of the present article; such radioactive material, devices or nuclear facilities shall be used only for peaceful purposes;

    (*b*)   Where it is not lawful for the State Party in possession of the radioactive material, devices or nuclear facilities to possess them, that State shall ensure that they are placed as soon as possible in the possession of a State for which such possession is lawful and which, where appropriate, has provided assurances consistent with the requirements of paragraph 1 of the present article in consultation with that State, for the purpose of rendering it harmless; such radioactive material, devices or nuclear facilities shall be used only for peaceful purposes.

4.   If the radioactive material, devices or nuclear facilities referred to in paragraphs 1 and 2 of the present article do not belong to any of the States Parties or to a

national or resident of a State Party or was not stolen or otherwise unlawfully obtained from the territory of a State Party, or if no State is willing to receive such items pursuant to paragraph 3 of the present article, a separate decision concerning its disposition shall, subject to paragraph 3 (*b*) of the present article, be taken after consultations between the States concerned and any relevant international organizations.

5.   For the purposes of paragraphs 1, 2, 3 and 4 of the present article, the State Party in possession of the radioactive material, device or nuclear facility may request the assistance and cooperation of other States Parties, in particular the States Parties concerned, and any relevant international organizations, in particular the International Atomic Energy Agency. States Parties and the relevant international organizations are encouraged to provide assistance pursuant to this paragraph to the maximum extent possible.

6.   The States Parties involved in the disposition or retention of the radioactive material, device or nuclear facility pursuant to the present article shall inform the Director General of the International Atomic Energy Agency of the manner in which such an item was disposed of or retained. The Director General of the International Atomic Energy Agency shall transmit the information to the other States Parties.

7.   In the event of any dissemination in connection with an offence set forth in article 2, nothing in the present article shall affect in any way the rules of international law governing liability for nuclear damage, or other rules of international law.

Article 19

The State Party where the alleged offender is prosecuted shall, in accordance with its national law or applicable procedures, communicate the final outcome of the proceedings to the Secretary-General of the United Nations, who shall transmit the information to the other States Parties.

Article 20

States Parties shall conduct consultations with one another directly or through the Secretary-General of the United Nations, with the assistance of international organizations as necessary, to ensure effective implementation of this Convention.

Article 21

The States Parties shall carry out their obligations under this Convention in a manner consistent with the principles of sovereign equality and territorial integrity of States and that of non-intervention in the domestic affairs of other States.

Article 22

Nothing in this Convention entitles a State Party to undertake in the territory of another State Party the exercise of jurisdiction and performance of functions which are exclusively reserved for the authorities of that other State Party by its national law.

Article 23

1. Any dispute between two or more States Parties concerning the interpretation or application of this Convention which cannot be settled through negotiation within a reasonable time shall, at the request of one of them, be submitted to arbitration. If, within six months of the date of the request for arbitration, the parties are unable to agree on the organization of the arbitration, any one of those parties may refer the dispute to the International Court of Justice, by application, in conformity with the Statute of the Court.

2. Each State may, at the time of signature, ratification, acceptance or approval of this Convention or accession thereto, declare that it does not consider itself bound by paragraph 1 of the present article. The other States Parties shall not be bound by paragraph 1 with respect to any State Party which has made such a reservation.

3. Any State which has made a reservation in accordance with paragraph 2 of the present article may at any time withdraw that reservation by notification to the Secretary-General of the United Nations.

Article 24

1. This Convention shall be open for signature by all States from 14 September 2005 until 31 December 2006 at United Nations Headquarters in New York.

2. This Convention is subject to ratification, acceptance or approval. The instruments of ratification, acceptance or approval shall be deposited with the Secretary-General of the United Nations.

3. This Convention shall be open to accession by any State. The instruments of accession shall be deposited with the Secretary-General of the United Nations.

Article 25

1. This Convention shall enter into force on the thirtieth day following the date of the deposit of the twenty-second instrument of ratification, acceptance, approval or accession with the Secretary-General of the United Nations.

2. For each State ratifying, accepting, approving or acceding to the Convention after the deposit of the twenty-second instrument of ratification, acceptance,

approval or accession, the Convention shall enter into force on the thirtieth day after deposit by such State of its instrument of ratification, acceptance, approval or accession.

Article 26

1. A State Party may propose an amendment to this Convention. The proposed amendment shall be submitted to the depositary, who circulates it immediately to all States Parties.

2. If the majority of the States Parties request the depositary to convene a conference to consider the proposed amendments, the depositary shall invite all States Parties to attend such a conference to begin no sooner than three months after the invitations are issued.

3. The conference shall make every effort to ensure amendments are adopted by consensus. Should this not be possible, amendments shall be adopted by a two-thirds majority of all States Parties. Any amendment adopted at the conference shall be promptly circulated by the depositary to all States Parties.

4. The amendment adopted pursuant to paragraph 3 of the present article shall enter into force for each State Party that deposits its instrument of ratification, acceptance, accession or approval of the amendment on the thirtieth day after the date on which two thirds of the States Parties have deposited their relevant instrument. Thereafter, the amendment shall enter into force for any State Party on the thirtieth day after the date on which that State deposits its relevant instrument.

Article 27

1. Any State Party may denounce this Convention by written notification to the Secretary-General of the United Nations.

2. Denunciation shall take effect one year following the date on which notification is received by the Secretary-General of the United Nations.

The original of this Convention, of which the Arabic, Chinese, English, French, Russian and Spanish texts are equally authentic, shall be deposited with the Secretary-General of the United Nations, who shall send certified copies thereof to all States.

IN WITNESS WHEREOF, the undersigned, being duly authorized thereto by their respective Governments, have signed this Convention, opened for signature at United Nations Headquarters in New York on 14 September 2005.

United Nations Security Council Resolution S/RES/1540 (2004): Non-proliferation of Weapons of Mass Destruction

(Adopted by the Security Council at its 4956th meeting, on 28 April 2004)

The Security Council,

Affirming that proliferation of nuclear, chemical and biological weapons, as well as their means of delivery,* constitutes a threat to international peace and security,

Reaffirming, in this context, the Statement of its President adopted at the Council's meeting at the level of Heads of State and Government on 31 January 1992 (S/23500), including the need for all Member States to fulfil their obligations in relation to arms control and disarmament and to prevent proliferation in all its aspects of all weapons of mass destruction,

Recalling also that the Statement underlined the need for all Member States to resolve peacefully in accordance with the Charter any problems in that context threatening or disrupting the maintenance of regional and global stability,

Affirming its resolve to take appropriate and effective actions against any threat to international peace and security caused by the proliferation of nuclear, chemical and biological weapons and their means of delivery, in conformity with its primary responsibilities, as provided for in the United Nations Charter,

Affirming its support for the multilateral treaties whose aim is to eliminate or prevent the proliferation of nuclear, chemical or biological weapons and the importance for all States parties to these treaties to implement them fully in order to promote international stability,

Welcoming efforts in this context by multilateral arrangements which contribute to non-proliferation,

Affirming that prevention of proliferation of nuclear, chemical and biological weapons should not hamper international cooperation in materials, equipment and technology for peaceful purposes while goals of peaceful utilization should not be used as a cover for proliferation,

Gravely concerned by the threat of terrorism and the risk that non-State actors* such as those identified in the United Nations list established and maintained by the Committee

---

* Definitions for the purpose of this resolution only:
Means of delivery: missiles, rockets and other unmanned systems capable of delivering nuclear, chemical, or biological weapons, that are specially designed for such use.
Non-State actor: individual or entity, not acting under the lawful authority of any State in conducting activities which come within the scope of this resolution.
Related materials: materials, equipment and technology covered by relevant multilateral treaties and arrangements, or included on national control lists, which could be used for the design, development, production or use of nuclear, chemical and biological weapons and their means of delivery.

established under Security Council resolution 1267 and those to whom resolution 1373 applies, may acquire, develop, traffic in or use nuclear, chemical and biological weapons and their means of delivery,

Gravely concerned by the threat of illicit trafficking in nuclear, chemical, or biological weapons and their means of delivery, and related materials,* which adds a new dimension to the issue of proliferation of such weapons and also poses a threat to international peace and security,

Recognizing the need to enhance coordination of efforts on national, subregional, regional and international levels in order to strengthen a global response to this serious challenge and threat to international security,

Recognizing that most States have undertaken binding legal obligations under treaties to which they are parties, or have made other commitments aimed at preventing the proliferation of nuclear, chemical or biological weapons, and have taken effective measures to account for, secure and physically protect sensitive materials, such as those required by the Convention on the Physical Protection of Nuclear Materials and those recommended by the IAEA Code of Conduct on the Safety and Security of Radioactive Sources,

Recognizing further the urgent need for all States to take additional effective measures to prevent the proliferation of nuclear, chemical or biological weapons and their means of delivery,

Encouraging all Member States to implement fully the disarmament treaties and agreements to which they are party,

Reaffirming the need to combat by all means, in accordance with the Charter of the United Nations, threats to international peace and security caused by terrorist acts,

Determined to facilitate henceforth an effective response to global threats in the area of non-proliferation,

Acting under Chapter VII of the Charter of the United Nations,

1. *Decides* that all States shall refrain from providing any form of support to non-State actors that attempt to develop, acquire, manufacture, possess, transport, transfer or use nuclear, chemical or biological weapons and their means of delivery;

2. *Decides* also that all States in accordance with their national procedures shall adopt and enforce appropriate effective laws which prohibit any non-State actor to manufacture, acquire, possess, develop, transport, transfer or use nuclear, chemical or biological weapons and their means of delivery, in particular for terrorist purposes, as well as attempts to engage in any of the foregoing activities, participate in them as an accomplice, assist or finance them;

3. *Decides* also that all States shall take and enforce effective measures to establish domestic controls to prevent the proliferation of nuclear, chemical, or biological weapons and their means of delivery, including by establishing appropriate controls over related materials and to this end shall:

    a.   Develop and maintain appropriate effective measures to account for and secure such items in production, use, storage or transport;

    b.   Develop and maintain appropriate effective physical protection measures;

    c.   Develop and maintain appropriate effective border controls and law enforcement efforts to detect, deter, prevent and combat, including through international cooperation when necessary, the illicit trafficking and brokering in such items in accordance with their national legal authorities and legislation and consistent with international law;

    d.   Establish, develop, review and maintain appropriate effective national export and trans-shipment controls over such items, including appropriate laws and regulations to control export, transit, trans-shipment and re-export and controls on providing funds and services related to such export and trans-shipment such as financing, and transporting that would contribute to proliferation, as well as establishing end-user controls; and establishing and enforcing appropriate criminal or civil penalties for violations of such export control laws and regulations;

4. *Decides* to establish, in accordance with rule 28 of its provisional rules of procedure, for a period of no longer than two years, a Committee of the Security Council, consisting of all members of the Council, which will, calling as appropriate on other expertise, report to the Security Council for its examination, on the implementation of this resolution, and to this end calls upon States to present a first report no later than six months from the adoption of this resolution to the Committee on steps they have taken or intend to take to implement this resolution;

5. *Decides* that none of the obligations set forth in this resolution shall be interpreted so as to conflict with or alter the rights and obligations of State Parties to the Nuclear Non-Proliferation Treaty, the Chemical Weapons Convention and the Biological and Toxin Weapons Convention or alter the responsibilities of the International Atomic Energy Agency or the Organization for the Prohibition of Chemical Weapons;

6. *Recognizes* the utility in implementing this resolution of effective national control lists and calls upon all Member States, when necessary, to pursue at the earliest opportunity the development of such lists;

7. *Recognizes* that some States may require assistance in implementing the provisions of this resolution within their territories and invites States in a position to do so to offer assistance as appropriate in response to specific requests to the States lacking the legal and regulatory infrastructure, implementation experience and/or resources for fulfilling the above provisions;

8. *Calls upon* all States:

   a. To promote the universal adoption and full implementation, and, where necessary, strengthening of multilateral treaties to which they are parties, whose aim is to prevent the proliferation of nuclear, biological or chemical weapons;

   b. To adopt national rules and regulations, where it has not yet been done, to ensure compliance with their commitments under the key multilateral non-proliferation treaties;

   c. To renew and fulfil their commitment to multilateral cooperation, in particular within the framework of the International Atomic Energy Agency, the Organization for the Prohibition of Chemical Weapons and the Biological and Toxin Weapons Convention, as important means of pursuing and achieving their common objectives in the area of non-proliferation and of promoting international cooperation for peaceful purposes;

   d. To develop appropriate ways to work with and inform industry and the public regarding their obligations under such laws;

9. *Calls upon* all States to promote dialogue and cooperation on non-proliferation so as to address the threat posed by proliferation of nuclear, chemical, or biological weapons, and their means of delivery;

10. Further to counter that threat, *calls upon* all States, in accordance with their national legal authorities and legislation and consistent with international law, to take cooperative action to prevent illicit trafficking in nuclear, chemical or biological weapons, their means of delivery, and related materials;

11. *Expresses* its intention to monitor closely the implementation of this resolution and, at the appropriate level, to take further decisions which may be required to this end.

12. *Decides* to remain seized of the matter.

United Nations Security Council Resolution S/RES/1373 (2001) Threats to international peace and security caused by terrorist acts
(Adopted 28 September 2001)

"*The Security Council,*

"*Reaffirming* its resolutions 1269 (1999) of 19 October 1999 and 1368 (2001) of 12 September 2001,

"*Reaffirming also* its unequivocal condemnation of the terrorist attacks which took place in New York, Washington, D.C., and Pennsylvania on 11 September 2001, and expressing its determination to prevent all such acts,

"*Reaffirming further* that such acts, like any act of international terrorism, constitute a threat to international peace and security,

"*Reaffirming* the inherent right of individual or collective self-defence as recognized by the Charter of the United Nations as reiterated in resolution 1368 (2001),

"*Reaffirming* the need to combat by all means, in accordance with the Charter of the United Nations, threats to international peace and security caused by terrorist acts,

"*Deeply concerned* by the increase, in various regions of the world, of acts of terrorism motivated by intolerance or extremism,

"*Calling* on States to work together urgently to prevent and suppress terrorist acts, including through increased cooperation and full implementation of the relevant international conventions relating to terrorism,

"*Recognizing* the need for States to complement international cooperation by taking additional measures to prevent and suppress, in their territories through all lawful means, the financing and preparation of any acts of terrorism,

"*Reaffirming* the principle established by the General Assembly in its declaration of October 1970 (resolution 2625 (XXV)) and reiterated by the Security Council in its resolution 1189 (1998) of 13 August 1998, namely that every State has the duty to refrain from organizing, instigating, assisting or participating in terrorist acts in another State or acquiescing in organized activities within its territory directed towards the commission of such acts,

"*Acting* under Chapter VII of the Charter of the United Nations,

"1.   *Decides* that all States shall:

"(a)   Prevent and suppress the financing of terrorist acts;

"(b) Criminalize the wilful provision or collection, by any means, directly or indirectly, of funds by their nationals or in their territories with the intention that the funds should be used, or in the knowledge that they are to be used, in order to carry out terrorist acts;

"(c) Freeze without delay funds and other financial assets or economic resources of persons who commit, or attempt to commit, terrorist acts or participate in or facilitate the commission of terrorist acts; of entities owned or controlled directly or indirectly by such persons; and of persons and entities acting on behalf of, or at the direction of such persons and entities, including funds derived or generated from property owned or controlled directly or indirectly by such persons and associated persons and entities;

"(d) Prohibit their nationals or any persons and entities within their territories from making any funds, financial assets or economic resources or financial or other related services available, directly or indirectly, for the benefit of persons who commit or attempt to commit or facilitate or participate in the commission of terrorist acts, of entities owned or controlled, directly or indirectly, by such persons and of persons and entities acting on behalf of or at the direction of such persons;

"2. *Decides also* that all States shall:

"(a) Refrain from providing any form of support, active or passive, to entities or persons involved in terrorist acts, including by suppressing recruitment of members of terrorist groups and eliminating the supply of weapons to terrorists;

"(b) Take the necessary steps to prevent the commission of terrorist acts, including by provision of early warning to other States by exchange of information;

"(c) Deny safe haven to those who finance, plan, support, or commit terrorist acts, or provide safe havens;

"(d) Prevent those who finance, plan, facilitate or commit terrorist acts from using their respective territories for those purposes against other States or their citizens;

"(e) Ensure that any person who participates in the financing, planning, preparation or perpetration of terrorist acts or in supporting terrorist acts is brought to justice and ensure that, in addition to any other measures against them, such terrorist acts are established as serious criminal offences in domestic laws and regulations and that the punishment duly reflects the seriousness of such terrorist acts;

"(f)   Afford one another the greatest measure of assistance in connection with criminal investigations or criminal proceedings relating to the financing or support of terrorist acts, including assistance in obtaining evidence in their possession necessary for the proceedings;

"(g)   Prevent the movement of terrorists or terrorist groups by effective border controls and controls on issuance of identity papers and travel documents, and through measures for preventing counterfeiting, forgery or fraudulent use of identity papers and travel documents;

"3.   *Calls upon* all States to:

"(a)   Find ways of intensifying and accelerating the exchange of operational information, especially regarding actions or movements of terrorist persons or networks; forged or falsified travel documents; traffic in arms, explosives or sensitive materials; use of communications technologies by terrorist groups; and the threat posed by the possession of weapons of mass destruction by terrorist groups;

"(b)   Exchange information in accordance with international and domestic law and cooperate on administrative and judicial matters to prevent the commission of terrorist acts;

"(c)   Cooperate, particularly through bilateral and multilateral arrangements and agreements, to prevent and suppress terrorist attacks and take action against perpetrators of such acts;

"(d)   Become parties as soon as possible to the relevant international conventions and protocols relating to terrorism, including the International Convention for the Suppression of the Financing of Terrorism of 9 December 1999;

"(e)   Increase cooperation and fully implement the relevant international conventions and protocols relating to terrorism and Security Council resolutions 1269 (1999) and 1368 (2001);

"(f)   Take appropriate measures in conformity with the relevant provisions of national and international law, including international standards of human rights, before granting refugee status, for the purpose of ensuring that the asylum seeker has not planned, facilitated or participated in the commission of terrorist acts;

"(g)   Ensure, in conformity with international law, that refugee status is not abused by the perpetrators, organizers or facilitators of terrorist acts, and that claims of political motivation are not recognized as grounds for refusing requests for the extradition of alleged terrorists;

"4. *Notes* with concern the close connection between international terrorism and transnational organized crime, illicit drugs, money-laundering, illegal arms-trafficking, and illegal movement of nuclear, chemical, biological and other potentially deadly materials, and in this regard *emphasizes* the need to enhance coordination of efforts on national, subregional, regional and international levels in order to strengthen a global response to this serious challenge and threat to international security;

"5. *Declares* that acts, methods, and practices of terrorism are contrary to the purposes and principles of the United Nations and that knowingly financing, planning and inciting terrorist acts are also contrary to the purposes and principles of the United Nations;

"6. *Decides* to establish, in accordance with rule 28 of its provisional rules of procedure, a Committee of the Security Council, consisting of all the members of the Council, to monitor implementation of this resolution, with the assistance of appropriate expertise, and *calls upon* all States to report to the Committee, no later than 90 days from the date of adoption of this resolution and thereafter according to a timetable to be proposed by the Committee, on the steps they have taken to implement this resolution;

"7. *Directs* the Committee to delineate its tasks, submit a work programme within 30 days of the adoption of this resolution, and to consider the support it requires, in consultation with the Secretary-General;

"8. *Expresses* its determination to take all necessary steps in order to ensure the full implementation of this resolution, in accordance with its responsibilities under the Charter;

"9. *Decides* to remain seized of this matter."

**

B. Nuclear Security Summits

Background

In his speech in Prague on April 5, 2009, U.S. President Barack Obama said that:

> ... we must ensure that terrorists never acquire a nuclear weapon. This is the most immediate and extreme threat to global security. One terrorist with one nuclear weapon could unleash massive destruction. Al Qaeda has said it seeks a bomb and that it would have no problem with using it. And we know that there is unsecured nuclear material across the globe. To protect our people, we must act with a sense of purpose without delay.
>
> So today I am announcing a new international effort to secure all vulnerable nuclear material around the world within four years. We will set new standards, expand our cooperation with Russia, pursue new partnerships to lock down these sensitive materials.
>
> We must also build on our efforts to break up black markets, detect and intercept materials in transit, and use financial tools to disrupt this dangerous trade. Because this threat will be lasting, we should come together to turn efforts such as the Proliferation Security Initiative and the Global Initiative to Combat Nuclear Terrorism into durable international institutions. And we should start by having a Global Summit on Nuclear Security that the United States will host within the next year.

As a result of President Obama's initiative, the first Nuclear Security Summit was convened in Washington, D.C. in April 2010. A second Nuclear Security Summit was held in Seoul in 2012 and a third in the Netherlands in March 2014. The Communiqués released at each Summit are reproduced below.

Additional information and documentation about the three Summits can be found at http://www.state.gov/t/isn/nuclearsecuritysummit/index.htm

Communiqué of the Washington Nuclear Security Summit (2010)

Nuclear terrorism is one of the most challenging threats to international security, and strong nuclear security measures are the most effective means to prevent terrorists, criminals, or other unauthorized actors from acquiring nuclear materials.

In addition to our shared goals of nuclear disarmament, nuclear nonproliferation and peaceful uses of nuclear energy, we also all share the objective of nuclear security. Therefore those gathered here in Washington, D.C. on April 13, 2010, commit to strengthen nuclear security and reduce the threat of nuclear terrorism. Success will require responsible national actions and sustained and effective international cooperation.

We welcome and join President Obama's call to secure all vulnerable nuclear material in four years, as we work together to enhance nuclear security.

Therefore, we:

1) reaffirm the fundamental responsibility of States, consistent with their respective international obligations, to maintain effective security of all nuclear materials, which includes nuclear materials used in nuclear weapons, and nuclear facilities under their control; to prevent non-state actors from obtaining the information or technology required to use such material for malicious purposes; and emphasize the importance of robust national legislative and regulatory frameworks for nuclear security;

2) Call on States to work cooperatively as an international community to advance nuclear security, requesting and providing assistance as necessary;

3) Recognize that highly enriched uranium and separated plutonium require special precautions and agree to promote measures to secure, account for, and consolidate these materials, as appropriate; and encourage the conversion of reactors from highly enriched to low enriched uranium fuel and minimization of use of highly enriched uranium, where technically and economically feasible;

4) Endeavor to fully implement all existing nuclear security commitments and work toward acceding to those not yet joined, consistent with national laws, policies and procedures;

5) Reaffirm the essential role of the International Atomic Energy Agency in the international nuclear security framework and will work to ensure that it continues to have the appropriate structure, resources and expertise needed to carry out its mandated nuclear security activities in accordance with its Statute, relevant General Conference resolutions and its Nuclear Security Plans;

6)   Recognize the role and contributions of the United Nations as well as the contributions of the Global Initiative to Combat Nuclear Terrorism and the G-8-led Global Partnership Against the Spread of Weapons and Materials of Mass Destruction within their respective mandates and memberships;

7)   Acknowledge the need for capacity building for nuclear security and cooperation at bilateral, regional and multilateral levels for the promotion of nuclear security culture through technology development, human resource development, education, and training; and stress the importance of optimizing international cooperation and coordination of assistance;

8)   Recognize the need for cooperation among States to effectively prevent and respond to incidents of illicit nuclear trafficking; and agree to share, subject to respective national laws and procedures, information and expertise through bilateral and multilateral mechanisms in relevant areas such as nuclear detection, forensics, law enforcement, and the development of new technologies;

9)   Recognize the continuing role of nuclear industry, including the private sector, in nuclear security and will work with industry to ensure the necessary priority of physical protection, material accountancy, and security culture;

10)   Support the implementation of strong nuclear security practices that will not infringe upon the rights of States to develop and utilize nuclear energy for peaceful purposes and technology and will facilitate international cooperation in the field of nuclear security; and

11)   Recognize that measures contributing to nuclear material security have value in relation to the security of radioactive substances and encourage efforts to secure those materials as well.

Maintaining effective nuclear security will require continuous national efforts facilitated by international cooperation and undertaken on a voluntary basis by States. We will promote the strengthening of global nuclear security through dialogue and cooperation with all states.

Thus, we issue the Work Plan as guidance for national and international action including through cooperation within the context of relevant international fora and organizations. We will hold the next Nuclear Security Summit in the Republic of Korea in 2012.

April 13, 2010

Seoul Communiqué - 2012 Seoul Nuclear Security Summit

We, the leaders, gathered in Seoul on March 26-27, 2012, renew the political commitments generated from the 2010 Washington Nuclear Security Summit to work toward strengthening nuclear security, reducing the threat of nuclear terrorism, and preventing terrorists, criminals, or other unauthorized actors from acquiring nuclear materials. Nuclear terrorism continues to be one of the most challenging threats to international security. Defeating this threat requires strong national measures and international cooperation given its potential global political, economic, social, and psychological consequences.

We reaffirm our shared goals of nuclear disarmament, nuclear nonproliferation and peaceful uses of nuclear energy.

Committed to seeking a safer world for all, we also all share the objective of nuclear security. We recognize that the Nuclear Security Summit is a valuable process at the highest political level, supporting our joint call to secure all vulnerable nuclear material in four years. In this regard, we welcome the substantive progress being made on the political commitments of Participating States since the Washington Summit.

We stress the fundamental responsibility of States, consistent with their respective national and international obligations, to maintain effective security of all nuclear material, which includes nuclear materials used in nuclear weapons, and nuclear facilities under their control, and to prevent non-state actors from acquiring such materials and from obtaining information or technology required to use them for malicious purposes. We likewise recognize the fundamental responsibility of States to maintain effective security of other radioactive materials.

We reaffirm that measures to strengthen nuclear security will not hamper the rights of States to develop and utilize nuclear energy for peaceful purposes.
Noting the essential role of the International Atomic Energy Agency (IAEA) in facilitating international cooperation and supporting the efforts of States to fulfill their nuclear security responsibilities, we further stress the importance of regional and international cooperation, and encourage States to promote cooperation with and outreach activities to international partners.

Noting the Fukushima accident of March 2011 and the nexus between nuclear security and nuclear safety, we consider that sustained efforts are required to address the issues of nuclear safety and nuclear security in a coherent manner that will help ensure the safe and secure peaceful uses of nuclear energy.

We will continue to use the Washington Communiqué and Work Plan as a basis for our future work in advancing our nuclear security objectives. At this Seoul Summit, we agree that we will make every possible effort to achieve further progress in the following important areas.

Global Nuclear Security Architecture

1. We recognize the importance of multilateral instruments that address nuclear security, such as the Convention on the Physical Protection of Nuclear Material (CPPNM), as amended, and the International Convention for the Suppression of Acts of Nuclear Terrorism (ICSANT). We therefore encourage the universal adherence to these Conventions. We urge states in a position to do so to

accelerate their domestic approval of the 2005 Amendment to the CPPNM, seeking to bring the Amendment into force by 2014. We acknowledge the important role of the United Nations (UN) in promoting nuclear security, support the UN Security Council Resolutions 1540 and 1977 in strengthening global nuclear security, and welcome the extension of its mandate. We will strive to use the IAEA Physical Protection of Nuclear Material and Nuclear Facilities (INFCIRC/225/Rev.5) document and related Nuclear Security Series documents, and reflect them into national practice.

2. We recognize the contributions since the 2010 Summit of international initiatives and processes such as the Global Initiative to Combat Nuclear Terrorism (GICNT) and Global Partnership against the Spread of Weapons and Materials of Mass Destruction, within their respective mandates and memberships. We welcome the wider participation in the GICNT and the Global Partnership and value its extension beyond 2012. Noting the importance of strengthening coordination and complementarity among nuclear security activities, we welcome the proposal of the IAEA to organize an international conference in 2013. We welcome contributions from the industry, academia, institutes and civil society that promote nuclear security.

Role of the IAEA

3. We reaffirm the essential responsibility and central role of the IAEA in strengthening the international nuclear security framework, and recognize the value of the IAEA Nuclear Security Plan 2010-2013. We will work to ensure that the IAEA continues to have the appropriate structure, resources and expertise needed to support the implementation of nuclear security objectives. To this end, we encourage States in a position to do so and the nuclear industry to increase voluntary contributions to the IAEA's Nuclear Security Fund, as well as in-kind contributions. We also encourage continued IAEA activities to assist, upon request, national efforts to establish and enhance nuclear security infrastructure through its various support programs, and encourage States to make use of these IAEA resources.

Nuclear Materials

4. Recognizing that highly enriched uranium (HEU) and separated plutonium require special precautions, we reemphasize the importance of appropriately securing, accounting for and consolidating these materials. We also encourage States to consider the safe, secure and timely removal and disposition of nuclear materials from facilities no longer using them, as appropriate, and consistent with national security considerations and development objectives.

5. We recognize that the development, within the framework of the IAEA, of options for national policies on HEU management will advance nuclear

security objectives. We encourage States to take measures to minimize the use of HEU, including through the conversion of reactors from highly enriched to low enriched uranium (LEU) fuel, where technically and economically feasible, taking into account the need for assured supplies of medical isotopes, and encourage States in a position to do so, by the end of 2013, to announce voluntary specific actions intended to minimize the use of HEU. We also encourage States to promote the use of LEU fuels and targets in commercial applications such as isotope production, and in this regard, welcome relevant international cooperation on high-density LEU fuel to support the conversion of research and test reactors.

Radioactive Sources

6. Taking into account that radioactive sources are widely used and can be vulnerable to malicious acts, we urge States to secure these materials, while bearing in mind their uses in industrial, medical, agricultural and research applications. To this end, we encourage States in a position to do so to continue to work towards the process of ratifying or acceding to the ICSANT; reflect into national practices relevant IAEA Nuclear Security Series documents, the IAEA Code of Conduct on the Safety and Security of Radioactive Sources and its supplementary document on the IAEA Guidance on the Import and Export of Radioactive Sources; and establish national registers of high-activity radioactive sources where required. We also commit to work closely with the IAEA to encourage cooperation on advanced technologies and systems, share best practices on the management of radioactive sources, and provide technical assistance to States upon their request. In addition, we encourage continued national efforts and international cooperation to recover lost, missing or stolen sources and to maintain control over disused sources.

Nuclear Security and Safety

7. Acknowledging that safety measures and security measures have in common the aim of protecting human life and health and the environment, we affirm that nuclear security and nuclear safety measures should be designed, implemented and managed in nuclear facilities in a coherent and synergistic manner. We also affirm the need to maintain effective emergency preparedness, response and mitigation capabilities in a manner that addresses both nuclear security and nuclear safety. In this regard, we welcome the efforts of the IAEA to organize meetings to provide relevant recommendations on the interface between nuclear security and nuclear safety so that neither security nor safety is compromised. We also welcome the convening of the High Level Meeting on Nuclear Safety and Security initiated by the UN Secretary-General, held in New York on 22 September 2011. Noting that the security of nuclear and other radioactive materials also includes spent nuclear fuel and radioactive waste, we encourage States to consider establishing appropriate plans for the management of these materials.

Transportation Security

8. We will continue efforts to enhance the security of nuclear and other radio-active materials while in domestic and international transport, and encourage States to share best practices and cooperate in acquiring the necessary technologies to this end. Recognizing the importance of a national layered defense against the loss or theft of nuclear and other radioactive materials, we encourage the establishment of effective national nuclear material inventory management and domestic tracking mechanisms, where required, that enable States to take appropriate measures to recover lost and stolen materials.

Combating Illicit Trafficking

9. We underscore the need to develop national capabilities to prevent, detect, respond to and prosecute illicit nuclear trafficking. In this regard, we encourage action-oriented coordination among national capacities to combat illicit trafficking, consistent with national laws and regulations. We will work to enhance technical capabilities in the field of national inspection and detection of nuclear and other radioactive materials at the borders. Noting that several countries have passed export control laws to regulate nuclear transfers, we encourage further utilization of legal, intelligence and financial tools to effectively prosecute offenses, as appropriate and consistent with national laws. In addition, we encourage States to participate in the IAEA Illicit Trafficking Database program and to provide necessary information relating to nuclear and other radioactive materials outside of regulatory control. We will work to strengthen cooperation among States and encourage them to share information, consistent with national regulations, on individuals involved in trafficking offenses of nuclear and other radioactive materials, including through INTERPOL's Radiological and Nuclear Terrorism Prevention Unit and the World Customs Organization.

Nuclear Forensics

10. We recognize that nuclear forensics can be an effective tool in determining the origin of detected nuclear and other radioactive materials and in providing evidence for the prosecution of acts of illicit trafficking and malicious uses. In this regard, we encourage States to work with one another, as well as with the IAEA, to develop and enhance nuclear forensics capabilities. In this regard, they may combine the skills of both traditional and nuclear forensics through the development of a common set of definitions and standards, undertake research and share information and best practices, as appropriate. We also underscore the importance of international cooperation both in technology and human resource development to advance nuclear forensics.

Nuclear Security Culture

11. Recognizing that investment in human capacity building is fundamental to promoting and sustaining a strong nuclear security culture, we encourage States to share best practices and build national capabilities, including through bilateral and multilateral cooperation. At the national level, we encourage all stakeholders, including the government, regulatory bodies, industry, academia, non-governmental organizations and the media, to fully commit to enhancing security culture and to maintain robust communication and coordination of activities. We also encourage States to promote human resource development through education and training. In this regard, we welcome the establishment of Centers of Excellence and other nuclear security training and support centers since the Washington Summit, and encourage the establishment of new centers. Furthermore, we welcome the effort by the IAEA to promote networking among such centers to share experience and lessons learned and to optimize available resources. We also note the holding of the Nuclear Industry Summit and the Nuclear Security Symposium on the eve of the Seoul Nuclear Security Summit.

Information Security

12. We recognize the importance of preventing non-state actors from obtaining information, technology or expertise required to acquire or use nuclear materials for malicious purposes, or to disrupt information technology based control systems at nuclear facilities. We therefore encourage States to: continue to develop and strengthen national and facility-level measures for the effective management of such information, including information on the procedures and protocols to protect nuclear materials and facilities; to support relevant capacity building projects; and to enhance cyber security measures concerning nuclear facilities, consistent with the IAEA General Conference Resolution on Nuclear Security (GC(55)/Res/10) and bearing in mind the International Telecommunication Union Resolution 174. We also encourage States to: promote a security culture that emphasizes the need to protect nuclear security related information; engage with scientific, industrial and academic communities in the pursuit of common solutions; and support the IAEA in producing and disseminating improved guidance on protecting information.

International Cooperation

13. We encourage all States to enhance their physical protection of and accounting system for nuclear materials, emergency preparedness and response capabilities and relevant legal and regulatory framework. In this context, we encourage the international community to increase international cooperation and to provide assistance, upon request, to countries in need on a bilateral, regional, and

multilateral level, as appropriate. In particular, we welcome the intent by the IAEA to continue to lead efforts to assist States, upon request. We also reaffirm the need for various public diplomacy and outreach efforts to enhance public awareness of actions taken and capacities built to address threats to nuclear security, including the threat of nuclear terrorism.

We will continue to make voluntary and substantive efforts toward strengthening nuclear security and implementing political commitments made in this regard. We welcome the information on the progress made in the field of nuclear security since the Washington Summit provided by the participants at this Seoul Summit. The next Nuclear Security Summit will be held in the Netherlands in 2014.

The Hague Nuclear Security Summit Communiqué (2014)

We, the leaders, met in The Hague on 24 and 25 March 2014 to strengthen nuclear security, reduce the continuing threat of nuclear terrorism and assess the progress we have made since the Washington Summit in 2010. In preparing for this Summit we have used the Washington and Seoul Communiqués as the basis for our work and have been guided by the Washington Work Plan.

Therefore,

1. We reaffirm our commitment to our shared goals of nuclear disarmament, nuclear non-proliferation and peaceful use of nuclear energy. We also reaffirm that measures to strengthen nuclear security will not hamper the rights of States to develop and use nuclear energy for peaceful purposes.

2. This Summit focuses on strengthening nuclear security and preventing terrorists, criminals and all other unauthorised actors from acquiring nuclear materials that could be used in nuclear weapons, and other radioactive materials that could be used in radiological dispersal devices. Achieving this objective remains one of the most important challenges in the years to come.

3. Our summit in The Hague builds on the Washington and Seoul Summits, and we note with satisfaction that most of the commitments that participants made during previous summits have already been fulfilled. We welcome the considerable progress made in strengthening nuclear security, while recognising that continuous efforts are needed to achieve that goal.

Fundamental responsibility of States

4. We reaffirm the fundamental responsibility of States, in accordance with their respective obligations, to maintain at all times effective security of all nuclear and other radioactive materials, including nuclear materials used in nuclear weapons, and nuclear facilities under their control. This responsibility includes taking appropriate measures to prevent non-state actors from obtaining such materials – or related sensitive information or technology – which could be used for malicious purposes, and to prevent acts of terrorism and sabotage. In this context we emphasise the importance of robust national legislation and regulations on nuclear security.

International cooperation

5. At the same time we emphasise the need to further strengthen and coordinate international cooperation in the field of nuclear security. Much can be done through the International Atomic Energy Agency (IAEA) and other intergovernmental organisations and initiatives, and through bilateral and regional cooperation.

6. International cooperation fosters the capacity of States to build and sustain a strong nuclear security culture and effectively combat nuclear terrorism or other criminal threats. We encourage States, regulatory bodies, research and technical support organisations, the nuclear industry and other relevant stakeholders, within their respective responsibilities, to build such a security culture and share good practices and lessons learned at national, regional and international level.

7. We support stronger international and regional cooperation with regard to education, awareness raising and training, including through nuclear security centres of excellence and support. We therefore welcome the expansion of nuclear security networks for education, and for training and support, by the IAEA and other international organisations.

Strengthened international nuclear security architecture

8. We recognise the need for a strengthened and comprehensive international nuclear security architecture, consisting of legal instruments, international organisations and initiatives, internationally accepted guidance and good practices.

Legal instruments

9. We encourage States that have not yet done so to become party to the Convention on the Physical Protection of Nuclear Material (CPPNM) and to ratify its 2005 amendment. We welcome the new ratifications of the CPPNM amendment since the Seoul Summit. As foreseen in Seoul, we will continue to work towards the entry into force of the 2005 amendment later this year. We stress the need for all contracting parties to comply fully with all its provisions.

10. We underline the importance of the International Convention for the Suppression of Acts of Nuclear Terrorism and stress the need for all contracting Parties to comply fully with all its provisions. We welcome the new ratifications and accessions since the Seoul Summit and encourage all States to become party to this Convention.

11. We welcome efforts aimed at developing model legislation on nuclear security, which could provide States with building blocks to develop comprehensive national legislation in accordance with their own legal systems and internal legal processes.

Role of the International Atomic Energy Agency

12. We reaffirm the essential responsibility and the central role of the IAEA in the international nuclear security architecture. We welcome the increased prominence of nuclear security in the Agency's work and its leading role in

coordinating activities among international organisations and other international initiatives. The International Conference on Nuclear Security: Enhancing Global Efforts of July 2013 demonstrated the IAEA's ability to enhance political awareness and to address policy, technical and regulatory aspects of nuclear security.

13. We attach great value to the Agency's support for national efforts to improve nuclear security. Its nuclear security guidance, contained in the IAEA Nuclear Security Series of publications, provides the basis for effective nuclear security measures at national level. We encourage all States to utilise this guidance as appropriate.

14. We welcome the Integrated Nuclear Security Support Plans (INSSP) with which the IAEA assists States in consolidating their nuclear security needs into comprehensive plans. We encourage States to use their INSSPs for making progress in nuclear security, as appropriate.

15. We underline the benefits of IAEA review and advisory services provided through mechanisms such as the International Physical Protection Advisory Service (IPPAS). To date, 62 IPPAS missions have been undertaken in 40 countries. While acknowledging the voluntary nature of these services, we encourage all States to utilise them and share the lessons learned without detriment to the protection of sensitive information.

16. The role of the IAEA will be crucial in the years ahead. Therefore we encourage greater political, technical and financial support for the IAEA, including through its Nuclear Security Fund, to ensure that it has the resources and expertise needed to carry out its mandated nuclear security activities.

Role of the United Nations

17. We welcome the significant contribution made by the United Nations to strengthening nuclear security – particularly in promoting the ratification and effective implementation of international conventions and protocols against terrorism, including nuclear terrorism – as well as the work undertaken by the UN Security Council Committee, established pursuant to resolution 1540. We urge States to fully implement resolution 1540 and subsequent resolutions, and to continue to report such efforts on a regular basis. We also recognise the important contribution of the United Nations to disarmament and non-proliferation.

Role of other international initiatives

18. We recognise the contribution made by the Global Initiative to Combat Nuclear Terrorism (GICNT) and the Global Partnership Against the Spread of Weapons and Materials of Mass Destruction since the 2010 and 2012 Nuclear Security Summits, within their respective mandates and memberships. Both have

expanded in membership and have become valuable platforms for coordination and cooperation on nuclear security.

19. We welcome regional initiatives, which play an important role in strengthening nuclear security collaboration within regions while supporting overall nuclear security goals. We welcome continued developments in this area.

Voluntary measures

20. We have identified a range of voluntary measures States may consider taking to show that they have established effective security of their nuclear materials and facilities while protecting sensitive information. Such voluntary measures may include publishing information about national laws, regulations and organisational structures; exchanging good practices; inviting IAEA review and advisory services and other reviews and following up on their conclusions; providing information through relevant existing reporting mechanisms and forums; further developing training of personnel involved in nuclear security by setting up and stimulating participation in training courses and applying domestic certification schemes. We note that many of the States participating in this summit already take such measures, in some cases in a regional context, and are using them to showcase their nuclear security efforts, thereby building national and international confidence in the effectiveness of their nuclear security regimes.

Nuclear material

21. We recognise that highly enriched uranium (HEU) and separated plutonium require special precautions and that it is of great importance that they are appropriately secured, consolidated and accounted for. Over the past four years we have made considerable progress in safe, secure and timely consolidation inside countries and in removal to other countries for disposal. Furthermore, a considerable amount of HEU has been down-blended to low-enriched uranium (LEU) and separated plutonium converted to mixed oxide (MOX) fuel. We encourage States to minimise their stocks of HEU and to keep their stockpile of separated plutonium to the minimum level, both as consistent with national requirements.

22. We encourage States to continue to minimise the use of HEU through the conversion of reactor fuel from HEU to LEU, where technically and economically feasible, and in this regard welcome cooperation on technologies facilitating such conversion. Similarly, we will continue to encourage and support efforts to use non-HEU technologies for the production of radioisotopes, including financial incentives, taking into account the need for an assured and reliable supply of medical isotopes.

Radioactive sources and materials

23. Radioactive sources are used in every country in the world, whether in industry, medicine, agriculture or research. At the same time, high-activity radioactive sources can be used for malicious acts. We have made progress in better protecting sources, *inter alia* through national registers. Considerably more States have amended their national legislation and regulations, taking into account the guidance in the IAEA Code of Conduct on the Safety and Security of Radioactive Sources and Nuclear Security Series recommendations. We are committed to promoting this guidance, first and foremost through the IAEA. We seek to secure all radioactive sources, consistent with international guidance.

24. We encourage States which have not yet done so to establish appropriate security plans for the management of spent nuclear fuel and high-level radioactive waste.

Nuclear security and safety

25. We recognise that nuclear security and safety have the common aim of protecting human health, society and the environment. We reaffirm that nuclear safety measures and nuclear security measures need to be designed and managed in a coherent and coordinated manner in the specific areas where nuclear security and nuclear safety overlap. In these areas, efforts to further improve nuclear security might benefit from experience gained with nuclear safety. We emphasise the need to develop a nuclear security culture, with a particular focus on the coordination of safety and security. Sharing good practices, without detriment to the protection of sensitive information, might also be beneficial. The principle of continuous improvement applies to both safety and security. In this regard we acknowledge the IAEA Nuclear Security Guidance Committee and the IAEA Commission on Safety Standards and their activities aimed at properly addressing safety and security interface issues.

26. We reaffirm the need to maintain effective emergency preparedness, response and mitigation capabilities in a manner that addresses both nuclear security and nuclear safety.

Nuclear industry

27. Nuclear operators have the primary responsibility to secure their nuclear material and as such have an important role to play in maintaining and strengthening nuclear security. Operators' security systems should be effective and place a strong emphasis on an effective security culture, physical protection and material accountancy. This needs to be demonstrated nationally by regular routine

tests and evaluations, including performance testing and self-evaluation where appropriate. We take note of the emerging interest in using performance-based regulations where appropriate. We support a more intensive dialogue between operators and government bodies, including the national regulator, which should be functionally independent, with a view to improving nuclear security regulations and regulatory effectiveness.

28. In this regard, we recognise the holding of the Nuclear Industry Summit organised as a side event to this Nuclear Security Summit as a positive engagement by the industry with nuclear security issues.

Information and cyber security

29. We recognise the growing importance of information security, including information held on computer systems, related to nuclear material and technology. Security is essential to preventing unauthorised actors from obtaining information, technology and expertise required for acquiring and using nuclear materials for malicious purposes. In these areas further cooperation between government, industry and academia is desirable. We promote a nuclear security culture that emphasises the need to protect sensitive expertise and information and discourages publication of such information in online media and in public forums.

30. In order to address the growing threat of cyber attacks, including on critical information infrastructure and control systems, and their potential impact on nuclear security, we encourage States and the private sector to take effective risk mitigation measures to ensure that the systems and networks of nuclear facilities are appropriately secured. Unauthorised access to these systems could compromise the safe and secure operation of the facility as well as the confidentiality, integrity and availability of the relevant information.

Nuclear Transportation

31. We reaffirm our determination to further enhance the security of nuclear and other radioactive materials while in domestic and international transport. We acknowledge that sharing good practices and lessons learned, without detriment to the protection of sensitive information, can be useful contributions to this goal. We encourage States, the relevant industries and centres of excellence to be involved in these efforts at both national and international level.

Illicit Trafficking

32. We underline the vital importance of using all tools at our disposal to locate and secure nuclear material out of regulatory control, including effective export control arrangements and law enforcement mechanisms, to regulate nuclear transfers and counter illicit transfers of nuclear material. In this context

legislative measures are necessary to enable national prosecutions. We underscore our commitment to sharing information, best practices and expertise, subject to States' national laws and procedures, through bilateral, regional and multilateral mechanisms in relevant areas such as nuclear detection, forensics, law enforcement, and the development of new technologies to enhance enforcement capacity of customs personnel. We urge States to participate in the IAEA Incident and Trafficking Database and to provide the IAEA with relevant information in a timely manner. In the interest of supporting law enforcement efforts, we encourage States, consistent with their respective national regulations and international obligations, to expand information-sharing, including through INTERPOL and the World Customs Organization (WCO), regarding individuals involved in the illicit trafficking of nuclear or other radioactive materials.

Nuclear Forensics

33. Nuclear forensics is developing into an effective tool for determining the origin of nuclear and other radioactive materials and providing evidence for the prosecution of acts of illicit trafficking and other malicious acts. We welcome the progress and recent development of several instruments that improve the use of traditional forensic methods, and emphasise the need to further develop innovative forensic methods and tools for investigating incidents involving nuclear and other radioactive materials. We encourage further international cooperation, within the IAEA and other relevant international organisations, aimed at connecting and enhancing traditional and nuclear forensics capabilities, where feasible, and establishing national nuclear forensics databases to enable better determination of the origin of material. We welcome the organisation by IAEA of a conference on advances in nuclear forensics in July 2014.

Future of Process

34. Continuous efforts are needed to achieve our common goal of strengthening the international nuclear security architecture and we recognise that this is an ongoing process.

35. Our representatives will therefore continue to participate in different international forums dealing with nuclear security, with the IAEA playing the leading role in their coordination.

36. The United States will host the Nuclear Security Summit in 2016.

The Hague, 25 March 2014